GRASS ROOTS
POLITICS

Grass Roots Perspectives on American History

Soldiers and Society: The Effects of Military Service and War on American Life
Peter Karsten

GRASS ROOTS POLITICS

Parties, Issues, and Voters, 1854 — 1983

Richard J. Jensen

With the assistance of Steven L. Piott and
Christopher C. Gibbs

Grass Roots Perspectives on American History, Number 2

GREENWOOD PRESS
WESTPORT, CONNECTICUT • LONDON, ENGLAND

Library of Congress Cataloging in Publication Data

Jensen, Richard J.
    Grass roots politics.

    (Grass roots perspectives on American history,
ISSN 0148-771X ; no. 2)
    Includes index.
    1. Political parties — United States — History.
2. Voting — United States — History.   3. United States —
Politics and government — 19th century.   4. United
States — Politics and government — 20th century.
I. Piott, Steven L.   II. Gibbs, Christopher C.   III. Ti-
tle.   IV. Series.
JK2261.J46   1983   324.973   82-23070
ISBN 0-8371-6382-X (lib. bdg.)

Library of Congress Catalog Card Number: 82-23070
ISBN: 0-8371-6382-X
ISSN: 0148-771X

First published in 1983

Greenwood Press
A division of Congressional Information Service, Inc.
88 Post Road West
Westport, Connecticut 06881

Printed in the United States of America

10 9 8 7 6 5 4 3 2 1

To D'Ann Campbell

CONTENTS

ILLUSTRATIONS AND TABLES

GRASS ROOTS
POLITICS

I

THE VOTERS, MODERN AND TRADITIONAL: ETHNICITY, RELIGION, RACE, AND CLASS

Why do individuals vote the way they do? An adequate explanation must take into account the relatively permanent disposition of the voter toward public affairs (itself a product of many social, cultural, and psychological factors); the alternatives offered by the parties in terms of candidates, issues, and promises; and the short-term impact of specific factors, like energetic campaigning or even the weather on election day. This chapter will focus on the predispositions of the voters. Party organizations and issues will be discussed in chapter two. We will ignore the weather.

Before discussing the causes of voter dispositions, it would be helpful to jump ahead a bit and explain how these dispositions determine behavior. The reader is reminded that we use the concepts "traditional" and "modern" in a special way, as a shorthand for two different psychological types of voters. It is important to keep in mind that "traditional" does not necessarily refer to past time, nor "modern" necessarily to recent years. At all times in the last century there have been modern and traditional voters living side by side. The "traditional" voter, as we shall define him, is loyal to his family, friends, neighbors, ethnic group, community, and most important, to his party. Whether Republican or Democrat, he supports his party like a spirited alumnus supports his alma mater. In politics this loyalty greatly simplifies decisions about how to vote, and it permits even poorly educated persons to make sense out of public events. "My party is right, deserves my trust, and will get my vote; the other guys are bums, or, at best, misled." The traditional voter, as we shall see in the next chapter, is like a soldier in an army: obedient to orders, exalting in victory regardless of the "causes" of the war.

The "modern" voter, on the other hand, is like a careful shopper deciding which products—candidates and issues—to buy. He has transcended blind partisanship and votes on the basis of his own evaluation of the issues and candidates. Although he probably agrees with his family, friends, and neighbors, the cause of this agreement lies in shared values, rather than deference to uncritical acceptance of their decisions. The modern voter, consequently, is more likely to think in terms of liberal and conservative than Democrat and Republican. He or she "votes for the man (or woman), not the party." Of course, the modern conservative will most often vote for Republicans, and the modern liberal for Democrats, but that is because the parties tend to stand for conservative and liberal positions, respectively. The modern voter pays a good deal more attention to issues than the traditional voter, and if the information available in a campaign is too inadequate for him to decide which side to favor, he may simply not vote.

The broadest interpretive framework for analyzing voters is the traditional-modern dimension, which encompasses psychological outlook, ethnic and religious affiliation, social status, and economic self-interest. This framework permits the historian to integrate many strands of social, political, and even economic change, and it helps explain otherwise peculiar or inexplicable events and modes of behavior.

The more "modern" American aspires to middle-class values — upward mobility through hard work, universalistic values whereby men are judged on their merits rather than by family connections, race, or "pull." Likely he is involved in the market economy, where money rules, and prices, supply, and demand are functions of a national or international market. Thus subsistence farmers, gentlemen living on inherited wealth, and persons on welfare are largely outside the modern economy, while white-collar workers, businessmen, cash-crop farmers, and wage laborers are inside it.

Religion was a key factor in voting in the nineteenth and early twentieth centuries simply because religious beliefs and the outlook on life they inculcated loomed so large in the determination of a person's values. The more "modern" religious outlook, which we shall call "pietistic," stressed that an individual must not rely on rote theology or established churches for salvation, but would have to confront Christ directly, via a conversion experience or at least a positive commitment to right behavior. That achieved, his duty was to help spread the message of universal salvation (through revivals or social gospel work at home, plus foreign missions) and to eliminate the temptations to sin in the society around him.

The more traditional religious outlook, which we will call "liturgical," taught that the way to salvation lay in following the prescribed rituals of the churches (like communion, confession, Mass attendance), in truly believing the dogmas of the church (the pietists had few dogmas and no heresy), and in obeying pastors, priests, and bishops.

Liturgicals in the nineteenth century, being outnumbered by pietists, thought the government had no right to dictate in matters of morality and bitterly resented the aggressive pietistic efforts to prohibit their traditional beer and wine. Pietists in government seemed to be dangerous fanatics who had to be stopped. Furthermore, the pietists ridiculed their liturgical formal-ities and tried to shut down their parochial schools. While by no means friendly to slavery, drunkenness, or ignorance, the liturgicals opposed moralistic crusaders who proposed to enact their incorrect moral code into law. As long as they were in a minority, the liturgicals favored a negative government that would leave them alone. (But in the twentieth century, when their power at the polls was great, Catholics sought to legislate their own opposition to "immoral" obscenity, birth control, divorce, and abortion.)

In the nineteenth century there were already over a hundred different denominations, each of which contained pietists and liturgicals in different mixtures. The pietists were the Methodists, northern Baptists, Presbyterians, Reform Jews, Quakers, Congregationalists, and Disciples of Christ. The most liturgical were Catholics, Mormons, Orthodox Jews, Episcopalians, and Southern Baptists. However, there were pietist-liturgical conflicts within each denomination, often leading to schisms or heresy trials. The Lutherans displayed the greatest confusion to outsiders. Scandinavian and Pennsylvania-Dutch Lutherans were heavily pietistic, while German Lutherans were intensely liturgical. Indeed, the Missouri Synod, the largest body of German Lutherans, to this day has fierce internal disputes on heresy and the proper interpretation of the Bible.

When Americans became converted to religion in the nineteenth century (in 1800 few were churchgoers), those people who were psychologically more modern chose pietistic denominations, while the traditionalists favored the liturgical churches. The latter included immigrants from Catholic Europe, mostly of peasant background, who developed a devotion to Catholicism far stronger than they had exhibited in the old country. Blacks lived traditional lives and practiced modern religion—chiefly because the central event in their experience, emancipation from slavery, was a profoundly modern, equalitarian demand that ripped apart the traditional fabric of southern life. Black religion and politics, then as now, focused on the past and future implications of emancipation. ("We shall overcome, someday!") The correlation between pietistic-liturgical beliefs and modern-traditional social and economic behavior, while not perfect, was quite strong.

Studies of actual voting behavior, while still incomplete, demonstrate conclusively that, in the North, pietists preferred the GOP and liturgicals the Democratic party. The correlation between denomination and party, according to our modern-traditional model, should not be perfect. *Within* each religious grouping, we expect that men with more modern or middle-class occupations were more Republican. Thus, businessmen, professionals, white-collar workers and skilled factory workers should have been more Republican, while unskilled and semiskilled workers should have been more Democratic after the effect of religion is controlled. Table 1, based on interview data from the 1870s bears this out exactly.

Table 1
PARTY BY OCCUPATION AND RELIGION: Illinois in the 1870s

Occupation	All	Grouping (read down)					
		Rep.	Ind.	Dem.	Pietistic	None	Liturgical
Business	21.1%	24.0%	25.5%	13.3%	23.3%	21.6%	15.3%
Professional	8.5	9.6	8.9	6.8	13.4	7.3	4.6
White-collar	6.8	6.9	7.3	6.3	5.8	7.6	5.3
Skilled blue-collar	32.7	36.0	30.4	30.9	33.8	35.2	21.4
All high and middle status	69.1	76.5	72.1	57.3	76.3	71.7	46.6
Unskilled (specific industry)	8.2	5.8	7.1	12.0	3.1	8.2	16.5
Unskilled (common labor)	15.2	10.2	13.6	22.9	11.0	13.2	30.4
Retired, unknown	7.5	7.5	7.3	7.8	9.6	6.9	6.5
Total	100%	100%	100%	100%	100%	100%	100%
Number of nonfarmers	1717	669	506	542	447	1009	261
Number of farmers	1129	467	105	557	374	553	201
Proportion of farmers among all men in category	39.7%	41.1%	17.2%	50.6%	44.5%	35.5%	43.5%

Source: Richard J. Jensen, The Winning of the Midwest: Social and Political Conflict, 1888-1891 (Chicago: University of Chicago Press, 1971), p. 313.

Farmers are somewhat harder to classify along a modern-traditional spectrum. Pietists voted mostly Republican and liturgicals Democratic, that much is certain. It also seems that market-oriented farmers (who sold most of their output) favored the GOP, while more isolated subsistence farmers voted the opposite. However, wheat farmers, who sold their crops on the world rather than just the national market, were often dissatisfied with the Republican high tariff doctrine, which hurt them, and frequently bolted to third parties (Populist in 1892, Farmer-Labor in 1920s).

A further complication comes from Appalachian farmers in Kentucky, Tennessee, Virginia, and North Carolina. Although extremely traditional in outlook, they strenuously opposed the Confederacy and paid little attention to white supremacy (few blacks lived in their areas). They began voting Republican in the 1860s and continue to do so to the present, even producing national Republican leaders like Senator Howard Baker of Tennessee. This is an instance of traditionalist opposition to proslavery, traditional ideology producing affiliation with the modernist party, regardless of economic situation.

The realignment of the 1850s placed the two major parties squarely on the modern-traditional axis. The Republican party represented the modern, ambitious, pietistic, middle-class voters, while the Democratic party represented the traditional, security-minded, liturgical, working-class (and upper-class aristocratic) end of the spectrum. Republican city machines, in Philadelphia, Chicago, and elsewhere solicited traditional votes, and a modernizing element existed in the Democratic party. In both instances the clash of values within the parties led to bitter disputes (the progressive-standpat battle in the GOP between 1910 and 1914 and the silver-gold conflict among Democrats in 1896).

Nevertheless the Republican party reflected modern values: an end to slavery, polygamy, and saloons; equal rights for blacks; and support for industrialization (through high tariffs, railroad land grants, favors to growth industries, a sound banking system, and hard money). The Democrats opposed "fanaticism" on the slavery and prohibition questions; supported white supremacy; and favored the consumer and the subsistence farmer in economic policy (low tariffs, low taxes and spending, free silver, and inflation for the benefit of debtors).

The Democrats tolerated, indeed positively encouraged, ethnic and cultural diversity; the Republicans insisted on a single standard of uniform, middle-class Americanism until McKinley in 1896 showed the GOP it had to tolerate the "peculiar" traditions of immigrant groups if it expected to win elections and promote rapid industrialization. Southern Democrats, even though they included some modern leaders like Woodrow Wilson, were totally committed to the principle that race relations be based on traditional norms, with the blacks kept in a strictly inferior position.

The modern-traditional spectrum had deep implications for the way parties were organized and campaigns conducted. The army style was basically traditional. It supposed that men were loyal to a code of beliefs and obedient to their political commanders. The GOP adopted the army style because it was the only way to win elections, yet middle-class Republicans were never reconciled to the blind loyalty it demanded. They were Republicans because the goals of the party, though not its tactics, were modern. But the middle classes harbored an antiparty animus and easily supported nonpartisanship in municipal politics and were swept into the progressive movement once the threat of Democratic triumphs was smothered by McKinley's great victories. Progressivism, as we shall see, set the goal of a universalistic, efficient government in which traditional practices were banished.

The Democratic party in the twentieth century, confronted with an increasingly modern, middle-class rank-and-file, adjusted by adopting the efficiency and good-government ideals of the middle class, while still emphasizing party loyalty and trying to maintain its city machines (Doc. 32). Thus Chicago's Mayor Daley, boss of the last great Democratic machine, could proclaim his devotion to good government, despite the gibes of reformers and the systematic effort of the GOP to expose and indict his top lieutenants for corrupt practices.

A serious dilemma inherent in traditional army-style politics involved the selection of major candidates. Traditional political leadership was basically local in outlook, caring more for the particularistic needs of specific constituents than for broad questions of policy. Yet major leaders—mayors, governors, and especially presidents—of necessity dealt with broad policy problems and could not govern effectively if they spent their energies on particularistic matters. Traditionalists could be effective in legislative offices, from city councils to the Congress. And that is where most of them ended up. The GOP in the army days resolved the dilemma by always nominating modernists to executive offices. They especially favored high army officers (Fremont, Grant, Hayes, Garfield, Harrison, Eisenhower) or lawyers and businessmen (Lincoln, Hoover, Harding, Landon, Willkie, Dewey, Goldwater) whose careers signalled to the middle-class electorate their ability to handle large affairs of state. (The occasional professional politician who won the GOP nomination usually had demonstrated executive abilities, like Theodore Roosevelt, Taft, and Reagan.)

The Democrats had a serious problem, for their best leaders were traditionalists who rose to power commanding city machines, but who were simply unqualified for the White House or the governor's mansion. Very few Democratic mayors have ever gone on to higher office (James Curley, the corrupt Boston boss who became governor, and Hubert Humphrey, the Minneapolis reformer, are conspicuous exceptions). Their experiment of nominating generals (McClellen in 1864, Hancock in 1880) worked poorly, so they fell back on either bona fide modernists within their ranks (Tilden in

1876; Cleveland in 1884, 1888, and 1892; Parker in 1904; Wilson in 1912 and 1916; Cox in 1920; Davis in 1924; Stevenson in 1952 and 1956; McGovern in 1972; and Carter in 1976 and 1980) or else traditional politicians with an aura of modernist executive ability or upper-class respectability about them (Bryan in 1896, 1900, and 1908; Smith in 1928; Truman in 1948; Johnson in 1964; Humphrey in 1968; and the aristocrats Roosevelt in 1932, 1936, 1940, and 1944; and Kennedy in 1960). Still, the Republicans always enjoyed a surplus of eligible, modern, executive-type candidates, while the Democrats always seemed short of appropriate talent.

Voter Realignments, 1880-1928

Although there were occasional deviations from the modern-traditional voting pattern between 1854 and 1928, there were only four major realignments: the German shift on prohibition, the urban and German shift of 1896, and two ethnic shifts in the 1920s.

The Germans comprised the largest ethnic group in the country over the last century, being more numerous than blacks. They concentrated in New York, Chicago, St. Louis, Baltimore, and other large cities, and in rural areas north and west of Chicago, as far as the Dakotas. The great majority were liturgical Catholics or Lutherans, with a pietistic Methodist minority (always Republican) and a small but extremely articulate agnostic or free-thinker contingent typified by Carl Schurz. The pietists and freethinkers were usually Republicans; the Catholics, Democrats. But a third or so of the liturgical Lutherans voted Republican because that party was seen as much more anti-Catholic than the Democrats. German Jews, being reform (pietist) in religion and playing very modern roles in the economy, apparently were Republican, though the data is too sparse to be certain. Most Jews today are of Eastern European origins, very modern, and very heavily Democratic.

In the 1880s, in state after state the Republican party was taken over by aggressive pietists who demanded prohibition and restrictions on parochial schools. The liturgical Germans reacted sharply. Mobilizing all their votes, pride, and money, they countercrusaded against the GOP, most notably in the Midwest in 1890 and 1892, which produced victory for Grover Cleveland and a host of local and state Democratic candidates. But one key element in the traditional German outlook was a deep hostility toward inflation. On this point they agreed with the modernists. In 1896, when Bryan crusaded for an inflationary silver policy, Germans surged back to the GOP, electing McKinley president.

Bryan's crusade in 1896 also shook the Republican loyalties of pietistic workers and farmers in the traditional sector of the economy and wheat farmers and metal miners in the West. Bryan was very clever about this. In addition to being the Democrats' standard bearer, he also secured the nomination of the Populists and a new ad hoc party, the Silver Republicans. He could thus appeal to men of all parties to vote for him without abandoning their partisan loyalties. Bryan did well among some pietists who could not accept McKinley's version of a modernized, industrial state. (Middle-class pietists considered Bryan's pietism not only phony, but blasphemous, as when in his "cross of gold, crown of thorns" speech Bryan likened himself to Christ. They intensified their Republicanism.) Radical prohibitionists also responded to his religious appeal, for McKinley promised toleration of liturgical drinking practices, while Bryan's moral vision more closely approximated prohibitionist absolutism. Southern pietistic Democrats responded enthusiastically to Bryan, for his style was pietistic and yet safely traditionalist on one key issue — Bryan explicitly condemned federal interference in state affairs, which, in the South, meant he upheld white supremacy. Southern traditionalists loved Bryan. His savage attacks on the evil modernizers in Wall Street proved he would never disappoint the hard pressed small farmer.

But Bryan's appeal ignored the traditional Northern Democrats who were bound up with the modern economy — factory workers, coal miners, and railroad employees especially (many of whom were Germans). McKinley exploited this weakness brilliantly. His supporters, when appealing to liturgicals, downplayed the pietistic ethos of the GOP, promised toleration for liturgical practices (that is, no more prohibition or efforts to shut down parochial schools), and emphasized Bryan's pietism meant he was not a true Democrat. The grinding poverty and unemployment during the depression of the 1890s was caused by Democratic malfeasance, McKinley claimed, and inflationary silver policies would bankrupt railroads, mines, mills, and factories, throwing millions more out of work. McKinley promised that the Republican gold and high tariff policy would end the depression. Liturgical Democrats in the modern sector switched to the GOP, where they would remain until prohibition enforcement and another depression belied Republican promises. Liturgicals with jobs not closely tied to the industrial order (like construction and petty trade), notably the Irish, stayed loyal to the Democratic party, much as they disliked Bryan's style. The Irish got their reward quickly, for in the wake of Bryan's defeat they took over the party leadership posts vacated by gold Democrats. (There were some Democratic modernizers, like Woodrow Wilson, who opposed Bryan, either by voting Republican or for an ad hoc "Gold Democrat" ticket.)

The third major realignment before the New Deal era took place in 1920 and affected liturgical traditionalist Democrats, especially in the large cities. They felt betrayed on several fronts by Wilson and overwhelmingly voted for Harding or simply did not vote. Prohibition, enacted by a coalition of pietistic Republicans and pietistic Southern Democrats, was blamed on the

Wilson administration. The League of Nations, the great Wilsonian effort to project modern universalism on the world scene, angered particularistic German, Irish, Jewish, and Italian voters, who felt their mother countries had been unfairly treated. The German-Americans, most of all, had come under vicious attack by the Wilson administration during the war — their proud culture was ridiculed ("Hun barbarism," the government said), their language was forbidden in schools and even on the telephone (in Iowa and Missouri), and they were treated as second-class citizens and potential saboteurs. In 1924 Germans supported LaFollette's third party candidacy, for he had been their most outspoken and fearless champion during the terrible war years. Not until Al Smith and Franklin Roosevelt came along to soothe their pride would the urban ethnics vote for a Wilsonian.

The last important change before the New Deal came in 1928, and it involved the full-scale emergence of traditionalist Catholics into the political arena. For the first (and only) time a devout son of Holy Mother Church won a presidential nomination. (John Kennedy was a distinctly modern Catholic; indeed his presidency helped spark a reaction against traditionalism within the Catholic church.) To affirm the dignity of their cultural heritage and to strike back at aggressive pietistic prohibition, Catholics overwhelmingly voted for Al Smith. Catholic women, whose avoidance of voting fitted their traditional subservient role, suddenly emerged as a new force in the electorate. Undoing Wilson's damage to the northern wing of the party, the Catholic vote carried New York, Boston, St. Louis, Cleveland, Milwaukee, and Newark into Smith's column. Hoover, the quintessential pietistic modernizer, however, won the vast majority of modern voters. He carried Chicago, Philadelphia, Los Angeles, and most other large cities. He even carried the more modern southern cities, becoming the first Republican before Eisenhower to break the solid Democratic South (Doc. 20). The Smith phenomenon was a one-shot affair, as the Catholics did not *permanently* surge into the Democratic ranks for several more years. In 1930, for example, heavily Catholic Allegheny County (Pittsburgh) registered a mere 7 percent of its voters as Democrats, about the same as half-Catholic Philadelphia. San Francisco and Buffalo, also largely Catholic, registered under 30 percent Democratic that year.

The New Deal Realignment, 1932 to the Present

Franklin Roosevelt engineered the rebuilding of the Democratic party, bequeathing it a majority status it still retains. The chief factor, obviously, was the Great Depression. Republican strength stemmed from their promise that modernization meant prosperity. By 1932 that image was shattered beyond repair, and for fifty years the Democrats would always bring up the spectre of Hoover-style modernization to frighten the insecure. Prohibition, another modernizing measure to which Hoover was firmly committed, likewise had proven a failure by 1932. Liquor was freely available in every city, where it bred illegal activity that corrupted municipal politics. Roosevelt's neotraditional stance (wet in the north, moderately dry in the South; low taxes, low tariffs; tolerance of white supremacy; suspicious of industrialization, anti-big bankers, and pro-farmer) swept virtually every group into his temporary coalition in 1932.

To build a permanent coalition, Roosevelt by 1936 had developed an aggressively traditionalist posture. Growth-oriented industrialization was disastrous, he proclaimed. Middle-class virtues of ambition and hostility to welfare were outdated. His New Deal agencies reduced the sway of bankers and talked about protecting consumers. They limited the managerial power of industrialists while strongly encouraging labor unions. Private thrift gave way to compulsory old-age pensions and deficit spending. Relief was doled out massively, not to people whose middle-class habits most merited it, but rather to the poorest, most traditional folk in greatest need. Catholic traditionalists received token government posts. Even more important to them was the rejection of the pietistic moral code signalled by the repeal of prohibition. Big-city machines in Chicago, the Bronx, Jersey City, Boston, Kansas City, and elsewhere were systematically strengthened, much to the annoyance of old progressives, who overwhelmingly opposed the New Deal.

The 1936 election was the greatest and last triumph of traditionalism in American politics. Northern Catholics and unskilled workers surged to the polls encouraged by efficient machine and union canvassing, and the charismatic appeal of Roosevelt. In 1932 Roosevelt won 62 percent of the city vote, in 1936 he polled 70 percent (losing only two cities of any size, Pasadena and Syracuse). Factory workers, no longer enchanted by the modernizing ideal, and increasingly unionized, joined the coalition, as did most farmers frustrated with the failure of the modern ideal to keep them from bankruptcy.

Roosevelt's coalition in 1936 was too large. Millions of voters with essentially modern, pro-Republican outlooks on social and economic issues had voted against their basic value orientation because it had failed and the energetic programs of the New Deal seemed to promise recovery. But recovery did not come. Roosevelt's economic policies, a hodge-podge of panaceas, proved unable to end the depression. In fact it got much worse in 1937 and 1938, and the militant sit-down strikes then underway threatened to further weaken the economy. The Democratic party, torn with strife, seemed paralyzed (Doc. 25). Key Southern Democrats shifted to the conservative opposition. In 1938 the Republicans won their most desperate victory, gaining eighty seats in the House and five in the Senate and regaining fourteen governorships.

For the next dozen years the Republicans won big majorities in the North

in off-year elections, when the people who actually voted were predominantly middle class. However, the Democrats concentrated their resources
on winning the White House, for their traditionalist supporters were much
easier to mobilize when the contest could be dramatized by their presidential candidates. Thus the Republicans did very well in 1938, 1942, 1946, and
1950—all off years—while the Democrats reelected Roosevelt in 1940 and
1944, and Truman in 1948, though by far smaller margins than 1936 (Doc.
26).

   In the traditionalist-modern spectrum, Catholic manual workers were at
one pole, and white-collar Protestants at the other. In 1936, the first group
was 86 percent Democratic and the second 34 percent, a dramatic 52 percent
differential. Table 2 shows how well the polarization held up year by year,
with little sign of diminishing, until the 1968 contest. In fact, polarization
was greatest in 1960, when a Catholic ran for president, but was still quite
high in 1958 and 1962, when religion as such was not an issue.

   The composition of the party coalitions was fairly stable between 1952
and 1976, even though the era witnessed landslides one way or the other.
The Republican vote was remarkably homogeneous. In the eight presidential elections from 1952 through 1980, an average of 99 percent of the
Republican voters were white; 91 percent lived outside the dozen largest
cities; 80 percent did not have a union member in the household; 77 percent
were Protestant, and 77 percent lived in the North. The uniformity of background gave the GOP a conservative tone, and also dampened the possibil-

Table 2
PERCENT DEMOCRATIC BY TRADITIONAL-MODERN STATUS, 1936-1972

Election	Traditional: Blue-collar Catholics	Modern: White-collar Northern Protestants	Difference
1936 Presidential	86	34	52
1940 Presidential	85	32	53
1944 Presidential	74	31	43
1948 Presidential	75	35	40
1952 Presidential	63	18	45
1954 Congressional	74	36	38
1956 Presidential	60	21	39
1958 Congressional	81	35	46
1960 Presidential	84	19	65
1962 Congressional	80	29	51
1964 Presidential	85	45	40
1966 Congressional	78	34	44
1968 Congressional	64	34	30
1972 Presidential	46	17	29

ity of ideological battles within the party. Although Republicans were a minority of all adults, they were more active politically and generally more united than the opposition.

By contrast, the Democratic coalition included highly diverse elements that were not easily brought together in national campaigns. On the average from 1952 through 1980, Catholics made up 36 percent of the Democratic vote; union members 33 percent; southerners (both white and black), 25 percent; residents of the twelve largest cities, 16 percent and blacks 13 percent. In contrast to the stable GOP coalition, the Democratic coalition fluctuated considerably. Blacks made up only 7 percent of the Stevenson supporters in 1952, but thanks to increased turnout, made up 22 percent of McGovern's vote in 1972, and 21 percent of Carter's vote in 1980. The Catholic share of the Democratic coalition fluctuated from a high of 43 percent in 1960, when fellow Catholic John Kennedy was the candidate, to only 32 percent in 1976, when southern Baptist Jimmy Carter was the nominee. On the other hand, Carter's appeal to his friends and neighbors in Dixie meant that 36 percent of his vote came from the South, compared to a fairly regular 23 percent average for Democrats in 1952 through 1972. The highly diverse Democratic coalition was regularly subject to disruption as one or another component resented the favored position that some other component seemed to enjoy.

Between 1938 and 1964, the Democrats repeatedly promised to extend more New-Deal-type federal aid to the various elements of their coalition, but were unable to do so. The chief reason was the strength of the conservative coalition, consisting of the great majority of Republican congressmen in alliance with most of the southern Democrats. As we will see in the next section, this coalition depended upon modern, middle-class families, who were opposed to taxes, and hence spending, except for national defense expenditures.

In 1964, however, the power of the conservative coalition was temporarily destroyed. President John Kennedy, despite the 23 percent of his vote drawn from the South, broke with the southern Democrats in Congress in an effort to pass "New Frontier" legislation favoring the other groups in his coalition. The conservative coalition stymied Kennedy, but his successor, Lyndon Johnson, was far more successful. The 1964 Democratic landslide reduced the dependence of Democrats upon southern white support, both for the presidential vote (only 15 percent of Johnson's vote in 1964 came from white southerners), and for voting majorities in Congress. (In 1965, 34 percent of the Democrats in the House were from the South, compared to 41 percent in 1963). The vigorous leadership of Lyndon Johnson and his northern Democratic allies made possible the spectacular "Great Society" legislative programs of the mid-1960s, but does not explain why they occurred when they did.

The combination of affluence and guilt on the part of modern voters explains the timing of the "Great Society." By 1964, the country had enjoyed a quarter-century of rapid growth, with prosperity widely shared among white-collar workers and skilled blue-collar workers. Average (mean) family income after taxes was double what it had been in 1936, even with inflation taken into account. The symbols of affluence were everywhere: 90 percent of all families owned a TV set, 75 percent had at least one car, and 24 percent owned two or more autos. Half the adults had graduated from high school, and 20 percent had attended college at least for a while. Taxes comprised 30 percent of the gross national product, a fraction that had not changed since World War II and which was much lower than in other industrialized countries, like Britain, Germany, and Japan. American affluence was secure, and there seemed to be more than enough money available for spending.

The guilt that modern voters felt came from the fact that the affluence was not shared by everyone. Half the black population lived below poverty levels in 1964, together with 40 percent of the people over age 65. Only 10 percent of white families lived in poverty, and most of them were either old or were broken by divorce. Even more guilt was generated by the denial of voting rights to most southern blacks, by the enforced segregation in public places throughout the South, and by the segregation of most black school children in both the North and the South. The media repeatedly emphasized these affronts to the equalitarian ideals of modernity. Even more effective was the vociferous demands of the civil rights movement for an end to the treatment of blacks as second class citizens. The civil rights movement was led by charismatic blacks, notably the Reverend Martin Luther King, but it also included many white liberals, labor union leaders, and churchmen. By the time Dr. King led a massive, but peaceful march on Washington in 1963, only the most traditional southern whites could oppose the justice of the civil rights cause. The outpouring of national grief at the assassination of Kennedy in 1963 permitted Johnson to channel the guilt feelings of society into an elaborate program of civil rights reforms and spending for the benefit of the Democratic coalition.

A series of civil rights laws involved federal seizure of the voter registration process in the South. As a consequence, the black southern electorate soared from 1.5 million in 1960, to 2.2 million in 1964 to 3.1 million in 1968. In Mississippi, the number of black voters multiplied by 13, from 22,000 in 1960 to 286,000 in 1968. Laws that outlawed discrimination in employment based on race had an immediate effect. Between 1960 and 1981 the proportion of blacks with white-collar or skilled crafts jobs jumped from 22 percent to 47 percent, a notable improvement, though still far below the comparable rates for whites (60 percent in 1965 and 67 percent in 1981). The ratio of average black family income to white income, which had held fairly steady at 55 percent from World War II to 1965 began to climb, reaching 61 percent by 1970, then slipped to 58 percent in 1980. However, when more radical blacks began demanding black power, including control of the civil rights movement itself, and a series of riots burned through hundreds of cities between 1964 and 1968, white support for more civil rights legislation evaporated. The black community itself became more conservative on social issues like "law and order" (Doc. 36).

The federal courts, however, continued their program to desegregate public schools. In 1961, 93 percent of black children in the South attended all-black schools. By 1972, however, only 30 percent of southern black children attended schools that were 95 to 100 percent black. In the North, by sharp contrast, 54 percent of black children still attended practically all-black schools in 1972. Desegregation involved mandatory busing throughout the South and in some northern cities such as Boston and Denver as well. White public opinion strongly opposed busing. Blacks were split on the issue, with many preferring black control over the community schools in lieu of desegregation, which usually left white superintendents and school board in charge. Many politicians, including President Nixon, announced their opposition to busing, but there was nothing they could do to reverse the situation. The federal judges were ordering desegregation, including busing as necessary, to carry out the Supreme Court's ruling that segregated schools violated the equal protection clause of the Constitution (the Fourteenth Amendment). Desegregation procedures were, therefore, a constitutionally necessary remedy for historic patterns of segregation that had traditionally been required in the South by law, and occurred in the North because blacks were not free to live anywhere they wished in a city.

The civil rights programs of the Johnson administration and the courts can be interpreted as a systematic effort to modernize laws and customs that had forced blacks to live in segregated environments without access to good jobs in the modern sector. Soon the ideal of modernizing legal, educational, and economic environments was extended to other groups, called "minorities," that in the 1960s still lived more or less traditional lives. The largest minorities were the Hispanics, that is, Americans of Puerto Rican or Mexican ancestry. Native Americans, though fewer in number, were also given the protection and advantages of prominority governmental programs. In political terms, however, the nonblack minority groups were quite weak because of very low levels of political activism or voting. In California, for example, where Hispanics comprise 16 percent of the population, they hold only 2 percent of the state's 20,000 elective posts in local government. Of 7 million Hispanics eligible to vote nationwide, only 38 percent are even registered, and most of them do not vote.

The question arose in the late 1960s whether women as a group should also be treated as a "minority," because historically they had been forced to remain in traditional roles. An equal rights amendment was passed by Congress in 1972, but soon encountered intense opposition from some women and religious groups (especially Catholics and Mormons) who argued that

ERA was not needed, but would instead hurt some women. Since the civil rights laws that protected the job rights of blacks also extended to women, there was general agreement that ERA would not have much additional impact on the growing success women were having in entering previously all-male occupations. However, feminists feared that the defeat of ERA would signal a reactionary step that threatened to undo all their gains of the 1970s. After intense lobbying and grass-roots political activity, the feminists succeeded in 1978 in extending the deadline for ratification of ERA by the states to 1982. Feminist activism proved unsuccessful in convincing state legislators in the hold-out states (chiefly in the South) to ratify ERA. In 1980, for the first time, a "gender gap" opened, as women began voting differently than men — they were more Democratic, more pacifist, and more liberal (Doc. 37). However, the increased feminist political activism had not, by 1983, resulted in a significant gain in the number of women holding major offices. (See map 1.)

Beyond its support for minorities, Johnson's Great Society also included large spending programs for the poor, the old, schools, and cities. Federal spending in these areas tripled between 1960 and 1970, then tripled again by 1978. The total share of the country's entire gross national product spent by federal, state, and local government for social welfare programs, including social security, education, medical care, relief, and housing, doubled from 10 percent in 1960 to 20 percent in 1975, then levelled off. By contrast, spending on defense budgets declined from 10 percent of the GNP in 1960 to 6 percent in 1982. In other words, social welfare and defense spending were about the same in 1960, but by 1975 the welfare spending was triple the defense budget. The differential was continuing to increase until President Reagan in 1981 turned the priorities around.

The Great Society's spending programs were criticized as wasteful and ineffective by conservatives. There is little doubt that a lot of money was spent in a big hurry, especially on big-city projects, with a great deal of mismanagement and waste. By the government paying most of the medical expenses of the poor and the elderly, for example, the cost of medical services for everyone else was forced up because of shortages. On the other hand, it must be remembered that millions of people received medical treatment they otherwise would not have obtained. Johnson's "war on poverty" was ridiculed as a hopeless, wasteful endeavor of lofty motives. Yet studies of poverty in the mid-1970s revealed that, once the new free services and low-cost benefits, like food stamps, were taken into account, fewer than 10 percent of the population still lived in poverty, compared with 22 percent in 1960.

The Great Society's critics, however, had the last word. Johnson's popularity in the polls dropped from 75 percent approval in 1964 to only 46 percent in 1966; it would sink still lower when his failure to end the war in Vietnam further eroded public confidence in his competence to run the

Map 1

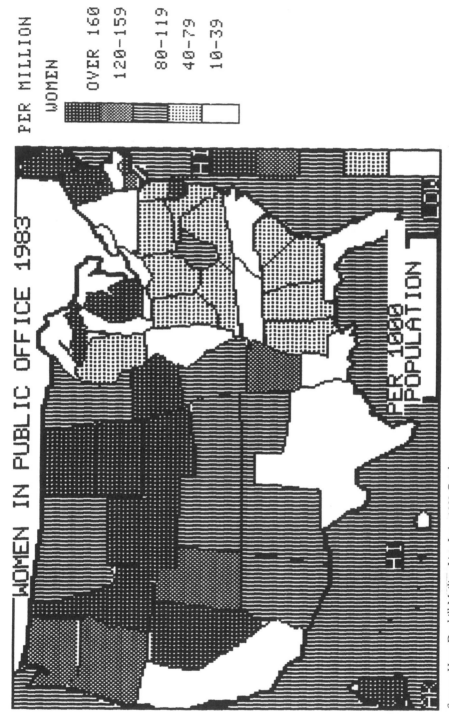

Source: Hugo Dunhill Mailing List, Inc., 1983 Catalog.

country. Most of Johnson's critics were conservatives and Republicans. They reflected modernist, middle-class views that feared "big government" for reasons we will explore in the next section. By 1980, furthermore, most Democrats had come to agree that the Great Society had gone too far. The issue for the 1980s would be whether Reagan and the conservatives would be able to repair the damage, or whether they would go too far in the other direction (Doc. 36).

Conservative Reaction, 1938-1980

A basic explanation for the permanent revival of conservative opposition to liberal spending programs since the 1930s was the transformation of the taxation system during World War II. Roosevelt's policy of "tax, tax, tax; spend, spend, spend; elect, elect, elect," as his top aide phrased it, may have angered devotees of middle-class values, but it worked because far more people benefited from the New Deal than paid for it. At one time or another in the 1930s, nearly one half of the country's families were beneficiaries of relief or federal employment programs, but only 10 percent of the families paid any federal or state income taxes. Washington raised more money from tobacco and liquor excises than from the personal income tax and paid for its spending programs by borrowing money. The war, which absorbed a third of the gross national product, required heavy new taxes. By 1944 virtually every household was paying income taxes. Coupled with social security taxes, this meant that a government wanting to "spend, spend, spend" would have to "tax, tax, tax" everyone. For the first time the majority of voters were forced to weigh the relative advantage of generous government spending versus a higher bite out of their take-home pay. Of course, in a grave wartime emergency, the people paid. When the war ended they wanted their taxes reduced.

Furthermore, the bite of strong centralized government also hit the average household in the guise of the draft and strict rationing for ordinary needs, like meat, shoes, sugar, and gasoline. After the war the draft was revived and continued until 1972 by a bipartisan coalition anxious to offset Soviet power in the Cold War. It never became a major partisan issue. However, rationing did. Liberal Democrats, strongly backed by labor unions, fought to preserve rationing and its stepsister, price controls. They believed, in neotraditionalist fashion, that the government should closely control the economy, especially to ensure that the poor and the weak (that is, those outside the modern market economy) were not injured by the untrammeled forces of modernization. This position came to be known as economic liberalism (Doc. 36).

The economic conservatives strenuously opposed neotraditionalism, government price and wage controls, and especially rationing, which distorted the free operation of the market economy. It generated inefficiency, especially when administered by academicians (John Kenneth Galbraith was a key figure in the rationing system) and government bureaucrats who had "never met a payroll" (that is, had never been part of the modern market economy). Republicans, demanding an end to controls, swept the 1946 elections in their greatest landslide ever. They ended controls (except in New York City, where rent control persisted for decades), cut taxes (over Truman's veto), and the economy leapt forward—despite the prophecies of the liberals that conservative laissez faire would cause another great depression.

Eisenhower's election in 1952 confirmed the conservative triumph on the economic issue with but few compromises (Doc. 28). Government policy favored the modern sector, especially large industry. A modest program of social security and welfare provided assistance to the elderly, blind, and handicapped, who, even the conservatives agreed, were unable to participate in the modern economy. Unemployment compensation existed as a cushion for workers temporarily dislocated by economic changes or the business cycle. In 1957-1958, however, a short, sharp recession strengthened the liberal argument that conservative programs were inadequate to meet human needs. The Democrats scored large gains, most of which evaporated when prosperity returned. At all times the conservative coalition stayed in control of Congress.

Lyndon Johnson's 1964 landslide provided enough new liberal strength in Congress for a dramatic shift in national economic policy. Like the Roosevelt of 1933, Johnson was a pluralist who promised something for everybody—tax cuts for the wealthy, expansionary fiscal policies for more rapid business growth, and a new program of welfare for the traditional sector (chiefly minorities, the old, and Appalachian whites). Johnson's Great Society welfare programs were designed to provide temporary aid to the poor and to modernize them permanently by pumping funds into education, manpower retraining, and urban renewal. However, the welfare spending grew far beyond expectations. Recipients of aid to dependent children, for example, skyrocketed from 4.4 million in 1965 to 11.1 million in 1972, and then levelled off. Total spending on relief programs rose from $6.3 billion in 1965 to 60 billion in 1978.

The effects of the Great Society's programs to modernize individuals through manpower retraining and education were disappointing. Manpower retraining helped some people, but soon it proved too expensive and too ineffective. Spending on elementary and secondary education shot up ($18 billion in 1960, $28 billion in 1965, $61 billion in 1972, $107 billion in (1980), yet the intellectual performance of students rose only slowly, then began to decline. Sociologists discovered, much to everyone's astonishment, that the amount of money spent on primary and secondary schools had virtually no impact on what students learned. Thus the attempted instant modernization of the traditional sectors of society, and the speed-up of the whole process of making everyone better educated, better trained, and freer to grasp opportunity, turned out to be an extremely expensive failure.

Reaction was inevitable. It first came in the form of the opposition of the lower-middle-class and blue-collar whites to special favors for minorities, especially in jobs. This reaction helped Nixon and Wallace in 1968, Nixon in 1972, Ford in 1976, and most dramatically, Reagan in 1980 (Doc. 36). Conservatism, especially when focused on the "hard hats" (that is, skilled, blue-collar workers) and other "forgotten Americans" was back in fashion: people should work for what they get, not have it handed to them on a silver platter. As George Meany, head of the AFL-CIO noted in 1969, labor union members were "becoming middle class." "When you have no property, you don't have anything, you have nothing to lose by these radical actions. But when you become a person who has a home and has property, to some extent you become conservative. And I would say to that extent, labor has become conservative."

Liberal Democrats, distressed by the conservative swing of the electorate, attempted to turn it to their advantage by attacking the privileged tax position of the rich and of corporations. Ralph Nader and other consumer advocates crusaded against the degeneracy of American business, as shown both by shoddy automobiles and by excessive profits. George McGovern wanted to soak the rich and give not only to the poor but to everybody else. His panaceas violated the modernist precepts and resulted in his complete repudiation (Doc. 31). Furthermore, McGovern's belief in the necessity of bigger and bigger government had become increasingly unpopular. In 1972, 60 percent of the citizens who considered themselves conservatives felt that government was "too big." More startling was the fact that liberals were starting to share this view. In 1964, only 25 percent of the liberals thought government was too big; by 1972, 57 percent thought so.

The people responded to the supercharged atmosphere of the late 1960s and early 1970s with cynicism and apathy. Americans heard new scandals every day; the Watergate episode was only the most dramatic. The media caught the mood by sending the brightest reporters to dig up every example of wrongdoing or impropriety they could find. Jimmy Carter, elected in 1976 as an outsider untarnished by the corruption of Washington, was himself embarrassed by the indiscretions of his "Georgia mafia." Bert Lance, Carter's closest aide, was hounded out of Washington within a few months. Voter turnout fell to historic lows as more and more people decided that all politicians were basically corrupt and that government inherently involved a gigantic waste of money (Doc. 33).

By the late 1970s there were signs that voters' distrust of government was so strong that they would rouse themselves from lethargy by a new form of politics, the grass-roots tax revolt. A forgotten reform of the Progressive era was the initiative, through which the people could make policy directly, without going through politicians. Tax revolts first appeared in local school bond referenda, when taxpayers suddenly stopped voting for bigger school budgets. Politicians ignored the simmering protest until 1978, when by a huge majority the California electorate slashed property taxes (Doc. 34). Suddenly in every state similar tax revolt movements appeared, threatening to chop away at the financial basis of local and state governments. Politicians hurriedly changed their tone, announcing themselves as genuine devotees of lower budgets. Nowhere was the overnight transformation more startling than in California, where liberal Democratic Governor Jerry Brown changed from bitter foe of "reckless" tax cuts to their most earnest champion.

Taxes, in fact, had grown only very slightly faster than the overall economy between 1960 and 1983. Government employment, including the military, had grown from 15 percent of the labor force in 1960, to 18 percent in 1970, then levelled off. But most of the cutbacks were at the federal level; state and local employment doubled between 1960 and 1977, while the labor force only grew by one third. Worse, the productivity of government seemed to be lagging: people paid more money to more people and felt they received less in return. The bureaucracy and insensitivity of government became ever more galling. The incumbency factor seemed to make elections hopeless as a way to reform the system. As a leader of the citizens' lobby Common Cause complained in 1973, "In Congress today we have neither a Democratic nor a Republican party. Rather we have an incumbent party which operates a monopoly." As civil service workers formed unions, went on strike regardless of disruption, and demanded higher salaries than the private sector paid, voters concluded that "public service" was no longer a noble ideal and no longer needed to be tolerated. How effective the tax revolts will prove to be is hard to predict. This author suspects that the political power of the postal, teachers', police, fire, and other public unions will be more lasting than grass-roots protests. In sum, he fears that government will grow more powerful, more autonomous, and less democratic in every decade for the forseeable future.

Despite the decline in voting, a new form of grass roots participation in politics began in the 1970s: cash contributions to parties, pressure groups, and ideological causes. Richard Viguerie, a leader of the new right, discovered in the late 1960s the secret of inducing millions of Americans to part with $10 or $100—direct mail. Massive data banks holding millions of names and addresses are sorted by computer and a "personalized" letter is sent out wholesale to people who have shown some interest in the cause or who might be interested. Sent over the signature of some prominent spokesperson, the tone of the letter is countercrusading: the "enemy" is on the verge of victory and only an outpouring of support from true believers can save the day! Send $20 or America as you know it won't be here tomorrow! While only 1 or 2 percent of the recipients actually send cash back (and their names are very carefully recorded for future use), all the readers receive a message that is much more compelling than a television commercial, for it is private and, if the sorting was done well, deals urgently with a matter of grave concern.

Conservative causes, especially opposition to gun control and to abortion, have proven quite successful in direct mail appeals, although environmental causes also do well. (See maps 2 and 3). Likewise, the Republican party has far more mail contributors than the Democratic. (See maps 4 and 5).

Is direct mail a manipulative threat to democracy or an extension of grass roots activism? The senders have discovered that they cannot change people's minds, but that they can manipulate emotions and activate the citizen's impulse to have a say in public affairs. The causes that actually do have mass support are the ones that flourish; unpopular appeals will not even pay the postage. (It should be emphasized that most of the money that comes in has to be used to cover the cost of the mailings.) As party loyalties continue to fade away, we can expect that direct appeals through the mailbox will grow in number and importance.

Map 2

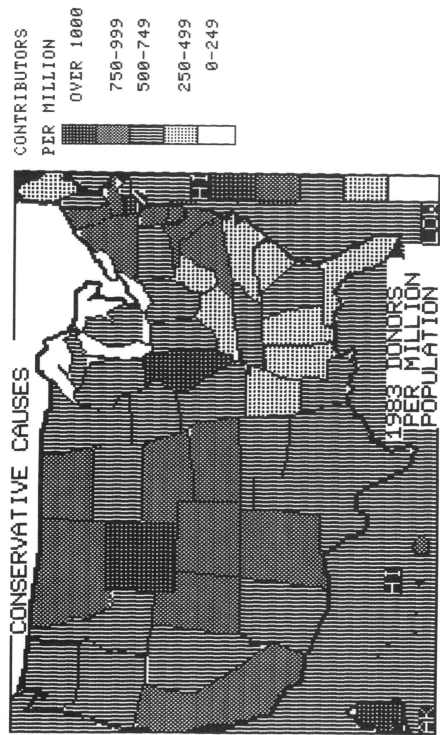

CONSERVATIVE CAUSES

CONTRIBUTORS
PER MILLION

OVER 1000

750-999

500-749

250-499

0-249

1983 DONORS
PER MILLION
POPULATION

Source: Hugo Dunhill Mailing List, Inc., 1983 catalog.

Map 3

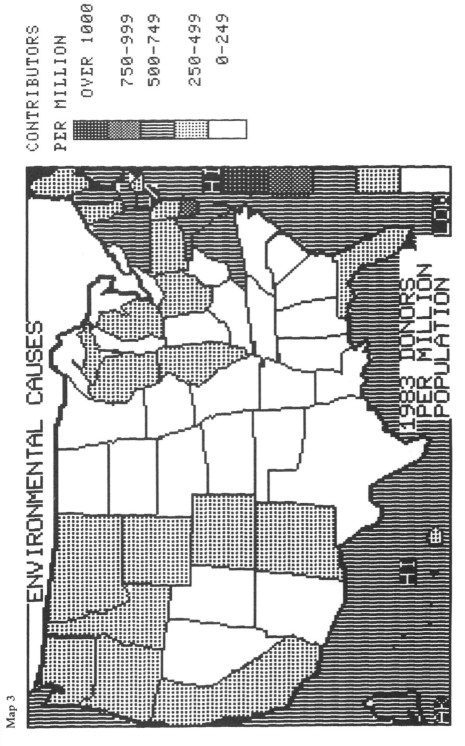

ENVIRONMENTAL CAUSES

CONTRIBUTORS
PER MILLION

OVER 1000
750-999
500-749
250-499
0-249

1983 DONORS
PER MILLION
POPULATION

Source: Hugo Dunhill Mailing List, Inc., 1983 catalog.

25

Map 4

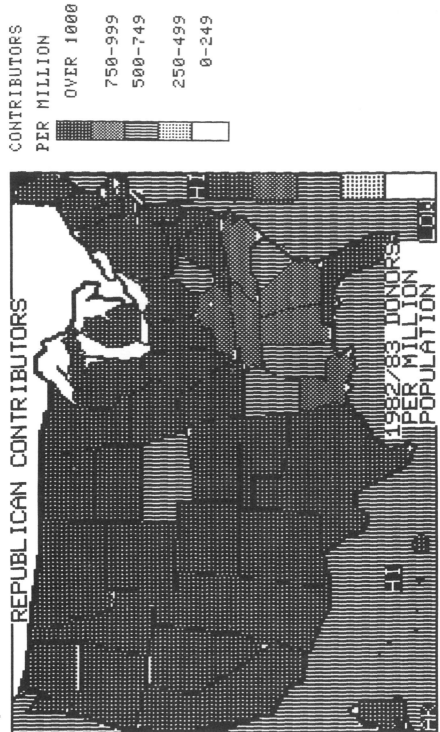

REPUBLICAN CONTRIBUTORS

CONTRIBUTORS
PER MILLION

OVER 1000

750-999

500-749

250-499

0-249

1982/83 DONORS
PER MILLION
POPULATION

Source: Hugo Dunhill Mailing List, Inc., 1983 catalog.

Map 5

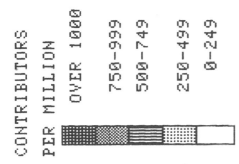

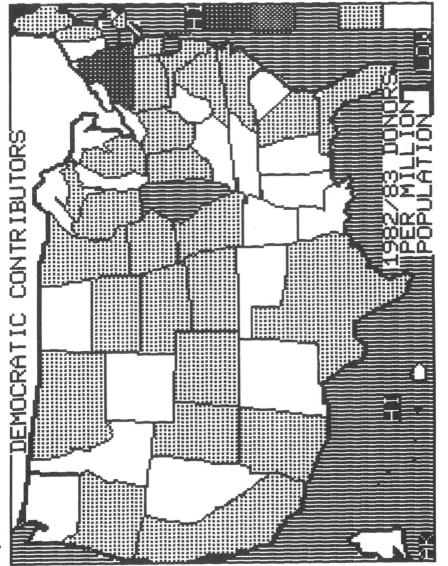

Source: Hugo Dunhill Mailing List, Inc., 1983 catalog.

27

II

THE POLITICAL PARTY: FROM TRADITIONAL TO MODERN BASE

Nineteenth-Century Party Organization

Few American achievements of the nineteenth century overshadowed the invention of the modern political party. The decrepit relics of today barely suggest the enthusiasm unleashed, the loyalty kindled, and the organizational revolution accomplished by the parties that emerged in the early nineteenth century. Of course, "parties" in the sense of loose groupings of politicians had existed everywhere in the eighteenth century. They were traditional organizations, built upon deference (that is, on loyalty to powerful and rich families) and incapable of permanently mobilizing the total population to take stands on great national issues.

The Jeffersonians, beginning in the late 1790s, invented modern organizational techniques to mobilize the electorate. The Federalists, too beholden to the idea that only gentlemen should involve themselves in affairs of state, limped far behind. By 1820, however, the Jeffersonian party faced a disorganized, demobilized opposition. It became consequently little more than a clique of officeholders, setting the stage for a new outburst of party-building in the late 1820s and early 1830s.

The party builders of the 1830s were modern organizers. Some, like General Andrew Jackson, knew how to raise and lead armies. Others, like Martin Van Buren, were adept at coordinating the work of thousands of local politicians and officeholders into a political army that could vanquish any foe on election day. They could run the affairs of government with discipline and dispatch.

Despite a lingering sense of loss at the decline of deference, and the replacement of aristocratic gentlemen by coldly efficient operators, the Whigs emerged with a counterforce that battled the Democrats on even terms throughout the 1840s. By the 1850s, however, a combination of democratic reforms, which further reduced the scope of deference in politics (notably, the direct election of judges), and the upsurge in modernistic reform move-ments (prohibition, nativism, and antislavery) ripped the Whigs apart.

In 1854 emerged a new movement, dedicated to social and economic modernization — the Republican party. From that year to the early twen-tieth century, two great parties mobilized the electorate with all the tech-niques of elaborate discipline, communication networks, and attention to detail that a modern organization could possibly muster (Doc. 1). Paradoxi-cally, while the techniques were modern, and the leading politicians were skilled organization men (usually with experience as army officers, editors, lawyers, or corporate businessmen), the voters they appealed to were basically traditional. Nearly all the rank and file of the Democratic party were traditionalists, and easily accepted the loyalty and discipline de-manded of them. Republican voters, as we have seen in chapter one, were psychologically more modern in outlook. They saw their party as the engine of modernization in society and gave their support to it as long as it pursued that goal. When the GOP began to veer toward traditionalism, signalled by corruption and bossism, the rank-and-file Republicans showed a willingness to revolt, most notably in 1912.

In terms of formal organization charts, today's parties closely resemble those of a century ago. Only a few rules of the game have changed (voter registration, primary elections). Each level of government, from precinct to the nation as a whole, was paralleled by a party formation.

Save in presidential campaigns, when the national organization stole the spotlight (if nothing else), the most powerful unit from the 1830s to the 1930s was the state organization, followed by the county. At each level the ruling body was the party convention. At the precinct level, self-declared partisans gathered to elect delegates to ward or township conventions, which in turn selected county, district, and state delegates. Four times in five, conventions were quiet, routine affairs without conflict (Doc. 5). Occasionally they provided a background for opposing party factions. Once in a great while, they were suddenly taken over by organized pressure groups intent on forcing their views or their candidate on a reluctant party. Thus prohibitionists swarmed some GOP local conventions in the 1880s, as did anti-Catholics in the 1890s. George McGovern used the same technique to win the 1972 Democratic nomination, as he copied Goldwater's precinct-by-precinct takeover of the GOP in 1964 (Doc. 31). Standing committees, selected by the conventions, ran party affairs on a monthly basis in quiet times or on a daily basis during campaigns. Conventions were responsible for nominating appropriate candidates (in the twentieth century, primary elections usually do this) and writing the platform (state platforms still are written, though nobody reads them anymore). The party committee was responsible for fund raising, communications, getting out the vote, and parcelling out the patronage if the party won, or blaming somebody else if it lost.

At election time leaders of each nineteenth-century party could count on the active work — say, 10 or 15 hours a week — of 2 to 5 percent of the adult male population: that is the equivalent today of all American golfers, tennis players, and skiers devoting all their recreation time to party work and enjoying it just as much. Half or more of the population were interested spectator-participants at speeches, rallies, picnics, and parades. That is the equivalent today of all the summer visitors to zoos, fairs, amusement parks, and outdoor sports events put together, with pleasure drivers added in!

The reasons party workers displayed so much enthusiasm were twofold: traditional devotion to party and, more concretely, rich patronage rewards (Doc. 5). Historians have yet to estimate the total amount of patronage available in the nineteenth century, but it was enormous. The federal government alone provided one patronage position per hundred voters or so, and state and local governments must have provided nearly as many. A typical patronage prize was a federal postmastership or a job as a city policeman or school principal. The postmastership required very little work (they did not *deliver* the mail in those days, you had to pick it up yourself), but even for a small city, it paid about five times what a full time factory-worker earned, and more than most doctors, lawyers, or railroad executives earned. The best five hundred or so patronage jobs — like consul at Liverpool, or clerk of the county court in Denver — paid more than all but the wealthiest factory *owners* or railroad presidents earned. And usually the work was performed by an assistant. Most *elected* offices, except for sheriff, paid far less, but still more than a hard-working professional man earned. Obviously the demand for patronage was high. Officeholders rotated rapidly — four years at the public trough was considered the norm. So effective was the system that tens of thousands of men clamored for the opportunity to electioneer. The parties never lacked for workers; indeed, one suspects that the great frequency of elections was a response to the surplus supply of talent ambitious to establish a claim on the spoils of victory (Doc. 7).

While the officeholder enjoyed most of his income (no income taxes, or sales taxes either!), a large fraction of the salary and a good deal of time, was routinely channelled back to the party. The Republicans and Democrats were almost completely self-financed. Candidates for office did not have to be rich to run, as their campaigns were paid for by the party. Until the end of the nineteenth century, there was little need to approach wealthy "angels," rich businessmen, or special interest groups to raise funds. There were plenty of scandals in the nineteenth century, but rarely did they involve efforts to buy candidates, or extort money from defenseless businessmen. In the cities, contractors kicked back profits to the machine, but that was basically a return of patronage money (Doc. 2).

American politics in the nineteenth century was thus publicly financed in effect, though not by law. Reformers bitterly protested that public moneys, raised by taxes, should be spent only for legitimate government purposes (Doc. 4). Efficiency in government was incompatible with excessive spending on superfluous patronage jobs and with the policy of appointing men on the basis of their party standing rather than their competence to do the job. After President Garfield was assassinated by a crazed office seeker in 1881, Congress passed a modest federal civil service law, thanks to the demands of reformers and the votes of Democratic congressmen who wanted to drain the patronage reservoirs of the GOP. (In 1893 the popular mayor of Chicago was assassinated by another disappointed man, as was the mayor of San Francisco in 1978. No reforms followed either event.) Civil service, itself a modernizing scheme, would have had little effect, except that the presidential elections of 1884, 1888, 1892, and 1896 each reversed the party in control of the executive branch, and each outgoing president froze thousands of his appointees by irreversibly extending civil service coverage to them. By 1900 half of federal jobs were outside the patronage network, and Congress saved a little money by letting their salaries slip behind the rising cost of living. Thus federal patronage largely disappeared as a major inducement to party workers. Simultaneously, states and localities began to adopt civil service, though several states (Pennsylvania and Indiana) and large cities (Chicago and Philadelphia) maintained very large patronage markets into the late twentieth century.

At first glance it might seem that lucrative nineteenth-century patronage would have the effect of boosting one party or the other into an unassailable position, as victory produced patronage that in turn generated more victories. The last link of the chain did not hold, however. Patronage had the curious effect of weakening the winning party, making it less rather than more likely to win the next election. Candidates invariably promised more rewards than they could deliver, no matter at what level. Presidents-elect spent the four months between the November election and the March inauguration trying to pacify the hundred men who thought they deserved a cabinet portfolio and the thousand who felt they merited an ambassadorship. The world lacked enough countries to go around. Secession crisis or no, Lincoln too focused mostly on the distribution of patronage to Republicans, who looked eagerly on all those Democratic jobs. Southern conviction that Lincoln's patronage appointees in their states would form the nucleus of an antislavery party hurried the process of secession. Bloody civil war only occurred once over patronage, but in tens of thousands of instances victorious local parties fell prey to feuding, factionalism, and frustration when they learned there simply was not enough gravy for every potato. The sharp drop in morale that resulted weakened the winner's chances at the next election, while all the opposition worked feverishly for their fair share of spoils. Since party workers dealt chiefly with their own partisan rank and file and read only very biased party newspapers, they always expected victory. Even if defeat was likely, exaggerated expectations of the patronage rewards that would result from eventual success spurred on the workers year in and year out. The patronage system was chronically in disequilibrium, facilitating frequent changes in party control and avoiding the twentieth-century tendency toward routine reelection of incumbents. Essentially, the selfish demands of the more traditional lower echelon of party workers frustrated any movement toward efficient, long-range planning on the part of the more modern high elected officials. Governors and presidents could not easily modernize government or society as long as they owed massive patronage rewards to the men who got them elected.

The highly organized nineteenth-century parties thought of themselves as armies going into battle on election day against an opposing army, with patronage as the spoils of victory (Doc. 7). The metaphor was natural in the antebellum era when most civilians were enrolled in militia units that elected their own officers who, likely as not, were politicians. Andrew Jackson gave up a seat in the United States Senate to become general of the Tennessee militia — in peacetime — and Lincoln's first leadership role came when he engineered his election as captain of a motley Illinois militia unit in the Black Hawk War. Most decisive was the Civil War itself, which demonstrated the efficacy of a disciplined military organization in uniting the efforts of thousands of men to a single goal.

In the political armies, the candidates were line officers, party functionaries were staff officers, lowly workers were precinct "captains," and the average voters comprised the rank and file. So intense and widespread was partisanship that nearly every voter considered himself enrolled in one army or the other, with less than 10 percent either independent, soldiers in a third party, or "mercenaries" whose votes were for sale. Successful armies require not only discipline but high morale. The function of giant parades, complete with uniformed bands and marching units, banners, flags, shouts, and long-winded speechfests, was to instill confidence in the rank and file by the visual and aural experience of being an integral part of a united and invincible movement that would inevitably crush the enemy (which was holding its own parades and picnics across town) (Doc. 14).

The army metaphor had further implications with direct bearing on how the country was governed. As long as the officers (candidates) were minimally qualified to hold government posts, their names and personalities were of secondary importance. The traditionalistic electorate was urged to vote loyally for the party, not for the man. Since the demand for elective offices was so high, few men were renominated more than once. After a term or two the vast majority of legislators voluntarily retired to let their fellow partisans have a turn in office. Voters seldom had a chance to judge the effectiveness of the men in government; at best, they could evaluate the party. Except where special constituency interests were involved, legislators routinely followed the party line, and rare was the maverick who so delights the modern voter (Doc. 5).

Strong internal communications were vital to army-style parties, and they met the challenge in the 1830s with a brilliant invention, the mass circulation newspaper. Every partisan who could read (nearly all could in the North) subscribed to a weekly (for farmers, and inhabitants of small towns) or a daily (for city dwellers). Even though the population was much smaller, newspapers proliferated far more then than now. In the 1880s, the ten thousand families of Dayton, Ohio, could select from among four daily and twenty-two weekly papers published locally. The three thousand families of Pottsville, Pennsylvania, could choose among three dailies and seven weeklies. To be sure, competition was not as high as it seems. Each paper focused on a specialized clientele. There were papers that catered to some combination of Republicans or Democrats, middle or working class people, city folks or farmers, English language or foreign speakers; and, in bigger cities, the larger factions inside each party sponsored their own papers. Most little towns of two hundred or more families had at least their own weekly newspaper. Circulations were small but the variety was remarkable. The low costs of operating a paper with one or two employees and a circulation of one thousand or two thousand made feasible five to ten thousand newspapers in a county with ten million voters. The real explanation for the remarkable development of mass media *before* advertising became the dominant factor was politics.

The nineteenth-century newspaper was a party organ. The parties sponsored the newspapers. They solicited subscriptions, contracted party printing, funnelled public contracts to the printshop, and occasionally covered losses. In return, the editor filled his columns with long political speeches, full texts of platforms, announcements of meetings, full coverage of rallies, details on the comings and goings of state senators, county chairmen, coroners, and other men of moment, and, above all, a stream of unqualified editorials glorifying the triumph of the party and warning of the treachery of the enemy. In a word, the newspapers fastened onto the traditional loyalties of the electorate. The news was biased, every bit of it, to the delight of red-hot partisans, who learned about the dismal turnout that humiliated the opposition while their own rally filled the largest hall to the rafters. The party did no wrong and was ever on the verge of a smashing victory. When victory came, the editors sang the praises of the God-fearing voters, Lincolnesque candidates (or Jackson-like, as the case may be), and farsighted, time-honored party principles. If perchance the late returns showed reverses, evil was afoot, the ballot boxes had been stuffed, unscrupulous mercenaries had sold their votes, or the rains were unnaturally heavy downstate. Not for two weeks did Republican readers of the prestigious *New York Tribune* learn that their man Blaine had lost in 1884 — and that sad news came in an interview with Blaine himself (Doc. 2, 5).

Blaine, like many leading politicians, began his career as an editor. Next to the county chairman, the party editors had the most honored roles in the army staff. The troops waited for the morning paper to learn how the enemy was to be ruined today, his arguments torn apart, his silly programs ridiculed. If the weekly *New York Tribune* did not arrive on time, a Republican farmer in upstate New York would be speechless around the hot stove in the village store (Doc. 10). Better he should repair his chicken coop.

Twentieth-Century Party Organization

Modern parties are pale reflections of their ancestors. What was cause and what was effect is still debated, but so many conditions drastically changed that no other outcome was possible. First, and most basic, partisan loyalty declined and the most traditionalist voters lost interest in politics. Politics became the arena of the modern voter. Second, civil service and the declining pay and prestige of patronage jobs undercut the motivation for active precinct work and corporations took over the financing of campaigns (Doc. 11, 15). Third, the newspapers abandoned their party roles. Fourth, the Progressive movement changed the rules of politics to undercut the party organization and upgrade the power of the independent voter. And finally, politicians adopted new campaign techniques that no longer required disciplined armies to win.

Beginning in about 1900, interest in politics began a sharp decline, partially reversed in the 1930s, but then resuming again. At the national level, the Republicans from 1896 to 1928, had such a preponderance of strength that presidential contests and most state races, for that matter, were usually foregone conclusions. The thrill of a close contest was increasingly found in baseball, boxing, or football, not politics. The decline in interest appears most graphically in turnout rates (Chart 1). In the 1890s in a dozen states, at least 90 percent of the eligible men voted. From 1952 through 1982, turnout averaged only 59 percent in presidential elections, and 42 percent in off-year congressional elections. The trend was downward, so that in 1980 only 54 percent voted, and in 1982 only 35 percent—two out of three adults simply did not bother to vote (Doc. 33). Having easy registration laws (and, perhaps, a native-son candidate on the national ticket) helps some. In 1976 Minnesota had its Senator Walter Mondale running for vice-president plus election-day registration. Seventy-one percent voted, the highest turnout in the country. Georgia boasted of its Jimmy Carter on the ballot, and registering there was as easy as getting a dog license (and free), but only 42 percent bothered to vote. Nationwide today, about three-fourths of eligible voters are registered to vote. Of those registered, three-fourths vote in presidential elections and only half in off-year elections.

Alienation from the status quo or cynicism about politicians seems not to have been the basic cause of turnout decline in the early twentieth century, (see chart 1) for people who knew enough about what was happening to be unhappy about it usually did register and vote. More likely, politics was seen as irrelevant or too confusing for a traditionalist to understand. The better educated, more modern voter, on the other hand, remained interested and came to dominate the twentieth-century electorate.

Under the army style, most people found politics the best entertainment in town. More important, they understood more of what was happening. The old-style politicians realized that the way to keep a voter loyal and active was to feed him with information, regale him with highly technical three hour speeches, and drill into him the principles involved (Doc. 8). The propaganda was biased of course, but the bias consisted of imposing on current events a framework for evaluating the goodness and badness of government action. Straight news is bland, unpalatable for traditional, poorly educated people who cannot follow the complexity of events well enough to figure out which action is right and which wrong. Local television stations today understand this principle, and feed viewers crime, fires, personalities, sports, and happy talk. The only analogue today to the devoted partisan of the nineteenth century who devoured political detail is the sports fan who, regardless of how little schooling he has, loves the game, knows all the players and their performance records, and roots avidly for his team. Today the sports pages are the most colorful, informative, and technically detailed part of every newspaper.

The newspapers abandoned their party role at the turn of the century, when publishers like Hearst and Pulitzer (both expoliticians) discovered that the route to fabulous profits was to go after huge circulations, which would bring in advertising revenue that was far more lucrative than political patronage. To reach a mass audience, the big-city press abandoned partisanship and began offering entertainment and shopping news. Sex, sports, and sensationalism, together with Ann Landers, comics, crosswords, fashions, and horoscopes sell more papers than the text of a governor's message. Today's newspapers, with five or ten times as much space as the four- to eight-page papers of a century ago, devote, at best, half the space that was once given to political news, no matter how vital it is. The news they do report, furthermore, usually comes from sanitized AP or UPI wires, completely devoid of partisanship.

As more and more citizens cast off their traditional partisan loyalties and casually drifted in and out of the active electorate, politicians realized that parties could no longer simply rally an army on election day and win a victory. The candidate had to sell himself to the voters directly—to merchandize his availability the way stores competed for customers. Early rumblings of the merchandizing style emerged late in the nineteenth century, and by 1920 it had largely replaced the army style, except in big cities (Doc. 17).

Chart 1

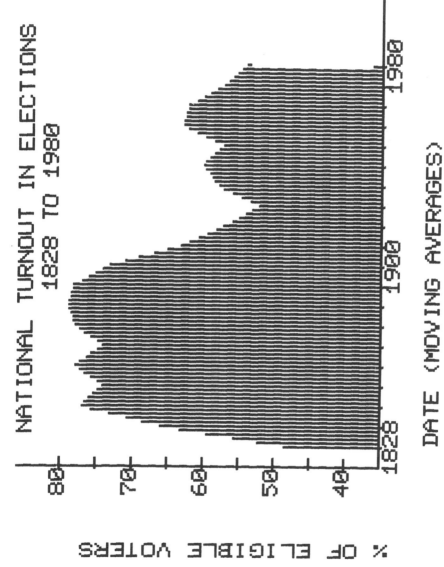

NATIONAL TURNOUT IN ELECTIONS 1828 TO 1980

% OF ELIGIBLE VOTERS

80 70 60 50 40

1828 1900 1980

DATE (MOVING AVERAGES)

Source: U.S. Bureau of the Census, *Historical Statistics of the United States* (Washington, 1976), and U.S. Bureau of the Census, *Statistical Abstract 1983* (Washington, 1983).

Advertising as a way of persuasion sold some soap and biscuits before the First World War, when it was drafted to sell the American people on President Wilson's war aims, to move billions of dollars of war bonds, and to conserve food. It worked, and ever since no American has been safe from Madison Avenue. The Republican National Committee engineered an advertising campaign to elect congressional candidates in 1918 and Harding in 1920. By then sharp candidates were already using paid commercials (movie shorts shown between feature films), direct mail, and even comic books. The Kinsey Institute found a 1944 pornographic comic book warning Ohio factory workers that Republican Senator Taft would molest their wives; the workers, however, decided to send Taft back to Washington. The first serious use of radio was to merchandize candidates, and television followed as soon as people had sets in the early 1950s. Unlike the nineteenth-century speech, in which an army commander would rally just his own troops, a radio or TV speech is beamed to everyone. The electronic media are not effective at disseminating complicated ideas, but they can reassure the audience that the candidate is an articulate foe of waste, a happy family man, and withal their best hope—and they do it in 60 seconds between a deodorant ad and a "shoot-em-up" (Doc. 27).

Candidates running on their own seldom furl themselves in the party banner. They need independent and opposition party voters, so they deemphasize issues, stress their personal qualifications, and saturate the media just before the election. Most television commercials, it should be noted, sell not expensive and valuable items like suits, furniture, or houses, but cheap, disposable frills like toothpaste, beer, cola, and aspirin. Since TV time and direct mail is extremely expensive, and since party coffers no longer are filled with patronage kickbacks, candidates must raise their own money from family, friends, and special interests who need access to government. It is remarkable that more scandals over fund raising have not occurred—even the scandals of the 1972 Nixon fund raisers drew far less attention than the Watergate escapade and cover-up.

Merchandizing politics affected government through the rise of special interest groups and through the professionalization of politics. In the nineteenth century most officeholders were amateurs who served a term or two and retired. That type is still prevalent in the suburbs, but in Congress and many legislatures, the career professional has become dominant. In Congress the change dates from the Progressive era, when a systematic effort to undermine army-style parties occurred. This was carried out by efforts to establish direct election of senators, direct primaries, initiative, referendum, recall, woman suffrage (to get pure voters), stiff literacy tests (to remove foreigners), registration laws (to stop election fraud), and prohibition (to banish saloon power from politics and allow voters to think soberly). Some of the congressional reforms intended to undercut tight party control were the reduction of the power of the speaker (a party man), an increase of power in the hands of committees, and strengthening of the seniority system. The result was that power in Congress fell to men with seniority, regardless of their party loyalty. Progressives like George Norris, Robert LaFollette, William Borah, and Hiram Johnson used the new seniority system brilliantly to undercut the force of party discipline and reorient the political spectrum from conflict between Republicans and Democrats to liberals versus conservatives. Southern conservatives, however, proved even more alert than northern liberals and, from the New Deal to the mid-1970s, controlled the major committees most of the time.

Today nothing succeeds like success in politics. Incumbents with two or three terms to enhance voter recognition are virtually invulnerable to defeat, even if the opposition candidates for other offices sweep in by a landslide. In elections since 1960, only 10 percent of incumbent congressmen were defeated for reelection. Ticket-splitting, obviously, is the explanation. Rare in the nineteenth century (partly because secret ballots were seldom used before 1890, but mostly because of the overwhelming strength of party loyalty), ticket-splitting is the norm today and grows more widespread every year. In 1972, for example, 42 percent of the congressional districts in the country voted Republican for president but Democratic for Congress. That year only 38 percent of the electorate voted a straight party ticket, while 62 percent voted for some Republicans and some Democrats. In the 1940s and 1950s, by contrast, about two-thirds of the voters cast straight one-party ballots.

By shaking thousands of hands, acting as ombudsman for his little constituents and as advocate before the federal bureaucracy for his powerful friends, and taking credit for every grant to his district, the incumbent congressman can easily build a secure bailiwick until retirement, largely immune to the whirligig of national swings (Doc. 29).

Politics has always been an expensive business (Doc. 11). Between 1952 and 1972, the total cost of all the campaigns for all the elective offices in the country rose from $140 million to $425 million. Yet, after taking inflation, the size of the economy, and the number of voters into account, the relative cost changed very little (from 42 cents out of every $1,000 in GNP in 1952 to 36 cents per $1,000 in 1972). Indeed, the relative costs had been about the same in 1896. Looked at another way, the cost of filling some 540 national offices, 13,000 seats in state legislatures, and 500,000 posts at the local level averages out to about two dollars per man, woman, and child per year.

Yet in many cases the costs are remarkably high. In 1978 Republican Senator Jesse Helms of North Carolina raised $6 million for his reelection campaign and ran a deficit! Twenty other state candidates across the country spent over a million dollars each. In 1982 the governor of Texas was defeated for reelection, and in 1983 the mayor of Chicago was defeated, despite campaign treasuries of over $10 million (Doc. 38). What accounts for these huge budgets? The merchandizing candidate must run his or her own campaign independently of party organizations, which in most states are too weak to do the effective job they once did. Smart candidates hire campaign consultants from New York or Los Angeles who advise on public opinion surveys, fund-raising, advertising, media coverage, policy research, and recruitment of volunteers (Doc. 30). They will tell a candidate how to dress, where to speak, and, if he is unsure of himself, what to say. Advertising is enormously expensive, since a single professional sixty-second commercial might cost $50,000 to prepare and several thousand dollars every time it is repeated on the air (Doc. 27). A series of commercials in a large state can easily cost hundreds of thousands of dollars. In West Virginia in 1978 Senator Jennings Randolph spent a quarter of a million dollars on TV commercials and won; in California the Republican candidate for governor that year spent nearly $2 million for TV and lost. Salaries for staff aides, speech writers, publicity experts, and local organizers, plus their telephone, airplane, and hotel bills, mount up rapidly. Raising the money to pay these expenses is itself very expensive. Senator Helms spent most of his $6 million to send out tens of millions of letters to conservatives around the country just asking for the money! Four times out of five the candidate who spends more money wins — but he is usually the incumbent to begin with, and therefore has easier access to generous contributions from all sorts of interest groups. Anyone challenging an incumbent needs a huge campaign budget just to become known and to neutralize the incumbent's years of free media publicity.

Congress wrestled with numerous campaign reform proposals in the 1970s. Beginning in 1976, the *presidential* nominating conventions and campaigns of both major parties became publicly financed. This will avoid future scandals such as clouded Nixon's 1972 campaign. It will also help the Democrats a little more than the Republicans, for the GOP previously had access to more cash. However, Congress refused to impose limits on spending in *congressional* campaigns or to pay for those campaigns out of the Treasury. Otherwise, challengers to incumbents would have had a hopeless time winning; as it stands now, they merely have a remote chance.

The Big-City Machine

Our analysis of merchandizing politics applies to most of twentieth-century America except for two outstanding bastions of traditionalism, the big-city machines and the solid South. In the cities army styles remained feasible much longer, for the largely traditional inner-city inhabitants are poor and need help (Doc. 21). Patronage jobs may seem worthless to the suburbanite, but they can mean a great deal to poor blacks, Chicanos, and Puerto Ricans. A city administration more interested in votes than in efficiency, business interests eager for special tax assessments or city-hall contracts, and a large voting population too poor to flee to the suburbs was the formula for the modern big-city machine. Furthermore, the appeal of party loyalty can still be strong for traditional ethnic and racial groups, composed largely of poorly educated manual workers, unemployed men, and welfare mothers (Doc. 38).

City machines developed in the nineteenth century, as soon as municipal spending was sufficient to provide enough patronage so that the politicians did not have to rely on state and federal largesse. Nearly every city of one hundred thousand qualified, as did many smaller ones. Invariably the machines built their voting power on poor, traditionally oriented groups, usually immigrants and blacks. Either party could play the game, though the Democrats did it best (except in Philadelphia, which was controlled by Republicans until the 1940s).

The basic unit in machine politics was the ward. The ward boss, orchestrating his votes by means of precinct captains on the public payroll, had his man in the city council and the state legislature, where coalitions could be formed with other bosses (Doc. 22). The modern middle-class wards, invariably hostile to machine politics, typically supported a reform candidate for mayor; but even if elected he rarely could overcome the machine coalition in the city council. Modernizing reform was possible only after ending ward representation in favor of city-wide elections, a cherished goal of the Progressive movement (Doc. 18).

In the machine wards, politics was particularistic – focusing on jobs, welfare, city contracts, little favors, inside tips, and help for people in trouble with the authorities. Issues as such were irrelevant – except for prohibition, which traditional Catholic voters bitterly opposed. The newspapers that propounded modernizing virtues were unread in the tenements. Authority instead rested with the local politicians, priests, petty businessmen, and pimps. The saloons provided the natural milieu for machine politics, and their closing in 1920 watered down machine power. (You could get a drink in a speakeasy, but hardly hold regular meetings there.) The millions of immigrants pouring into the cities in the late-nineteenth and early-twentieth century provided more than enough replacement votes for the modernized second and third generations that grew up and moved to more prosperous neighborhoods. The machines were corrupt and inefficient by middle-class standards and often subject to criminal control. Nevertheless they did serve the useful function of cushioning a little the transition of traditional European peasants encountering the rich, baffling, modern world.

The modernist middle class bitterly fought machine politics (Doc. 20). First, the corruption and excessive patronage generated high taxes, inefficiency, and unresponsive bureaucracies. At a deeper level, the corruption and particularism of the machines violated the modern values of public honesty and impartial rule of law. All men should be treated alike, via fixed laws and disinterested judges and administrations. Whether or not the tax-payer actually lost money because of illegal speakeasies, kickbacks from contractors, or fixed traffic tickets, he was confronted with a government that bent the laws to favor special interests that often included the most depraved, criminal, and ignorant sectors of society. The suburb offered a haven for tender sensibilities, but was not economically feasible for most of the middle class until the rise of commuter suburbs after World War II.

Beginning at the turn of the century, middle-class progressives, anxious to cleanse government of corruption, waste, and blind partisanship, started working mightily to destroy city machines (Doc. 20). They are still at it, though most have fled to the suburbs. By the 1920s it seemed that progres-sivism was on the verge of triumph. Most cities of twenty-five thousand or more abandoned partisan government in favor of city managers or commis-sioner forms and civil service (Doc. 18). Some traditional voting blocs, mostly Catholic, had either adopted middle-class norms or lapsed into apathy, thus draining off machine votes. Then came prohibition, and the machines discovered that they could mobilize the traditional spirit once more by demanding a return of beer, wine, and whiskey. In 1928, the can-didacy of Al Smith further boosted the power of predominantly Catholic machines. (In 1927 machine bosses in Chicago formed a permanent coali-tion, taking control for at least a half century of the Cook County Demo-cratic party, the city council, the county board, the mayor's office, most legislative and congressional seats, and all the patronage goodies.) The New Deal cooperated closely with machines (except FDR's old enemy, Tammany Hall in Manhattan), even so far as naming machine men to the rank of Democratic national chairman and vice-president (Truman). The technique was simple: Channel relief through the machines, and build up labor unions to cooperate with them (Doc. 24).

After World War II, the machines were in precarious balance, as their loss of newly modernized voters to the reform cause was neutralized by the exodus of reformers to the suburbs. The massive influx of traditional-minded poor blacks from the South did not at first accrue to the machine's benefit, because old-line Irish and Italian ward bosses hesitated to encour-age the blacks to vote. The result was that hundreds of black wards in the largest cities were controlled by white machine politicians, who often made handsome profits as urban renewal bulldozed the decrepit housing, while further disorganizing the black population.

Suddenly, in the mid-1960s, the lower-class blacks in virtually all the large northern cities (not in the South, for machines were weak there) revolted against the white machines. Perhaps they were angry because the new civil rights laws pushed through Congress with unanimous machine support were designed to help disfranchised southern blacks and middle-class northern blacks, who could afford good housing and could compete for middle-class jobs. There was nothing for lower-class northern blacks, and they unleashed their hostility by symbolic three-day riots that, for the first time, made their presence, plights, and power visible to all. (Unlike early race riots, in which whites and blacks battled one another in the streets, the riots of the 1960s consisted of arson and looting attacks on white-owned property. Most deaths that occurred were inflicted by white police or troops.)

The riots displaced the civil rights movement with the Black Power movement. Lower-class blacks began voting and demanded offices for other blacks. Soon Cleveland, Gary, Newark, Detroit, Atlanta, and Los Angeles had black mayors, together with militant congressmen, legislators, and councilmen. (However, in New York, where the old machine was weakest and the white power structure benevolent, there were no major riots and blacks won little power.) The emergence of powerful, traditionalistic black-controlled machines led by militant blacks working closely with their lower-class constituents became more and more likely as whites continued to migrate to the suburbs into the 1980s. The black revolt paid off not only in political power, but in vastly enlarged welfare programs and an increased share of government jobs (Doc. 29).

Representation of blacks in legislatures, city halls, county court houses, and on school boards soared from 603 in 1967 to 1,460 in 1970 and 5,200 in 1983 (map 6). Half of this representation was in the South. Black representation in Congress moved from zero between 1901 and 1928 to one between 1929 and 1944, two between 1945 and 1954, six in 1965, and twenty in 1983. The numbers are destined to increase, despite the stiff resistance of ethnic whites remaining in the central cities. With the upsurge in black power, voter turnout in the ghettos became nearly the same as in white areas, particularly in the South (Doc. 38). As a result, the old order of white supremacy finally crumbled in the South in the 1970s. Even former die-hard segregationists, like Senator Strom Thurmond of South Carolina and Governor George Wallace of Alabama, began to appeal to black voters with amazing success.

The One-Party South

Southern politics closely resembled the North until the eve of the Civil War. Defeated by "damn Yankees" on the battlefield and humiliated during Reconstruction, the white South reacted by creating a unique political culture, thoroughly traditional in style, that remained distinct into the 1960s.

With the outbreak of war, the Confederacy spontaneously abandoned partisan politics. Elections were held, to be sure, but party organizations vanished and partisan labels were not used. The idea was that a great national crisis of survival was no time for divisiveness; instead of petty squabbling among politicians, the new nation's leaders were expected to devote

Map 6

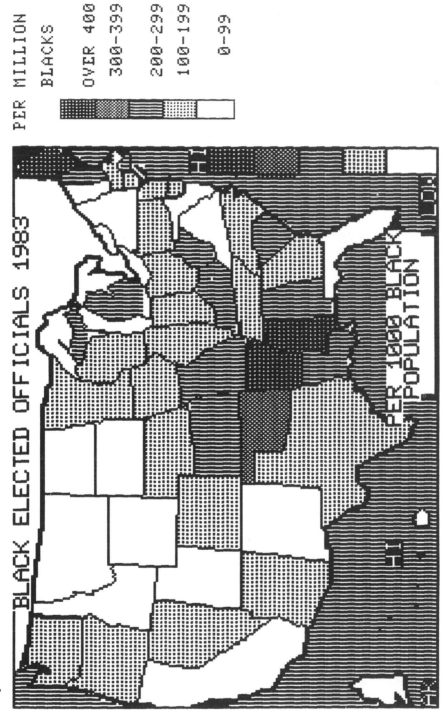

PER MILLION
BLACKS

OVER 400
300-399
200-299
100-199
0-99

BLACK ELECTED OFFICIALS 1983

PER 1000 BLACK POPULATION

Source: Hugo Dunhill Mailing List, Inc., 1983 catalog.

themselves exclusively to the public good. The Confederate Constitution facilitated nonpartisanship by limiting the president to one term, putting most jobs under civil service, and stripping Congress of patronage and pork-barrel opportunities. The North experimented briefly with bipartisan conduct of the war, then, realizing the advantages of parties, reverted to normalcy by 1862.

The strong Republican organization proved highly advantageous to the Union war effort, as local party leaders took the lead in recruiting companies and regiments of volunteers, thus guaranteeing their loyalty (the regular army was not trusted, and played a minor role in the war). Republican contractors made fortunes supplying munitions, food, horses, uniforms, transportation, and barracks for the army. Even more important, staunch support of Lincoln's war policies became mandatory for the rank and file. Without the commitment of Republican party loyalty behind the draft, emancipation, and the policy of unconditional victory, the North could not have sustained the heroic sacrifices entailed by total warfare against fellow Americans.

By contrast, the Confederacy suffered from its prematurely modern nonpartisanship. Without the whip of party loyalty to contain grumbling and discontent, Jefferson Davis's administration became the target of simmering hostility. Recruitment and fund raising became functions of individual willingness to make personal sacrifices for the survival of the new nation, leading to an unequal distribution of burdens. As the war progressed, the central administration relied more and more upon the army for support (and upon congressmen who represented districts overrun by Yankees and thus who were out of contact with their constituents). The Confederate central government found itself increasingly frustrated by state governors and legislatures not tied to Richmond by partisan loyalties. The upshot was that when the war did end, it was the Confederate army officer corps, represented by Robert E. Lee, and the opposition politicians who emerged as the undisputed leaders of the white South. Jefferson Davis not only lost the war, he lost the peace as well.

Victorious Republicans, however, were not reassured by Lee's surrender that the South had truly abandoned its rebel spirit. Slavery was abolished in name, though black codes soon reestablished a sort of quasi-slavery that deeply troubled Republicans who feared a subversion of their war aims. President Andrew Johnson compounded the contradiction by allowing ex-Confederates to control the new civilian governments he established. A final, true victory over the rebels necessitated equal civil rights for the freed blacks (thus permanently abolishing slavery) plus control of the South by loyal elements (thus exterminating all chances of a revival of Confederate nationalism). These goals were achieved by a series of reconstruction laws and constitutional amendments. They gave power in the South to a Republican coalition led by northern immigrants and loyal southerners ("carpetbaggers and scalawags," sneered the ex-Rebels), and based on the new black vote.

Radical reconstruction, which lasted an average of three to four years in the southern states, was an unstable amalgam of modernizing efforts in an intensely traditional society. Republican modernizers attempted to institute not only universal male suffrage, but also free public education, democratic representation, and Yankee business practices. An agrarian region economically devastated by war could not afford the reforms, either financially or psychologically. The highly traditional black voting base of the Republican coalition allied itself increasingly with spoilsmen, and when the blacks around 1870 began demanding their share of offices, the coalition was ready to fall apart. Conservative southerners, appealing to the traditional values of racial unity and white supremacy, lured away most white Republicans and in some areas began terrorizing the blacks. President Ulysses Grant's efforts to suppress Ku Kluxism finally wearied the North, which by 1874 was already convinced that slavery and rebellion were dead and that further federal intervention would only benefit corrupt regimes (Grant's included). Democratic victories in the 1874 election presaged a quick end to Reconstruction, which was finally achieved in 1877, when Rutherford Hayes was counted in as president after promising to withdraw the federal troops maintaining the last Republican regimes in the South. Hayes also tried to form a coalition with the modernizing whites (mostly ex-Whigs) in the South but was unable to do so when the overriding demand for white unity precluded the formation of a significant white Republican movement.

The end of Reconstruction did not itself produce segregation or drive all blacks out of politics. For another quarter century (to about 1900), blacks continued to vote and hold a few offices, although they had no real power and their economic condition steadily worsened. By the 1890s wealthy southern politicians came under heavy pressure from poor white agrarians, led by Thomas Watson, the Georgia Populist, and Ben Tillman, South Carolina Democrat. Undoubtedly the severe distress caused by low cotton and tobacco prices in the 1890s stimulated the agrarian revolt, but it also represented a turning away from the modernizing ideal, with its implications of industrialization, urbanization, and equal rights (Doc. 6).

Southern agrarianism in the 1890s took the form of vicious attacks on President Cleveland and his modernizing businessmen allies. "He's an old bag of beef," fumed Governor Tillman, "and I'm going to Washington with a pitchfork and prod him in his old fat ribs"—or so runs the bowdlerized version of what Tillman proposed to do. The poor farmers Tillman spoke for resented Cleveland's hard money policy that seemingly favored crafty bankers over honest farmers. The agrarian South, cooperating with agrarians and miners in the North, seized control of the Democratic party in 1896. But old-line southern politicians, hastily repudiating Cleveland, managed to defeat a traditionalist coalition of poor Populist farmers and black Republicans, leading to an uneasy stalemate in southern politics that lasted until the Progressive movement in the early years of the new century.

Southern Progressives, like their northern counterparts, were modernizers. Educators, clergymen, editors, lawyers, physicians, and middle-class businessmen united in a program to weed out traditionalist corruption (such as saloon power and, especially, the wholesaling of black votes to conservative planter-politicians), and to modernize the schools, prisons, roads, hygiene, and local governments of the South without undergoing the ordeals of forced industrialization. Disfranchisement of blacks and Jim Crow (legal segregation) were thus modernizing movements designed to "purify" politics by removing the blacks (and many poor, traditional whites as well), and to alleviate the culture of violence by separating the races legally. Jim Crow assigned very specific rules of behavior to both blacks and whites, permanently consigning blacks to an inferior, traditionalist role while concentrating public resources on the modernization of the white population.

The party structures of the solid South disintegrated under the blows of Progressivism. Although southern congressmen were staunch Democrats in Washington, they operated at home without benefit of party organization or even party labels (since all serious politicians were Democrats, outside of remote Appalachian areas). The one-party South effectively became the home of nonparty politics. Without party organizations or media to guide them, most white farmers and workers became apathetic, leaving a close balance in the active electorate between three forces: the conservative, traditional rich planters; the middle-class modernizers; and the remaining traditional poor farmers. These groupings provided the matrix for all politics in the South down to the 1960s.

Three basic political styles, all traditionalistic, emerged in the South: class-based factionalism, friends-and-neighbors free-for-alls, and full-scale machines. The class factions flourished in Mississippi and South Carolina, where demagogues rallied the poor "rednecks" and "crackers" against the plantation conservatives, and the middle classes providing stormy and (in Huey Long's Louisiana) bloody confrontations. In friends-and-neighbor systems (Texas, Arkansas, North Carolina), candidates by the dozen competed for office not so much on the basis of platforms as on personality. A network of courthouse friends and a good base at home propelled ambitious young men to office, while leaving the electorate in confusion about what was happening. In several states (Virginia, North Carolina, and Tennessee), a conservative machine managed to cement enough courthouse cliques into a winning machine, such as flourished in Harry Byrd's Virginia until the 1960s. In Louisiana, Huey Long built a machine based on patronage, strong arm power, ethnic white minorities, and poor white farmers; but he and his family heirs never quite completely controlled the state.

Black southerners never completely disappeared from politics. Many demagogues repeatedly claimed to be the only true white supremacists

(which they weren't), promising to maintain inviolate the traditional, subordinate role of the black man (which they did). Republicans never won
offices in the South (with a curious exception or two), but did play a large
role at national conventions. In 1912, for example, William Howard Taft
narrowly defeated Teddy Roosevelt's progressive Republicans by calling
upon black delegate support. Forty years later his son, Robert Taft, tried
the same tactic, but failed, for in Texas and elsewhere a new breed of
middle-class white Eisenhower supporter seized control of the moribund
state Republican organization. In 1964 Goldwaterites, the dominant force in
the South, removed the last of the black Republican leaders. Since then
southern blacks have cast 90 to 95 percent of their votes for the Democrats.

The 1928 election split the solid South. Hoover, the engineer-modernizer
par excellence, attracted not only the middle classes, but also the farmers
who saw Al Smith's Catholicism and opposition to prohibition as anathema
to their values. Only in the deep South, where plantation conservatives
supported Smith on the basis of white supremacy forever, did the New
Yorker gain electoral votes (Doc. 19).

In 1932, however, Franklin Roosevelt undid the damage of 1928, reunit-
ing the solidly Democratic South for another two decades. Roosevelt represented himself as a traditionalist trying to right the havoc Hoover's inept
engineering-style leadership had wreaked on the economy. Personally
sympathetic to southern traditions (including segregation), Roosevelt won,
for a while, the support of the conservative plantation types. With a program for modernizing the Southern economy (through TVA and cotton
price supports), he regained the loyalties of the middle classes as well. They
still fondly remember FDR down in Dixie—"The clod-busters in this neck of
the woods will probably remain as loyal to the President as a Methodist
minister to fried chicken," a Texas editor commented.

Southern conservatives soon found the New Deal "a combination of wet
nursin', frenzied finance, downright Communism an' plain
dam-foolishness," as Governor Eugene Talmadge of Georgia once put it.
The trouble was that the New Deal was modernizing the southern economy
—with TVA, crop payments, the WPA, old-age pensions, new credit agencies and a myriad of relief programs, all of which enrolled blacks. The
county seat elites—the banker-merchant-judge-planter-lawyer-landowner-
sheriff-doctor governing class saw their power passing into a nationalized
bureaucracy, while mill owners, utility executives, and other industrialists
were threatened by unionization, minimum wages, and public power.
Roosevelt's immense popularity, plus the lack of a viable Republican alternative, guaranteed the region's electoral votes for as often as Roosevelt
chose to run. The counterattack of the conservative elite came in Congress,
just after Roosevelt's tremendous 1936 landslide.

The president made the mistake of trying to pack the Supreme Court,
thereby unleashing pent up conservative frustrations in the guise of defend-

ing the sanctity of the courts. Roosevelt's position further weakened in 1937-1938 when the economy took a sudden tailspin caused by inept New Deal programs, like heavy new taxes, and a renewed lack of business confidence. Recovery had not been reached after all. Roosevelt's next mistake was to personally join in efforts to purge conservative Democrats in the 1938 elections. He succeeded in the North, while his interference in the South redounded to the conservative benefit.

By 1938 a majority of southern congressmen, many of them committee chairmen, had formed a working alliance with northern Republicans (who meanwhile were purging most of their liberals). The conservative coalition proved virtually invincible for a quarter century—not until Lyndon Johnson broke its power in 1964-1965 did a major piece of legislation win congressional approval against the opposition of the coalition. Thanks to the southerners' chairmanships (they entered Congress younger and seemed to live longer than northerners), almost all the important committees in both houses were coalition controlled for practically the entire time from 1939 to 1972.

Crusades in the Nineteenth Century

The essence of modernizing, pietistic Protestantism in the nineteenth century was a deep revulsion against the presence of sin in American society. The pietists were those Protestants—Methodists, Presbyterians, and Baptists especially—who rejected the traditionalism of established churches, with their fancy liturgy and complex theology. Pietism demanded of its members a conversion experience—a deep transformation wherein a person felt the guilt of his sins and the redeeming love of Christ. Conversion was the only way to salvation, and the emotional revival meeting was the favorite way of converting sinners. In 1800 few Americans were pietistic, but wave after wave of revivals converted half the population by the end of the century. Well organized, enthusiastic, and deeply committed to their mission, the pietists crusaded to rid American society of the established evils left over from the bad old days and to check the spread of traditionalist forces, especially Catholicism. The pietists felt themselves to be the spirit of modernity, destined in God's name to eliminate traditional vices and lead society to a new plateau of civilization. Significantly, the new modern middle classes were heavily pietistic, while backward farmers and laborers (and some upper-class socialites or would-be aristocrats) hewed to traditional values in work, religion, and politics.

The great pietistic crusades of the nineteenth century—against liquor, slavery, Catholicism, sabbath-breaking, and polygamy (Mormonism)— released enormous amounts of energy into the political system. Women, being somewhat more religious than men, played the larger role. The antislavery crusade was the only pietist movement that was not nationwide. Southern pietists, while not formally committed to the proposition that owning slaves was a positive good, argued that it was a labor system and a race-relations system essential to the southern way of life, and broke off relations with their northern coreligionists. Thus the Baptists, Methodists, and Presbyterians split along North-South lines before the Civil War. (The Catholics, Episcopalians, Lutherans, and other liturgical-traditional denominations stayed together.)

The debates over the morality of slavery, liquor, and Catholicism have been discussed in the first chapter. Here we must emphasize how the crusading religious spirit of the pietists spilled over into American politics.

In the 1850s pietists were still a minority, but were so well organized, articulate, and highly motivated that they reshaped the political system. Most were Whigs. But that party seemed so subservient to office seeking that when its long-term victory chances dimmed in the 1850s, the pietists moved rapidly into a new crusade, the Know-Nothing movement. The American party, to use its official name, has the reputation of narrow-minded bigotry. Actually, it was a good-government movement hostile to patronage-hungry politicians, corrupt city machines, and the tide of Irish and German immigration, which threatened the preeminence of pietistic values. In 1854, most large cities elected Know-Nothing governments, as did several states. Prohibition laws were simultaneously enacted throughout the country in response to pietistic demands.

The Know-Nothings and prohibition movements were short-lived, for in 1854-1856 a new pietistic party emerged in the North, the Republicans. Absorbing the other movements, the Republicans crusaded in 1856 to destroy slavery. Politicians such as Lincoln soon took control of the new party and adopted a more pluralistic stance, designed to attract necessary German and nonpietistic voters, so that by 1860 the crusading fervor had passed and abolitionists complained about Lincoln's pussyfooting.

What motivated the crusader was the unshakable conviction that evil ones hold power (slaveholders, Catholics, and so on), and only by bringing God's wrath to bear in public affairs could the nation be purified. Their sudden appearance overwhelmed professional politicians — but by bending to the wind and claiming that only they could coordinate a victorious campaign, the politicians invariably took control of the crusades. To neutralize a crusade, its opponents denounced the crusaders as fools, fanatics, and amateurs, who would wreck the country if they got the chance. Thus Democrats in 1856 darkly warned that civil war was inevitable, should the Republicans win, and further advised Catholics that their religion was in jeopardy.

A second great crusade came in 1896, when young William Jennings Bryan promised to drive the money changers from the government and to install a millennium of justice by means of the panacea of free silver (that is, inflation) (Doc. 9). Bryan's silverite utopia thrilled the pietistic Democrats of the South and made heavy inroads among the economically traditional but religiously pietistic farmers in the Plains states. Bryan's antimodern thrust, threatening to wreck the industrial and financial sectors of the economy to benefit farmers, alarmed the middle-class pietists. They not only gave solid support to McKinley but have remained loyal to his party ever since. McKinley realized he needed more than middle-class votes to stop Bryan. He labelled the Democrats the party of depression and won over factory and railroad workers by promising to end unemployment through a protective tariff (the country was then in a deep depression, and a Democrat was president). Shrewdly sensing that religiously traditional German farmers and craftsmen were fully committed to a modern economy, McKinley promised tolerance and pluralism within the GOP for all who joined him in repelling the silverite menace (Doc. 12).

Crusaders breathed the heady air of utopianism. In 1900, during Bryan's second campaign for free silver, Frank Baum, one of his Chicago supporters, published a "modern fairy tale" that ingeniously captured the yearnings of the Bryan crusades. *The Wonderful Wizard of Oz* told of the great cyclone which hit parched, poverty-stricken Kansas and transported the innocent heroine to a land overflowing with milk and honey, yet controlled by wicked witches. The cyclone landed Dorothy's house on the Wicked Witch of the East, killing her and freeing the Munchkins from bondage. (That is, the agrarian revolution will destroy the power of the industrialists and free the little people.) Protected by a magic kiss (electoral mandate) from the Good Witch of the North and clad in magical silver slippers (they were ruby in the movie version), Dorothy set out on the yellow (golden) brick road to reach the Emerald City (Washington) where the Wizard (president) would help her. Along the way she met the silverite coalition — the scarecrow (farmer) who could not frighten anyone and who mistakenly thought he was stupid (the hayseed image); the tin woodsman (industrial worker) cursed by the Wicked Witch of the East so that every time he swung his axe he sliced off part of his body and was all tin now (dehumanized by industrialization); and the Cowardly Lion (Bryan himself). After many perils, they entered the phoney Emerald Capital, and were awed by the weak charlatan who used the powers of his office to trick them. Dorothy finally redeemed the land of Oz by drenching the Wicked Witch of the West (draught) with water, only to discover the Wizard (President McKinley) was a fraud. No matter — the Scarecrow now realized he had brains, the Woodsman that he had a heart, and the Lion courage. After installing the Woodsman as ruler of Oz, Dorothy learned from the Good Witch of the South that her magical silver slippers were all powerful and they carried her back to Kansas. The moral was clear — farmer, worker, and politician, cooperating together could use free silver to transform society and redeem it from evil.

The fairy tale was literary fantasy, but Bryan's speeches were deeply serious when he identified himself with David battling Goliath, with the Good Samaritan, with Paul spreading the Gospel, with the honest man crucified on a cross of gold. A deeply religious people, alienated by hardship and the failure of the old leadership, had found its messiah (Doc. 8).

Twentieth-Century Crusades

Crusades proved possible in the merchandizing era, as the growth of the modernized electorate counterbalanced the decline of old-time pietistic religious fervor (Doc. 14 and 15). In 1912 Teddy Roosevelt shouted "I stand at Armageddon and I battle for the Lord!" His sacred vehicle, the Progressive party, comprised the modern sector of the GOP, while his archfoe, Taft, was left with the more traditional Republicans and the professional politicians. The latter picked up the pieces, and by switching over to merchandizing techniques and adopting the middle-class efficiency strain of progressivism, put the GOP back into power by 1920. In 1936 Franklin Roosevelt crusaded against unspecified "malefactors of great wealth," while Willkie tried in 1940 to rally the middle classes with a crusade against the inefficiency of the New Deal. Truman echoed Roosevelt's crusade in 1948 — marking only the first time since 1828 that a full-fledged crusade proved successful on the national level (Doc. 26).

By 1950 the country was thoroughly modernized and party loyalty was rapidly decaying. Joe McCarthy proved that newly middle-class Catholics, as well as conservative Republicans, could be responsive to an anti-Communist crusade. In 1952, Eisenhower dumped Taft in a crusade for party purity and then forced the Democrats out of the White House with a vague crusade against "Communism, Korea and Corruption." Once in office, however, Eisenhower practiced a tolerant conservatism that cooled crusading fevers in both parties for a dozen years, perhaps lulling the country into the conviction that if no one got excited, then nothing could or would be terribly amiss (Doc. 28).

After John Kennedy's assassination in 1963, America began losing its self-confidence. Southern whites were sure something was terribly wrong when their traditional racial order came under heavy assault. A prolonged foreign war in Vietnam with unclear aims and all too clear casualty totals played against a foreground of hundreds of massive big-city black riots. Lyndon Johnson tried to keep everybody happy in a Great Society in which everyone could share in the great barbecue. The middle classes, disgruntled by Johnson's wheeler-dealer style and sure they would have to pay the bills, revolted at the polls as early as 1966. Then the college students began proclaiming a new postmodern morality, which jettisoned middle-class ideals of self-discipline and ambition in favor of sex, drugs, radical politics, and the perpetual search for personal liberation. The scene was set for an outburst of crusading fervor that took a decade to play out.

The antiwar crusade on college campuses followed closely Martin Luther King's crusades for civil rights. Eugene McCarthy forged a middle-class anti-Johnson and postmodern antiwar coalition that helped topple Johnson in 1968. George McGovern tried to repeat the tactic in 1972, this time without paying close attention to the sensibilities of the middle class (Doc. 31). On the right, George Wallace organized a crusade against government paternalism (in the South, it looked more like a countercrusade). Unsuccessful in 1964 and 1968, his near martyrdom in 1972 moved him into the mainstream of Democratic politics, and Jimmy Carter absorbed much of Wallace's support in 1976. (The next best thing to martyrdom, or maybe even better, is near martyrdom). Barry Goldwater, who had started the new crusading spirit with his campaign to uphold middle-class virtues in 1964, was echoed, with greater success, by Ronald Reagan in California (1966) and by "law and order" candidates everywhere. Reagan's continuing crusading rhetoric gave him the 1980 Republican presidential nomination.

Reagan and Martin Luther King were the only successful crusaders in the period, with Reagan growing more flexible while in office. King, true still to his crusading fervor, became more and more frustrated in his latter efforts. Nevertheless the nation did respond, if belatedly, to the crusaders' demands. Civil rights laws passed and were enforced, the Vietnam war ended, women gained more equality, and potential (though not actual) citizen participation in government widened with the eighteen-year-old vote, the decentralization of school boards, and the opening of the Democratic party machinery to rank-and-file influence (Doc. 32). As the psychic crises of the 1960s passed, the people became absorbed in economic crises — dizzy inflation, severe shortages in food and energy, and rising taxes. When the Watergate scandal unfolded, the crusading fervor had died out. No mass rallies, no excited orators, no long petitions. Instead, conservative exemplars of old middle-class, modern values — men like Judge John Sirica, Senator Sam Ervin, Attorney General Elliott Richardson, prosecutors Archibald Cox and Leon Jaworski, and Congressman Peter Rodino — struggled to ensure that justice was done.

Crusades have brief life expectancies — rarely more than eighteen months in politics. The first frenzied months breed confidence that anything is possible, that a veritable revolution in morals is at hand. Yet the complicated structure of American government, and especially the ultimate role of nonelected federal judges and bureaucrats in regulating fundamental changes, means that permanent success requires permanent activity. Most crusaders drift off after a few defeats into private concerns, perhaps with utopian or mystical overtones. Abolitionists in the nineteenth century gravitated toward spiritualism, and a century later student antiwar crusaders drifted toward drugs and the occult. Permanent pressure groups, when properly adjusted to the political milieu, were more successful in shaping public policy.

Pressure Groups, Third Parties, and Special Interests

Nineteenth-century army-style politics could not tolerate the disruptive efforts of special interest groups. Organizations seeking major reforms either had to capture the party outright through crusades or operate as third parties. The latter route was followed by abolitionists until the Republican party formed. Emancipation came about strictly as a war measure rather than as a response to ideological pressure. Labor and farm movements also found it impossible to work within major parties. In 1890, for example, the Farmers' Alliance worked to elect its members running on major party tickets, only to discover their "allies" hewed to party rather than Alliance discipline once in office. Temperance advocates set out in the 1880s to capture the Republican party by packing township and precinct conventions. They succeeded in several states, causing disastrous defeats for the GOP. Republican professionals did battle with the prohibitionists at the local level, expelling them from power and withdrawing the party's support for prohibition.

The third party route, on the other hand, was doomed by the faithful adherence of the vast majority of voters to the Republican or Democratic banner. The Greenback party in 1878, and the Populist party in 1892-94 raised important issues but failed to create viable organizations (Doc. 8). They sent out hundreds of paid organizers and founded thousands of newspapers (which went bankrupt in a year or two), but proved unable to switch the loyalties of the farmers' groups and labor unions on which they were based. The only success the Populists had came when they fused with a major party that could not win on its own. Thus Kansas and Nebraska Populist victories represented in fact a Populist-Democratic coalition, while in North Carolina a Populist-Republican coalition won the governorship and legislature. In 1896, silver Democrats, led by Bryan, absorbed the Populists in the North. In the South the third party faced a hopeless dilemma, for it was allied with the GOP for state and local races and with the Democrats for the presidency. A white-supremacy campaign destroyed the North Carolina coalition in 1898, and after that Populism was dead. Its membership (perhaps 5 percent of the American electorate) returned to their original parties, became apathetic, or in some cases joined the new Socialist party.

Third parties were easier to start in the twentieth century, since partisanship was weaker and the merchandizing style was amenable to crusading. Permanent success, however, required winning offices. In 1912 Roosevelt's Progressives ran many candidates, thus splitting the Republican vote and electing Democrats. After their dismal showing in 1914, the Progressives returned to the major parties. In 1924, Robert LaFollette ran for president under the Progerssive label, relying on AF of L, socialist, and German votes. Significantly, the new party ran no candidates for any other offices. In 1968 George Wallace's American Independent party did field a few other candidates, none of whom received a fraction of Wallace's vote. When Wallace returned to the Democratic party in 1972, his former party soon collapsed.

Third parties have sometimes been hailed as harbingers of reform — the ideas they bring into the political arena are supposedly later adopted and enacted by major parties. This notion, however, is specious. True, third parties have advocated ideas later enacted. However they rarely if ever have initiated these schemes, preferring to advocate plans that already had a strong (but minority) following within the major parties in the hope of thereby winning over some of these voters. Invariably the major parties countercrusaded against the upstart party, attacking its leaders as fanatics and fools and ridiculing their ideas. The effect was to *suppress* advocacy of reforms and to postpone enactment until the memory of the crusade and countercrusade died out. Nearly all the leading Progressives of the early twentieth century, for example, were bitter opponents of Populism in the 1890s. Reform ideas the Populists advocated were either permanently discredited (free silver, public ownership of railroads) or postponed for years (the initiative, direct election of senators).

Merchandizing politics, by contrast, encourages pressure groups to advertise their ideas and line up their supporters behind favorable major party candidates, as women did in their drive for the right to vote (Doc. 16). The Anti-Saloon League was the most effective pressure group of the twentieth century. Financed and supported by the pietistic churches, it specialized in bipartisan pinpoint lobbying, with promises of massive electoral support for legislators who went along with it on just one or two votes, regardless whether the man was a drinker or not. The League avoided the crusading moralism of nineteenth-century prohibitionists and led counties, states, and finally the nation to total legal prohibition of the manufacture and sale of wine, beer, and liquor.

The American Federation of Labor followed a parallel course, with more permanent if less spectacular results. In the 1930s, however, a schism erupted within union ranks. The Congress of Industrial Organizations, smaller but more aggressive, broke with the AF of L and formed a close alliance with New Deal Democrats (Doc. 25). By contributing millions of dollars to depleted Democratic campaign chests, and more importantly, by engaging in army-style get-out-the-vote campaigns in industrial centers, the CIO came to dominate the Democratic party in states where it had previously been weak, like Michigan, California, and Pennsylvania. After the AF of L and the CIO merged in the 1950s, it achieved a very powerful, if not dominant role in nominating Democratic candidates in the industrial states and was the largest base of power of candidates like John Kennedy, Lyndon Johnson, and Hubert Humphrey. When George McGovern refused to cooperate on equal terms with the giant labor federation in 1972, it concentrated its resources on congressional and state races, confident that McGovern's humiliation would teach all future Democratic presidential nominees an unforgettable lesson. (The strategy worked, as Democrats won control of Congress and most legislature and state houses, despite Nixon's crushing personal victory.)

Other special interest groups active in twentieth-century politics have concentrated their efforts on lobbying, propaganda, and campaign funding, without attempting the voter mobilization used by the unions or the Anti-Saloon League. The number of pressure groups today is legion. The most important are industry, commerce, utilities, medicine, and agriculture with teachers, environmentalists, blacks, and consumers especially active since the 1960s.

Do the lobbyists and interest groups control the government? To a certain extent, yes. Major legislation on issues like education, civil rights, transportation, aid to cities, and so on, is written only after extensive negotiation and bargaining among legislators and lobbyists. The point is that the economic, social, and cultural interests of most Americans are represented by different lobbyists. The problem is that some people are much better represented than others and that millions of Americans feel that they are "forgotten" about in the corridors of power. Nothing is more likely to create alienation from our system of government. On the other hand, the lobbyists and special interest groups reply that they are usually on the defensive. They see their role as watchdogs to protect their clients from higher taxes, unwise administrative rulings, or dangerous legislation. In the early 1970s a citizen's lobby, Common Cause, claiming to represent only the general interest, emerged as the biggest lobby in Washington. Yet it quickly became just another cog in the system — its positions were predictable and its claim truly to represent the "national interest" was heavily discounted.

Beginning in 1974, a new kind of political agency, the Political Action Committee (PAC), assumed importance. The PAC is not so much a lobby as a funding device that solicits money from large numbers of individuals and gives it to candidates favorable to a particular position. In 1974 there were only 114 PACs, half of them connected with labor unions. The idea caught on, however, so that by 1982, 3,479 PACs raised over $200 million and contributed $90 million to congressional campaigns. Four types of PACs emerged. Trade and professional membership groups (teachers, realtors, physicians, used-car dealers) need to back their Washington lobbyists with punch. Corporate PACs raise contributions from their senior- and middle-level managers (*not* from their corporate treasury) and direct them to campaigns in the districts where the firm operates; both parties and both liberals and conservatives usually benefit. Labor unions raise funds voluntarily from their members so as to exercise a little more clout with liberal Democrats. Finally, ideological or special-interest groups raise money partly to fund their mass mailing efforts and partly to zero-in on unfriendly congressmen by supporting their opponents. Each PAC has an executive committee that decides how to spend the money. Since the maximum that can be given by one PAC to one candidate is only $5,000, the funds are widely spread.

How important are PACs in American democracy? No one yet knows. Certainly they are less important than lobbyists, because the lobbies provide explicit information and advice on specific legislation, while PACs only help their friends in general during the campaign. Since nine out of ten congressmen are routinely reelected and since all candidates get some money, the chief impact may be just to escalate the total spent on campaigning. Ultimately, PACs will be influential only to the extent that they reflect the general wishes of millions of Americans who realize that a $50 cash contribution produces more of a voice than a vote in the ballot box. The grass roots are still alive, even if the forms of democracy keep changing.

III
DOCUMENTS

1. EARLY PARTY RHETORIC

Below are two samples of party rhetoric of the 1850s and early 1860s. Note the Republican tendency to try to legislate morality and the Democrat's reaction to this "coercion."

Source: William Salter, *The Life of James W. Grimes* (New York, 1876), pp. 49, 65. Horatio Seymour, *Public Record* (1868), pp. 77, 9-10.

James W. Grimes was one of the founders of the Republican Party in Iowa. His letters and speeches point to many of the central issues that concerned the party at that time. In an 1854 speech to his constituents on slavery Grimes said:

Fellow-citizens, shall this attempt to induce you to support this measure by the force of party ties and affinities succeed? Is there no moral and high political responsibility resting upon you in this matter? . . . . No imputations or false charges shall force me to be false to my convictions of duty and right. I will not surrender the right of private judgment on this or any other subject, to avoid a false clamor, or a willful perversion of my sentiments.

In a letter to his wife Grimes wrote of the successes of the state legislature. The "Maine law" involved the prohibition of liquor.

The Legislature has done an immense amount of business, more than has been done by any two Legislatures before. The Constitution bill; Maine Law; Insane Asylum; Blind Asylum; Deaf and Dumb Asylum; Sunday law — that will prevent the dancing on the Sabbath that so much annoys us and our neighbors in the summer — Geological Survey bill — all have passed and become laws.

While Grimes appealed to a law higher than the Constitution, Horatio Seymour, a leading New York Democrat, urged strict compliance with the Constitution and regarded the legislation of morality as "political meddling" and governmental coercion.

My friends, we have always been opposed to the doctrine of "higher law" — that doctrine that men had a right to set up their own views, their own passions, their own prejudices against the laws of the land and the decrees of regularly-constituted authorities acting within their constitutional limits. We held that if men were displeased with the laws they should have them repealed — they should not be resisted; we held if men were opposed to those in authority, the rightful remedy was given by our Constitution — . . . . We contended for this principle of loyalty — this doctrine of obedience to law — this principle that you are bound to respect authority. [1862]

The cause of temperance was irresistible in the State of Maine while it was upheld by reason and persuasion. It was broken down by legislation. The authors of the bill, in the narrowness of their intellect, could not see that truth was stronger than statutes. . . . . Let the advocates of temperance see what spirit this enactment has evoked. . . . . Persuasion requires virtue, ability, and sincerity. Coercive laws are best enforced by the violent, vindictive, and base. Hence these are now taking the lead. . . . . The wise and the thoughtful are overruled by men raging with the delirium tremens of fanaticism; who assail the most sacred offices of religion; who see foul serpents coiling upon the sacramental altar, infusing their venom into the sacred elements, and hissing amid the solemnities of the last supper.

Governments emanate from the people, and merely represent their morality or intelligence. The folly which looks to governments to evolve the virtues, is like the ignorance which regards the thermometer as a regulator of temperature, or the barometer as the controller of the weather. [1856]

2. FUNDING POLITICS BEFORE
THE CIVIL WAR

In March 1860, with the union on the verge of collapse, a committee of the House of Representatives met to investigate the use of government money and patronage in political campaigns. The committee's investigation revealed much about the inner workings of American politics. Both the members of the committee and the witnesses they interviewed took it for granted that political parties operated like armies. For example, the committee's report asserted that "all office holders are but enlisted soldiers of the administration by which they are sustained." One witness referred to campaign funds as "munitions." Another, in referring to a loyal party worker, said that he had "fought, bled, and died for the cause."

Source: U.S. Congress, House, *House Reports*, 36th Cong., 1st sess., 1859-1860, Vol. 5, 1860, pp. 294-95, 495-501, 506, 552-56, 622-23.

In June 1860, Horace F. Clark, congressman from New York City, was asked about the importance of money in political campaigns.

Question: I wish to ask you with regard to the practice in the State of New York of using money in elections, so far as it has come to your knowledge, either personal knowledge or by reputation. I do not confine myself to one party, but refer to all parties.

Answer: There is no question, gentlemen, but that money is employed in and about elections in the city and State of New York by all parties. I should think it would be fair to say that each party gets all the money it can for that purpose, the only difference being that the democratic party employs the money to bring out democratic votes and the other parties to obtain votes of their own description. . . . The practice is regarded as a great and growing evil.

Question: You consider that practice universal in the State of New York?

Answer: So far as I know it is universal. I am not very well acquainted with the local politics of the western part of the State. But for the ten last years I have been sufficiently acquainted with political affairs to know that the employment of money for election purposes is one of general practice. And I think that any candid man with any information upon the subject must admit the fact. There are very many legitimate expenses attending elections. Those legitimate expenses are very great, and must be borne either by the candidate or by his friends. . . . The printing and the circulation of documents for the information of the people, and the providing safeguards about the polls, are all the subjects of large expenditures, and they are legitimate. . . .

I am satisfied that all parties obtain contributions of money for election purposes; I do not say otherwise than legitimately. I differ from some gentlemen as to the morality of such transactions. I do not think that the employment of money to enlighten the public as to the political issues of the day, or to ensure the ends of good government, is wrong. I think it is right, and I know it to be necessary. The evil is, perhaps, incident to our election system, and is probably beyond the reach of Congress.

It took a great deal of money to run a political campaign, even in the 1850s. Isaac West, a federal employee, testified about one method of getting that money.

Question: Were you at one time engaged in the custom-house at Philadelphia?

Answer: Yes, sir.

Question: When were you appointed?

Answer: The first of June, 1853, I think.

Question: How long did you remain in office there?

Answer: About five years.

Question: Were you there at the time of the election of 1856, when Mr. Buchanan was elected?

Answer: Yes, sir.

Question: What do you know about moneys being raised off the employés of the custom-house on that occasion?

Answer: There was a certain tax levied upon the persons connected with the custom-house.

Question: What amount on each person?

Answer: A certain percentage. On a person receiving $1,095 a year, I think the tax for the presidential election was from $30 to $33.

Question: Do you mean for the presidential election alone, or for both presidential and congressional elections?

Answer: I mean the presidential election alone.

Question: What about the other election?

Answer: The amount was not so great for the State election.

Question: How much was that?

Answer: That I do not recollect. It strikes me that it was from $5 to $7, something like that.

Question: The two, then, would amount to in the neighborhood of $40?

Answer: Yes, sir, in that neighborhood.

Question: Upon what salaried officers was that?

Answer: Those of $1,100, or, rather, $1,095 a year.

Question: Were the others assessed in proportion to their salaries?

Answer: Yes, sir.

Question: To whom was that money paid?

Answer: It was generally deposited. That portion which I collected in my department I gave to the deputy collector, Mr. Harbeson — I believe he was the treasurer, so far as the custom-house was concerned — and he paid it over to the executive committee, I believe.

Question: A political committee?

Answer: Yes, sir.

Question: Did all the employés pay?

Answer: I never knew one to refuse.

Question: What was the impression — that it was rather obligatory upon them to pay?

Answer: That seemed to be the impression; they all felt it their duty to pay that more promptly than some of their debts; that was the impression, but I do not know about whether they would have been removed, if they had not paid; but it was considered obligatory, I believe.

Question: Why did you quit working in the custom-house?

Answer: I was dismissed because I did not chime in with the course of the administration entirely.

Newspapers served as the most important means by which a political party could make its views known to voters. Newspapers served as party organs and in return received lucrative government printing contracts — if their party won. In 1857 John W. Forney of Philadelphia sought to establish a Democratic paper in that city. Note how careful Forney was to see that the paper's policy coincided with Administration policy. At the time he testified, Forney was Clerk of the House of Representatives.

I was compelled to call upon a few friends that I had to assist me in raising the means to establish my paper. Mr. Buchanan himself, when he saw that I was resolved to do it, said: "You cannot establish a democratic paper in Philadelphia and sustain it." I told him I thought I could; if I had any ability in the world it was for that. Up to that period we had had many good papers, but we had not had a progressive democratic paper there; and never anticipating any difficulty with him, I had hopes that I might so conduct the paper myself as to be enabled to secure the patronage of the administration and the confidence of the party. The money that was subscribed for that paper was raised by gentlemen outside of the administration. Mr. Buchanan himself offered, through Judge Black, one or two thousand dollars, which I declined, not desiring to be under any obligations to him. Now, that I was an applicant for public printing in the departments is wholly unfounded. That I would have taken the post office blanks at that time is true. I was at that time a practical printer. I was reared in a printing office; and I thought if that were offered to me, as it was constantly offered, it would be perfectly consistent with my trade and my paper to take it; but as to my ever asking for it, or taking any steps to secure it, with my present recollection the charge is most unfounded. Before starting my paper I prepared my introductory address . . . and so cautious was I not to get into difficulty with the administration and the party that I submitted that address to Judge Black in proof-sheets, telling him that if my allusions to Mr. Buchanan were not strong enough he should make them stronger; and he did amend that opening article; so I started my paper.

Competition between printers for government contracts was often heavy.

Mr. Rice was desirous of procuring a portion of the printing, to sustain the "Pennsylvanian," and Mr. Wendell was equally desirous of having it for the "Union," because the "Union" had no sustenance from Congress. The editor or proprietor of the organ generally had been the printer of one or the other house of Congress, and also had all the Executive patronage. I thought that, not being printer to either House, and having to pay the editors put upon the "Union," I was entitled to what patronage the President had, which would be about one-half of what the organ had; so that I strenuously objected to its being diverted to Mr. Rice. But I was not strong enough to sustain it. The influence of Mr. Rice and the fact of his being the editor of the home organ of Mr. Buchanan induced this order to give him the printing.

Question: Do you know of any other motive or reason being suggested for giving this contract to Mr. Rice, except to support him and his party organ?

Answer: None; that was Mr. Rice's reason that he "had fought, bled and died" for the cause. I recollect that he made a strong argument of his having been indefatigable in the party cause, and that he had, therefore, as good a claim to this printing as I or anybody else had.

In addition to contracts, public money also went to cover "electioneering" expenses. James O'Reiley, a federal employee in New York City testified about his political work.

Question: Have you been employed at any time in the custom-house in New York?

Answer: I was in the public stores.

Question: By whom were you employed?

Answer: There was a message sent to me that if I would go down there I would get employment.

Question: At what time was that?

Answer: Three days before the election; I mean three working days, not including Sunday, at the time Gen. Ward ran for Congress.

Question: The election of 1858?

Answer: Yes, sir.

Question: Did you go to work?

Answer: Yes, sir; I worked for a short time one day, and then I got excused until the day after election, with pay.

Question: What were you excused to do?

Answer: I believe for the purpose of going out to do what I possibly could for Gen. Ward.

Question: Are you a working politician; an active politician?

Answer: They say I am middling smart in that way, and for the last three or four years I have always been placed there to challenge the republican party.

Question: Do you yourself know of any others having been so employed?

Answer: I do.

Question: What did you do when you got your leave of absence? Did you go out and work for your party?

Answer: I did, sir.

Question: And remained at that work until after the election?

Answer: Yes, sir.

Question: What then did you do? Did you go back to work in the custom-house?

Answer: The day after the election I went back.

Question: Did you go to work in the custom-house?

Answer: I did a little, for that day.

Question: Did you continue at work there?

Answer: That evening I was told that my services were no longer required.

Question: Were you paid off that evening?

Answer: No, sir.

Question: Where were you paid off, and how?

Answer: I was paid off on the Saturday evening after.

Question: I want to know whether you and the others who were employed in this way were paid off in the regular way....

Answer: Yes, sir; and I have no doubt that we were paid with the government money.

Question: Do you know of a large increase of force being taken into the public stores a few days before the election?

Answer: I heard that there was.

Question: Do you know of your own knowledge?

Answer: I do not know of my own knowledge. I have no knowledge about that but what I have heard.

Question: Did it appear to be generally understood that there was a large increase of force at that time?

Answer: Yes, sir.

Question: And you went out to electioneer?

Answer: Yes, sir.

Question: And you were paid for five days' work?

Answer: Yes, sir.

Question: How long did you work in the custom-house?

Answer: I was there the first day only a short time. I did not go down early, and was there but a short time.

Question: Then your labor did not amount to much?

Answer: What I did there was nothing.

Question: You were paid for your political services?

Answer: Yes, sir.

3. ELECTION FRAUD IN NEW YORK
AFTER THE CIVIL WAR

After the Civil War, New York City contained a large foreign-born population concentrated in a small area and manipulated by the Democratic party for its own political ends. Democratic dominance meant that Republicans either went along with the machine ("Tammany Hall Republicans") or were overwhelmed. John I. Davenport, U.S. Commissioner and Chief Supervisor of Elections for the Southern District of New York, describes the fate of several antimachine Republicans.

Source: John I. Davenport, *The Election Frauds of New York City and their Prevention* (New York: Published by the author, 1881), pp. 181, 183-87.

There had probably been no election for years in which, to a greater or less degree, ballot-boxes had not been "stuffed," and the votes fraudulently canvassed and returned. The election of 1868 was not exceptional in this respect, as will appear.

By law there were four inspectors of election who received the votes on election day, and two canvassers of votes, who counted the ballots after the polls were closed. One half of each of these officers were appointed as Republicans, the other half as Democrats. . . .

In the Ninth Election district of the Sixth ward, on the day of election, the two Democratic inspectors refused to allow the oath to be put to any challenged voter, whereupon, finding remonstrance to be vain, the two Republican inspectors left the polling place and went to Police headquarters to complain of the conduct of their associates and have them removed. This broke up the Board of Inspectors, the law providing that no vote should be received without the presence of a quorum, nor unless at least three of the Board were satisfied and agreed to receive the vote. Notwithstanding these provisions of law, the two Democratic inspectors continued to accept the votes of all who presented themselves during the absence of their colleagues. Over 580 votes were cast in the district, of which about four to one were upon naturalization papers.

In the Third Election district of the Eleventh ward, on election day, a young man, a son of one of the deputy sheriffs, stationed himself behind the counter where the inspectors were receiving votes, and was furnished by one of the Democratic inspectors with his copy of the registry. As a voter would come up, this young man would call out, "all right," and before the Republican inspector could find the name of the would-be voter upon his register, the Democratic chairman of the Board would receive the ballots and deposit them in the boxes. During a portion of the day this young man received votes and deposited them in the boxes, acting as an inspector without even the color of law. Protesting was of no avail, and after the poll was closed it was found that votes had been received from persons not registered, while some names had been voted upon twice.

In the Fifth Election district of the Fourth ward, many illegal votes were received by the two Democratic inspectors against the protest of their Republican colleagues, and without a concurrence of a majority of the Board, as required by law.

In the Seventh Election district of the twenty-first ward, one of the Republican inspectors who had previously marked upon his book a large number of names of persons whom he desired to challenge, not believing them entitled to vote, was arrested upon a false charge on the morning of election day when on his way to the polls, and kept confined some five hours, when he was released on bail. Upon arriving at the poll of his district, he found that the votes of the persons he had so marked for challenge had all been offered to and received by the other members of the Board of inspectors.

In the Third Election district of the Fourth ward eighty-five names of persons who did not vote were added to the poll-list during the day of election. Late in the evening, but before the canvass was begun, the Republican canvasser became intoxicated, and eighty-five full sets of Democratic ballots were obtained, thrown upon the table with the contents of the boxes as they were emptied, and were canvassed and returned.

In the Fifth Election district of the Thirteenth ward the returns of the canvass of votes cast for Representative in Congress, gave George Francis Train, who was running as an independent candidate, one (1) vote.

After the election, Clark Bell, Esq., Mr. Train's attorney, procured a large number of affidavits from registered persons in that district, "who swore that they voted for Train." Peter Hale, a resident of No. 242 Division street, in that district, subsequently testified that he voted there for Mr. Train, and personally put into the hands of some forty voters ballots for Train, and "saw such votes deposited in the box."

In many districts in the city, on the day of election, it was almost impossible for the challengers to discharge their duties. Special deputy sheriffs, repeaters and roughs thronged the polls and threatened the lives of those who attempted to challenge illegal voters. In this work of preventing challenging, prominent Democratic politicians as well as Democratic inspectors of election frequently aided and encouraged the outside disturbing elements. A few instances will make the facts clear to the minds of all.

In the Sixteenth Election district of the Sixteenth ward, the Republican challenger was ordered out of the room early in the day, by the Democratic Chairman of the Board of Inspectors, and was compelled to leave.

In the Third Election district of the Eleventh ward, the Republican challenger protested to the Board against the reception of votes by the chairman, before the name of the voter was found on the registry by the inspector in charge of the "check" copy. For this, the chairman — a Democrat — ordered the police officer present to arrest the challenger, but the latter showed his authority to act, and the officer declined to remove him. He was then repeatedly threatened by the chairman of the Board, and outsiders, and told that if he "should attempt to challenge," his life would be forfeited. Intimidated, but determined not to be driven off, he made no direct challenges, contenting himself with noting the facts, and protesting against the action of the Board, but no attention was paid to his objections, other than to inform him that he must keep his mouth shut. In speaking of the affairs of the day, the challenger has testified "My friends told me that I had better not challenge anybody; and it was said in my hearing, that if I challenged anybody, the — — — — — — life should pay for it: my friends advised me to stay there and take observations. I have not the least doubt that if I had challenged, personal violence would have been inflicted upon me. I left fifteen or twenty minutes before the polls closed; . . . I had been picked out as a victim, and so I thought I had better go away."

4. CORRUPTION DIVIDES THE GOP IN THE 1870s

In 1873, in a letter to his old friend James A. Garfield, B. A. Hinsdale expresses his concern that the once reform-minded Republican party has become corrupted by too many years in power. He refers to the scandals of the Grant administration. His fears of growing factionalism were no doubt intensified by the revolt of the Liberal Republicans in 1872, in which a group of reformers sought, unsuccessfully, to sieze control of the party.

Source: Mary Hinsdale, ed., *Garfield-Hinsdale Letters* (Ann Arbor, 1949), pp. 235-37. Copyright 1949 by The University of Michigan Press.

Hiram, April 10, 1873

Dear Gen'l:

The other day I stated that the popular feeling growing out of the Salary Bill had a side well worth studying. My object in writing is to redeem my promise to say something about it.

The outcry has not been caused so much by the fact that Congress voted up a few salaries, including their own, as by the growing conviction that we are fairly entered on an era of reckless, prodigal expenditures and official corruption, in the States and especially in the Nation. The presidential election laid the popular apprehensions asleep for a time, but the disclosures of the Winter, Credit Mobilier, the Senatorial elections in various States, etc. called the matter up again and went far to convince the people that their old fears were well grounded. The Salary increase, and especially the Back Pay, coming at the close of the session, have for the time being at least satisfied the majority of men that we have fallen upon evil times. It is not, then, the increased Congressional pay that infuriated men so much as the discovery, real or fancied, that the increase was caused by greed and dishonesty. There is no disguising it that public men — I mean the class, not certain individuals — have fallen immensely in the public estimation in a half year. I make bold to say there has never been a time in the history of the Republic when Washington — I use the word figuratively as representing the various governing forces there centered — stood so low in the national mind as now. Some people rarely say Washington without a sneer, and they seem actually to think all things are venal in the National Capital.

To my mind the various corruptions referred to are indicative of the decay of the Republican party. They point back to a time of immunity growing out of the great strength of the party and the peculiar condition of the country, and forward to a time of hastening dissolution. One part of the answer to your question I am sure is this: the ribs of the ship are beginning to start — the planks to yawn — and through the opening seams we are getting a better view of some of the freight in the hold and of some of the men in the forecastle.

My opinion is that the Republican party has lost more ground since last Fall than Washington is aware of. In fact, I do not think it will ever regain it. Republicans have been greatly weaned from the party during the Winter. As staunch a one as there is in town told me the other day that he was amazed at the developments of the Winter, and that he was ready for a Reform movement. It is now clear that Grant's second administration is to be no better than the first, and if the Democrats are really out of the way why should one remain a Republican any longer?

I have speculated of late a little on this question: What will be the verdict of History on the Republican party? That History will award it the credit of destroying slavery and maintaining the Union, we may safely assume; but how outside of that? Have you ever thought of the matter?

To bring my letter to a close, I think a considerable share of the hostility you encounter just now can be explained and must in harmony

with what I have said above. You ought not to be so much absorbed in
the personal elements of the storm as to fail to consider its impersonal
bearings. As you seek to make your own craft ride the waves, be careful to study philosophically both wave and wind.

Truly,

B. A. Hinsdale

5. THE SCHOOLING OF A POLITICIAN

In a passage that might be titled "Innocence Abroad," Dr.
Charles C. P. Clark, writing in the late 1870s, describes his first
venture into local politics.

Source: Charles C. P. Clark, *The Commonwealth Reconstructed* (New York,
1878), pp. 77, 88-89.

I well remember the first Caucus that I ever went to, now some twenty
years ago. I went with the innocent hope of helping to get a better officering
of my ward. Arrived, at the hour appointed, in a dimly lighted and foul
smelling room, I found an expert of Political Organization already in possession of the gavel, tellers appointed, and a raft of idlers and the retainers
of politicians, with hardly a worthy citizen among them, crowding about
the polls, with printed ticket in hand; and, before an unprepared voter
could think what to do, the hat was turned, the result of the count of ballots
declared, the lights blown out, and the Caucus ended. Some years later I
was desirous of being made School Commissioner, with a view to help
improve public education in quality and abate its cost. The undertaking
looked the more feasible because the Commission had been constructed
with a special view to escape the influence of partisan politics. Besides, I
was a tax-payer, and an old resident of respectability, had quite a drove of
children to educate, and was known to be a man of some schooling myself. I
spoke to a number of my neighbors about it, who all agreed that I was the
very sort of man they wanted for the office. I looked upon myself as already
as good as nominated; and, the way things were situated, nomination was
equivalent to election. But when I got to the Caucus I found a ring of men,
each with his clique of personal friends and dependents, already surrounding and engrossing the polls, —one of whom had books and stationery to
sell to the Board of Education, —another desks, furnaces or other furniture
for school-houses, —another fuel, and so on, and who had already arranged
among themselves which of them should be the nominee. The result was,

that we got a man who had neither children, property, education nor public esteem.

As he became more experienced, Clark soon learned the importance of the press as an "ally of Political Organization."

This modern creation owns all the faculties of ancient fable: a hundred hands, uncounted eyes, untiring strength, immortal youth. It adds to these the illusion of the ventriloquist: — when it speaks we seem to hear the people speak, forgetful that its words issue from its own belly. The newspaper is the familiar of every fireside, and furnishes more than half our reading. It is therefore the master of reputation in democratic politics, both for persons and ideas. To possess its favor is to be called great and good; to lack it, oblivion at the best. This tremendous engine, once looked upon as the chief security of freedom, has now become in an enormous degree, as demagogue and party priest, the instrument of our enslavement. Political Organizers, observing its power, have taken it into their employ, till now the number of public journals in the country that they do not control by subsidy or promise may almost be counted on the fingers. Especially have they seduced this virtuous daughter of liberty to be their mistress by bestowing upon her great part of the many sinecures and easy berths in the public service. In the State of New York, for example, full half of the easy and profitable administration of the internal revenue was distributed among the editors and proprietors of newspapers. In my own town at the present moment [1876] the administration journal is served by three federal functionaries, who get their pay from the public treasury. It is the same with its democratic adversary, whenever and so far as its party gets power in city, country or State. In the various spheres of politics incredible sums are wasted in unnecessary and extravagant printing for the support and subjugation of the press. The pay roll of Tweed & Co. contained the names of eighty-nine of the newspapers of the city of New York, —hardly three righteous being left. From 1867 to 1871 official printing and advertising cost the tax-payers there above a million dollars a year, while for all proper purposes a tenth of the sum was ample. And yet that ring of plunderers was broken, it is said, because it did not pay editors enough to suppress the exposure of its transactions. The case is about the same, in Rochester, San Francisco, Savannah and every other city. It is notorious that at Albany, Harrisburgh, Columbus, Indianapolis and other State capitals political patronage has always been a mine of wealth to party journals. The new established government of the District of Columbia, Benjamin of our politics, has surpassed all its older brethren in this field of debauchment.

To these official subsidies are to be added the purse of the party out of office, and the personal patronage and douceurs of political aspirants. With this and with that, it is no slander to say that the body of newspaperdom is to-day the ally and servitor of Political Organization.

6. THE POLITICS OF THE NEW SOUTH

In the aftermath of the humiliation and ruin suffered during the 1860s, a new generation of southern white leaders emerged. They called for a "New South" based on a modern, industrialized economy. South Carolina politician M. P. O'Connor spoke in 1880 of the importance of federal funds for rapid economic modernization. His position marked a total reversal of Senator John C. Calhoun's warning that federal money would mean federal intervention, modern values, and an end to the traditionalism of the state.

Source: Mary D. O'Connor, ed., *The Life and Letters of M. P. O'Connor* (New York, 1893), pp. 533-34.

In the Forty-third and Forty-fourth Congresses, wherein our party had no representation from this State, examine and see what the representatives of our State accomplished for us then. While our sister State, Georgia, in one session of the Forty-fourth Congress, had appropriated, for public works of improvement over $150,000; the pitiful sum of $5,000 was doled out to South Carolina, with an Atlantic front wider than any State from Narragansett Bay to the Gulf; and with rivers, which, for centuries, have rolled their floods to the ocean, as broad as any east of the Mississippi. It has only been recently that the hand of public improvement has been reached out to us; and it is to the credit of our senators, and the delegation in Congress, that we were able to obtain of appropriations during the last session, the sum of $226,000 for the improvement of our rivers, and of Charleston harbor. We have outlived the age of poetry; and the practical realities of life are what should now engage and concern us. We have too long clung to our idols of political faith, and rejected the fostering hand of a paternal government. Our necessities have awakened us to their importance, and our material development demands that we should insist upon our proper distributive share of the public revenue for the building up of our commerce, and the development of our still hidden and manifold resources. In the discharge of my public duty, I have endeavored to serve my whole people as well as I might; and I have not considered for a moment the political complexion of any one of my constituents, in responding to any demand made upon me in the proper line of my duty. To this course I shall continue to adhere, believing that in the course of time, many who now differ with me in politics, will agree with me in subordinating their political predilections, for their own material welfare and benefit.

7. THE CITY MACHINE IN THE 1880s

Theodore Roosevelt got his early training in politics in New York City in the 1880s. In the following excerpt from *American Ideals and Other Essays, Social and Political*, he discusses the organization and operation of urban machine politics. Note how the machines created in the 1850s have been perfected and that the army style of politics, the concern with patronage, and the importance of money have persisted.

Source: Theodore Roosevelt, *American Ideals and Other Essays, Social and Political* (New York: G. P. Putnam's Sons, 1897), pp. 108-10, 112-13, 120-22.

The organization of a party in our city is really much like that of an army. There is one great central boss, assisted by some trusted and able lieutenants; these communicate with the different district bosses, whom they alternately bully and assist. The district boss in turn has a number of half-subordinates, half-allies, under him; these latter choose the captains of the election districts, etc., and come into contact with the common healers. The more stupid and ignorant the common healers are, and the more implicitly they obey orders, the greater becomes the effectiveness of the machine. . . .

These henchmen obey unhesitatingly the orders of their chiefs, both at the primary or caucus and on election day, receiving regular rewards for doing so, either in employment procured from them or else in money outright. Of course it is by no means true that these men are all actuated merely by mercenary motives. The great majority entertain also a real feeling of allegiance towards the party to which they belong, or towards the political chief whose fortunes they follow; and many work entirely without pay and purely for what they believe to be right. . . .

All of these men, whether paid or not, make a business of political life and are thoroughly at home among the obscure intrigues that go to make up so much of it; and consequently they have quite as much the advantage when pitted against amateurs as regular soldiers have when matched against militiamen. . . .

In every election precinct — there are probably twenty or thirty in each assembly district — a captain and from two to a dozen subordinates are appointed. These have charge of the actual giving out of the ballots at the polls. On election day they are at their places long before the hour set for voting; each party has a wooden booth, looking a good deal like a sentry-box, covered over with flaming posters containing the names of their nominees, and the "workers" cluster around these as centres. Every voter as he approaches is certain to be offered a set of tickets; usually these sets are "straight," that is, contain all the nominees of one party, but frequently crooked work will be done, and some one candidate will get his own ballots bunched with the rest of those of the opposite party. Each captain of a district is generally paid a certain sum of money, greater or less according to his ability as a politician or according to his power of serving the boss or machine. . . .

The money thus furnished is procured either by subscriptions from rich outsiders, or by assessments upon the candidates themselves; formerly much was also obtained from officeholders, but this is now prohibited by law. A great deal of money is also spent in advertising, placarding posters, paying for public meetings, and organizing and uniforming members to take part in some huge torchlight procession — this last particular form of spectacular enjoyment being one peculiarly dear to the average American political mind. . . . A curious incident . . . came to my knowledge while happening to inquire how a certain man became a Republican. It occurred a good many years ago. . . . I may preface it by stating that the man referred to, whom we will call X, ended by pushing himself up in the world, thanks to his own industry and integrity, and is now a well-to-do private citizen. . . . But at the time spoken of he was a young laborer, of Irish birth, working for his livelihood on the docks and associating with his Irish and American fellows. The district where he lived was overwhelmingly Democratic, and the contests were generally merely factional. One small politician, a saloon-keeper named Larry, who had a great deal of influence, used to enlist on election day, by pay and other compensation, the services of the gang of young fellows to which X belonged. One one occasion he failed to reward them for their work, and in other ways treated them so shabbily as to make them very angry, more especially X, who was their leader. There was no way to pay Larry off until the next election; but they determined to break his influence utterly then. . . by supporting the Republican ticket. . . . It was a rough district, and usually the Republican booths were broken up and their ballot-distributors driven off early in the day; but on this occasion, to the speechless astonishment of everybody, things went just the other way. The Republican ballots were distributed most actively, the opposing workers were bribed, persuaded, or frightened away, all means fair and foul were tried, and finally there was almost a riot, — the outcome being that the Republicans actually obtained a majority in a district where they had never before polled ten percent of the total vote. Such a phenomenon attracted the attention of the big Republican leaders, who after some inquiry found it was due to X. To show their gratitude and to secure so useful an ally permanently (for this was before the days of civil service reform), they procured him a lucrative place in the New York Post Office. . . .

8. THE POLITICS OF THE POPULIST MOVEMENT

The Populist movement in the early 1890s was a traditional response to the economic hardships that rapid modernization imposed on cotton and wheat growers and miners. Intense discussions took place at tens of thousands of local meetings. Although the Populists were never very numerous — fewer than 5 percent of the voters — they did articulate the frustration of simple folk trapped in a modern world not of their making.

Source: Greeley (Colorado) *Tribune*, February 11, February 18, January 21, 1891.

Greeley Tribune Alliance Column, February 18, 1891

"Strong Arm" Alliance is one of the first, if not the first, organization of the Alliance in old Weld County [Colorado], and is progressing well . . . it is a wonder to the surrounding community to witness old Coal Bank Draw come to the front . . . and take the initial step towards advancing the interests of her community. Not only have we formed an Alliance to take steps toward alleviating our financial conditions, but we have carried on semi-monthly literary and musical entertainments very successfully through the winter months, but spring draws near and we will adjourn to meet in early fall.

Greeley Tribune Alliance Column, January 21, 1891

In no country in the world is paternal government so much decried or denounced as here, yet in no other country is there so much of it. The Republican party is, par excellence, the most loud mouthed and obstreperous antagonist of paternal government, yet the Republican party has been its chief promoter and to this day its chief, almost its only support. Paternal government...means a paternal regard for the people, the common people. As exemplified by the Republican party it is a contempt for the common people, and an overweening care of...the rich. Through the paternal care of the Republicans, there is as well defined a plutocracy in this country as there is an aristocracy in Europe.... All that is necessary to secure the paternal care of the government is to prove that you have many millions of dollars.

The people, the common people, want the government to issue greenbacks direct to them, and a thousand bankers appear before the august government and with looks and sounds that betray holy horror roar out so that the startled world hears it, "Why, that would be paternalism! We have a thousand millions invested in banks—take care of us. Issue money to us and we will attend to it."

And the government does so.

The people ask the government to take possession of the railroads and run them in their interest. A thousand railroad men roar, "Hold on for Heaven's sake, that is paternalism. We can take care of the railroads."

And the government holds on.

It calls the railroad men together and says, "Dear children, here is a tract of land forty miles wide, running from the Mississippi to the Pacific ocean; I'll give it to you to build a railroad on it, and I'll give you $20,000 for every mile you build...and you can charge the common people and their freight all that the traffic will bear."

And it was so.

The common people wanted a parcels post, to carry their packages as the mail carries their letters. But the expressmen came down on the government like the wolf on the fold, and yelled, "No, no, that won't do—that would be paternal government and would be robbing us of a hundred millions a year."

And no parcels post was established.

The people asked the government to convert the postoffice into savings banks...but a thousand gold-winged harpies yawped, "No! Never, that would be paternal. Besides, we make millions and millions out of the workingmen's earnings."

And there were no postoffice savings banks.

Greeley Tribune Alliance Column, February 11, 1891

The facts are, that all party platforms for the last ten years have been made up of planks hewn out of the forests of agriculture and industrial timber. They have appealed to the working man in every utterance and promised to attend . . . to his peculiar wants, but so far, not one single line has been written in our laws that gives even a small measure of relief to this class of voters. 'Tis true we have the interstate commerce law, but a supreme court steps in and robs the commissioners of all power to control the roads under it. . . . Now we are getting weary of party promises, and knowing from past experience that a change in the administration is simply a change of masters, we propose to try what we can do in a party by ourselves.

There are certain reforms that neither of the old parties have ever even promised, and they alone will satisfy the working class. One of these is our banking system. We cannot be brought to see the justice of the government in loaning money to a certain class at 1 per cent., in order to allow them to loan it to the people at any rate of interest their greed or the people's necessity may enable or allow them to ask. Another is the enormous tribute demanded and exacted by railroads in the way of dividends on watered stock. Another is that the present system of taxation, by which means all the poor man's property is assessed and taxed and the rich man's property overlooked, shall be so amended as to tax all men equally. But why enumerate? Both the old parties are responsible for the growth of these and many other similar abuses, and some of us have grown gray and baldheaded in trying to reform them in the old parties, with the result that the year 1891 finds them still growing in injustice as well as strength. It is simply the part of lunatics or slaves to look for reform in either of the old parties.

9. THE CULTURE OF THE POPULIST MOVEMENT

Rural life on the High Plaines in the 1890s was hard, and Populists took their politics seriously. But, as Berna Hunter Chrisman shows, they tried to enjoy themselves as much as possible. Her account of campaigning for the People's Party in Nebraska indicates that the movement represented more than just a political party to its members.

Source: Berna Hunter Chrisman, *When You And I Were Young, Nebraska!* (Broken Bow, Nebraska: Purcell's Inc., 1971), pp. 174-79. Reprinted by permission.

At the time father first became interested in the political movement, just before we moved to Broken Bow, Judge Francis Hamer, judge of the district court, in an arbitrary judicial ruling, effectively stopped the farm foreclosures by individual loaners and bankers that had been going on in the region. Judge Hamer thereby incurred the enmity of many of the large financial interests in the area. Hamer's bold act brought about better understanding of what could be done by Law, through our political system, and aided the growing solidarity of the farmers and the working people in the towns. The politicians, ever alert to determine where people are going, so they can get in front and lead them there, soon joined this farmer-labor bandwagon. And the Populist party was born.

The new agrarian movement was first called The Farmers Alliance, but it soon took on the name "Populism," and began to cross over political lines, welcoming concerned farmers and ranchers from both old political parties to support it. In the beginning, at least in Custer County, it was a rather clandestine affair, with meetings of just a few men to discuss the issues and pass around some of the literature that had originated with the founding groups in Kansas and Oklahoma. . . .

Our family orchestra had commenced to play before many of the political groups organized by the "Pops." We now had five pieces — father playing the viola; Delphy and I changing off with 1st and 2nd violins; Charley Wachter helping father and an older man, Mr. Boone, who changed off from piano to organ, or harmonica to guitar, whatever was needed to beef up the group. This work was better, and more lucrative than playing dances, for the "Pops" always believed in paying a "fair wage for a fair day's (night's) work," even if they were only bankrupt, poverty-stricken farmers and laborers. I learned from them the Biblical adage that "the laborer is worthy of his hire," and what it meant economically and socially to an entire nation to pay decent wages so folks could buy back the manufactured items and the products they had created by their labor. Of course, we often played for nothing, just to help draw the crowd to the meeting, and considered that a donation to the cause.

I believe the first "open" political meeting at which we played was when the fiery-speaking, red-haired O. M. Kem ran for Congress as an Independent in 1890. The Republican Party had dominated Nebraska politics since statehood, yet the figures from father's old journal show that Kem gave both the GOP and the Demos a terrific shellacking, at least so far as Custer County was concerned. . . .

Mr. Kem's candidacy was, of course, not that important or his victory so wide-sweeping. But he was, indeed, the first man ever elected to Congress who was born in a soddy [sod house], and his election was an earnest of things to come as the rising tide of Populism swept the mid-west.

In 1892, the election results strengthened the Pops, and Mr. Kem again was victorious. . . .

In these fierce political campaigns, "Hunter's Orchestra" continued to play at many of the meetings, caucuses and rallies. Though we were popular performers there was another, a politically vociferous group, that far exceeded us in popularity. This was The Cat Creek Band. The Cat Creekers was a group of young men that, as father said, "called a spade a spade." Though he enjoyed their music and songs, he forbid us to copy their style or sing that type of political verses. One of the Cat Creek Band's songs consisted of twelve verses, sung to a catchy and lively tune, with a snare drum appeal, that went like this:

> I have heard H. V. Allen preach, and I've heard O. M. Kem tell,
> There may be a place like Paradise, but there's no such place as Hell —
> HALLELUJA! And we'll meet you in the Bye and Bye!
> Oh the campaign is a comin', the fact you all know well,
> The Republicans will do the best they can, but you bet we'll give them Hell —
> HALLELUJA! And we'll meet you in the Bye and Bye!
> English capitalists are taking this country, you've often heard them tell,
> And the Fifth of Next November, you can bet we'll give them Hell —
> HALLELUJA! And we'll meet you in the Bye and Bye!
> Come all you Republicans, from valley, hill and dell,
> You'll have to change your evil ways, or else you'll land in Hell —
> HALLELUJA! And we'll meet you in the Bye and Bye!
> Oh, say NO, Billy Bryan, this fact you know so-o-o well,
> You'll have to leave the Democrats, or else you've gone to Hell —
> HALLELUJA, BILLY! And We'll meet you Bye and Bye!

Despite the advice to "Billy Bryan," the Pops did, at the last, let themselves divide on the issue of bi-metalism, which Bryan used to capture their fancy. The Populists literally signed their own death warrant when they followed the Bryan Democrats into the political battles just before the turn of the century. Father, and of course his two daughters, strung along with the Free Silver Crowd, and Delphy and I appeared, together with Maude Kem, the Congressman's red-haired daughter, and fourteen other young ladies of Broken Bow in a tableau presented at political meetings all over the county. We sixteen, dressed in silver dresses and with silver dollars dangling from our necks, represented Silver as Queen. Miss Maude, her red hair and golden costume, and with a gold Double Eagle dangling from her neck, represented Sound Money — Gold, backed by 16 Silver Dollars.

Another verse we heard from the die-hard Pops as we campaigned for Bryan, but one which we never chanted was:

> Boiled rats and fried cats,
> Are good enough for the Democrats!

Father frowned on such language, and we went through the several campaigns, never attempting to out-do the Cat Creek Boys, singing our own modest campaign songs such as, "Goodbye, Old Party, Goodbye!" One evening we were rewarded, when playing at the Opera House before a full house, by Mr. Kem. He made a special point to come up on the stage where we were assembled. He shook father's hand.

10. THE PRESS AND THE PARTY

Whitelaw Reid, prominent Republican and editor of the *New York Tribune*, lamented the decline of party influence in journalism. In an essay presented before the Editorial Association of New York in Rochester on June 17, 1879, Reid asserted the importance of political parties and criticized total nonpartisanship on the part of modern newspapers. A glance at the small-town press of the period will show the reader that Reid's concern was premature, although the big-city press was abandoning its earlier partisanship.

Source: Whitelaw Reid, *American and English Studies*, Vol. II (New York: Charles Scribner's Sons, 1913), pp. 258-60. Reprinted with the permission of Charles Scribner's Sons.

What shall be the relations of this new journal of the future toward parties? I may claim to have been one of the apostles of independent journalism, but the zeal of the new converts has quite left me among the old fogies. It never occurred to me that in refusing to obey blindly every behest of a party it was necessary to keep entirely aloof from party — to shut off one's self from the sole agency through which, among a free people, lasting political results can be attained. A government like ours without parties is impossible. Substantial reforms can only be reached through the action of parties. The true statesman and the really influential editor are those who are able to control and guide parties, not those who waste their strength in merely thrusting aside and breaking up the only tools with which their work can be done. There is an old question as to whether a newspaper controls public opinion or public opinion controls the newspaper. This at least is true: that editor best succeeds who best interprets the prevailing and the *better* tendencies of public opinion, and, who, whatever his personal views concerning it, does not get himself too far out of relations to it. He will understand that a party is not an end, but a means; will use it if it lead to his end, —will use some other if that serve better, but will never commit the folly of attempting to reach the end without the means. He may not blindly follow a party; in undertaking to lead it he may get ahead of it, or even against it; but he will never make the mistake of undervaluing a party, or attempting to get on permanently and produce lasting results without one. Far less will he conceive that his journalistic integrity can only be maintained by refusing to believe good of his own party save upon demonstrative evidence; while for the sake of "fairness," he refuses to believe evil of his opponents save on evidence of the same sort. What his precise relation to a party is to be, must be determined by his own character, the character of the party, and the circumstances affecting both; but some relation is inevitable, unless he would be impotent. Of all the puerile follies that have masqueraded before High Heaven in the guise of Reform, the most childish has been the idea that the editor could vindicate his independence only by sitting on the fence and throwing stones with impartial vigor alike at friend and foe.

11. ESCALATING COST OF NATIONAL CAMPAIGNS

The cost of a full-scale national campaign escalated exponentially in the last third of the nineteenth century. As professional politicians honed their techniques for reaching each voter in each precinct in the land, they also discovered how the nation's new wealth could be tapped.

Source: World's Work (November 1900), pp. 77-81.

Campaigning has become a fine art, and costly. It is well within bounds to say that it will cost more than $5,000,000 to elect a President this year. This sum will be spent by the National Committees of the two great parties, and does not include the funds collected by the several State Committees, Congressional Committees, and smaller agencies.

The use of large sums in presidential campaigns was begun by the two committees which managed General Grant's canvasses in 1868 and 1872; but Mr. Tilden more than any other one man is to be credited with the perfecting of the political methods now in vogue. He had genius for the management of men on a large scale. He saw that the mere discussion of great issues which arouse the enthusiasm of the masses, though essential, does not in itself insure success, but that much work must be done in secret, and that every voter must be brought into direct personal contact with some campaign management. Such a plan requires a comprehensive system, great volumes of correspondence, and an almost limitless use of printed matter —

in a word, an organization which touches almost every voter in the land. Mr. Tilden's business methods have replaced the old methods of hurrah and sentiment.

In 1876 more than $800,000 were collected and spent by the campaign managers of the two parties. Four years later they had at their disposal more than $1,000,000, and in 1884 the campaign disbursements were half as much again. In 1888 the Harrison-Cleveland campaign cost not less than $1,800,000; and in the campaign of 1892 the expenditure of the two National Committees were quite $2,000,000. Finally in 1896 more than $4,000,000 passed through the hands of Chairman Hanna and Chairman Jones and their associates. . . .

What use is made of the money raised by the National Committees? The answer is not always easy. First on the campaign expense account stands the cost of maintaining committee headquarters. Before 1896 campaign headquarters were established in the city of New York, but in that year both parties, though maintaining branches in the metropolis, had their chief headquarters in Chicago, and the same plan has been adopted this year. The headquarters of a National Committee must be as extensive as a great railroad's executive offices, and the cost of their maintenance, including clerk hire, will exceed rather than fall below $3,000 a day. Moreover, a great many of the parades and meetings in New York City and in Chicago are arranged and paid for by the two National Committees; and these cost large sums. A torchlight parade in New York costs from $12,000 to $20,000, and a large public meeting costs from $3,000 to $4,000 for rent, music, speakers, decorations, advertising, printing, et cetera.

The chairman of a Campaign Committee is selected by the presidential candidate himself, and is always a man in whom the candidate places implicit confidence, both as to his loyalty and his political wisdom. The first work of the Committee is to prepare campaign literature. These documents not only inform the people, but give to orators and writers a mass of facts and arguments. This year the two National Committees have probably spent $500,000 in the preparation, publication, and distribution, through the medium of State, county, and city committees, of campaign documents.

Then each headquarters maintains throughout the campaign a news bureau, which, under the direction of experienced political writers, supplies partisan news and arguments to the smaller newspapers. A good many newspapers are subsidized—newspapers in foreign tongues, and certain class journals. There are hundreds of these kinds in the larger cities and town, nearly every one of whose editors is ready to support either party for a consideration. They do not say so openly, but they announce early in a campaign that unless they are "helped" in some way by the National Committee to which they appeal, it will be inconvenient for them to devote a proper amount of space to "booming" the candidate. Payments to these political soldiers of fortune usually take the form of standing orders for a certain number of papers of each issue, the orders ranging from three thousand to ten thousand copies.

The campaign orator does not now cut the figure that he did in former years, but his influence is still great, and must be taken into account by the managers. This year hundreds of speakers are under the direction of the National Committee, especially in the doubtful States. Their expenses are paid, but the services of most of them are given without pay. A great number of attractive speakers, however, — men who have no particular fame or who cannot afford to neglect their business without compensation, — are paid during the entire campaign. Some receive $100 a week and expenses, a few as much as $1,000 a week. They get cues from headquarters and are cautioned as to the peculiarities of each locality. They talk differently to the farmers and to the city people; and as a rule those speakers are preferred who tell many anecdotes, and know how to point a political argument with a joke. The result of this flood of oratory which costs a National Committee from $100,000 to $200,000, is doubtful. As Republican mass meetings are attended mainly by Republican voters, and Democratic mass meetings by Democratic voters the number of converts made by them must be small. But they serve to create enthusiasm and to maintain and to improve party discipline. Useful for the same purposes are the campaign clubs and societies, whose organization and equipment cost in the aggregate a large sum.

How is the money raised for all these expenses and for others even greater? The work has developed shrewd and successful beggars of money. As a collector of campaign funds Mr. Marshall Jewell, who was for several years chairman of the Republican National Committee, perhaps never had an equal. When others failed he succeeded and it is told of him that in Boston in a single day he collected $170,000. President Arthur was a charming beggar, and when he was an active politician his services as a money-getter were always counted as of the first importance. He had much to do with the collection of the funds disbursed by the Republican National Committee in 1880. So had Governor Levi P. Morton, who it is generally believed, within twenty-four hours collected $300,000 or thereabouts for purely technical politics. His powers were again put to the test in 1888. He followed a method of his own. He prepared a list of men whom he knew, and put down opposite their names the sums he thought they ought to give, and he went to see them. Few words were spoken. The businessmen looked upon the matter as a business transaction, and felt confident that Mr. Morton had good business reasons for calling upon them.

"Do you think I ought to put my name down for so much, Mr. Morton?"

"If I had not thought so, I shouldn't have named that amount."

Most men paid without further ado.

The fund used to elect Mr. Cleveland in 1884 came, in the main, from a dozen men. Mr. William L. Scott, Mr. William C. Whitney, and Mr. Oliver H. Payne each gave, it is believed, quite $100,000. It is thought that Mr. Edward Cooper and Mr. Abram S. Hewitt each contributed an equal amount. Senator Benjamin F. Jones was chairman of the Republican National Committee in that year, and with the aid of Senator Stephen B. Elkins he collected in round figures $800,000. But this sum did not pay all the bills, and there was a deficiency at the end of the campaign of $115,000. This Senator Jones made good out of his own pocket. . . .

Campaign managers say that it is under most conditions easier to raise money for the party which is out of power than for the party that is in office. Be this as it may, it is certain that the Democratic managers in 1892 had a larger fund at their disposal than the Republicans. And in 1896, when the Republicans were out of office, the commitee headed by Chairman Hanna collected a campaign fund almost twice as large as the fund of the managers of the Bryan canvass. It is an open secret that the largest subscriber to this fund was Mr. William K. Vanderbilt, who sent his check for $150,000. It was not sent in answer to any appeal, but was a deliberate and voluntary gift late in the campaign. The largest subscription from a corporation came from a purely savings and benevolent association, whose directors voted $25,000, "to protect their depositors from loss of their savings."

This fact brings us to the source of most of the campaign funds in recent years — the great corporations. The so-called "business interests" contribute most freely to the party that is in power; for they wish no change in the conduct of affairs; but many large concerns contribute to both sides, to have friends at court in any event. Office-holders are another certain source of revenue to the National Committee of the party in power, and a third source is a considerable class of men who, anxious to secure political prominence or to occupy high positions, give lavishly as a means of advancing their personal interests. Finally comes the aggregate of small popular subscriptions, which, especially in contests of unusual enthusiasm, is a large sum. . . .

There is always a sum, large or small, spent in "secret" work, which is charged on the books of the Committee to some general account, where it could never be traced, just as the contributions of corporations are charged on the books of these corporations to some account where a stockholder, for instance, could never find it. There are many uses of campaign money that the managers think prudent to keep secret which are not illegitimate. Indeed, the money that is used at last in buying votes on election day may have been properly charged on the books of a National Committee as a legitimate expenditure, and it may have been perverted from its legitimate use on the last day by the last man who received it; or — it may have come from some "secret" fund which had in the beginning been provided for uses that would not bear investigation. How much is spent in buying votes can never be guessed at. But since the secret ballot law went into effect in many States, bribery has been lessened. . . .

The most expensive work of a national campaign is done during the last three weeks before the election. Every doubtful State and city is closely watched by men prompt to discover every change in the political tide, and money is transmitted in large sums to the localities in which it is believed it will produce the best results. A few days before the election in 1888 West Virginia received $44,000 from the Democratic National Committee, and the Republicans sent $50,000 to the same State. About the same time the Democrats sent $100,000 into Indiana; and three nights before the election Chairman Quay, of the Republican National Committee, sent $300,000 from New York, to trusted lieutenants in Fort Wayne, Indiana. A fortnight before the election of 1896 the Republicans became doubtful about Iowa. Chairman Hanna at once resolved upon a personal canvass of every doubtful voter in the State. He proposed that every voter not classed on the polling lists either as a downright Democrat or a downright Republican should be visited by some zealous and tactful member of the Republican party. Before election day the thousands of such men in towns, in cities, and in the country were sought out and appealed to by the Republicans most likely to win them; and this canvass is said to have cost the Republican National Committee more than $200,000. Political parties are now so thoroughly organized and national campaigns are so skillfully conducted, that the vote of every State can be foretold with reasonable accuracy at least ten days before election, but the loss of a presidential election by 1,200 votes proves the lurking perils that beset the pathway of the wariest political strategist.

Reckoning all the expenses in all the States, it may be roughly estimated that a presidential campaign, including also Congressional, gubernatorial and lesser campaigns, causes the total expenditure of perhaps $20,000,000.

The work of campaign committees, National, State, Congressional, and even county and ward, is not done when the election is held; for the whole vast machinery is kept in existence, even if it have periods of inactivity, and work begins again, long before the public suspects it, in preparation for the next nominating conventions. . . .

Thus an irresponsible oligarchy has grown up. But it differs from almost every other oligarchy in history in this — only a few, and they the vulgarest, of the oligarchs receive public credit, or money, or dignity, or great offices, or any reward, except the excitement of the game. Indeed, many of them spend large private fortunes in the work. But it is such exciting exercise that few men who once engage in it ever lose a keen interest in it. Most of them for the fun of it — the exhilaration that comes of producing worldwide results. Some work for purely patriotic reasons.

Chart 2

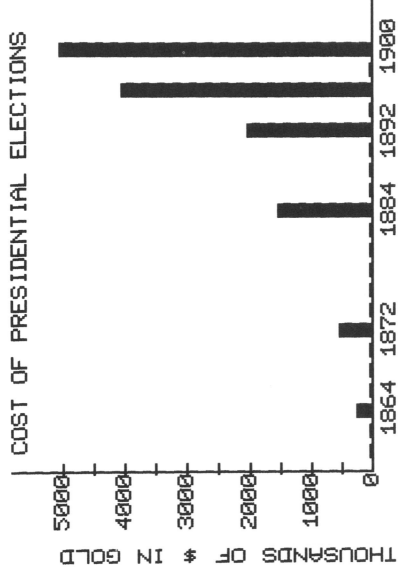

COST OF PRESIDENTIAL ELECTIONS

THOUSANDS OF $ IN GOLD

12. MR. DOOLEY COMMENTS ON
PRESIDENTIAL CAMPAIGNS

Mr. Dooley, creation of Finley Peter Dunne, political satirist
and one of the highest paid journalists at the turn of the century,
comments on the contests between William Jennings Bryan and
William McKinley. The highly popular Mr. Dooley lectures his
friend Mr. Hennessy on the important differences between the
Democratic and Republican platforms. He describes the activities of the candidates in the race and pokes fun at some of the
leading issues of the day.

Source: Finley Peter Dunne, Mr. Dooley's Philosophy (New York: Harper and
Brothers, 1906), pp. 100-102, 229-34.

"Years ago, Hinnissy, manny years ago, they was a race between th' dimmycrats an'th' raypublicans f'r to see which shud have a choice iv principles.
Th' dimmycrats lost. I dinnaw why. Mebbe they stopped to take a dhrink.
Annyhow, they lost. Th' raypublicans come up an' they choose th' 'we commind' principles, an' they was nawthin' left f'r the dimmycrats but th' 'we
denounce an' deplores.' I dinnaw how it come about, but th' dimmycrats
didn't like th' way th' thing shtud, an' so they fixed it up between thim that
whichiver won at th' iliction shud commind an' congratulate, an' thim that
lost shud denounce an' deplore. An' so it's been, on'y the dimmycrats has
had so little chanct f'r to do annything but denounce an' deplore that they've
almost lost th' use iv th' other wurruds.

"Mack sets back in Wash'nton an' writes a platform f'r th' comity on riso-
lutions to compose th' week afther. He's got a good job — forty-nine ninety-
two, sixty-six a month — an' 'tis up to him to feel good. 'I — I mean we,' he
says, 'congratulate th' counthry on th' matchless statesmanship, onshrinkin'
courage, steady devotion to duty an' principle iv that gallant an' hon'rable
leader, mesilf,' he says to his sicrety. 'Take that,' he says, 'an' elaborate it,'
he says. 'Ye'll find a ditchnry on th' shelf near the dure,' he says, 'f ye don't
think I've put what I give ye sthrong enough,' he says. 'I always was,' he
says, 'too retirin' f'r me own good,' he says. 'Spin out th' r-rest,' he says, 'to
make about six thousan' wurruds,' he says, 'but be sure don't write annything too hot about th' Boer war or th' Ph'lippeens or Chiny, or th' tariff, or
th' goold question, or our relations with England, or th' civil sarvice,' he

says. "'Tis a foolish man,' he says, 'that throws a hunk iv coal fr'm his own window at th' dhriver iv a brick wagon' he says.

"But with Billy Bryan 'tis diff'rent. He's out in Lincoln, Neebrasky, far fr'm home, an' he says to himsilf: 'Me throat is hoarse, an' I'll exercise me other fac'lties,' he says. 'I'll write a platform,' he says. An' he sets down to a typewriter, an' denounces an' deplores till th' hired man blows th' dinner horn. Whin he can denounce an' deplore no longer he views with alarm an' declares with indignation. An' he sinds it down to Kansas City, where th' cot beds come fr'm."

"Oh, ye're always pitchin' into some wan," said Mr. Hennessy. "I bet ye Willum Jennings Bryan niver see th' platform befure it wint in. He's too good a man."

"He is all iv that," said Mr. Dooley. "But ye bet he knows th' rale platform f'r him is: 'Look at th' bad breaks Mack's made,' an' Mack's platform is: 'Ye'd get worse if ye had Billy Bryan.' An' it depinds on whether most iv th' voters ar-re tired out or on'y a little tired who's ilicted. . . .

"Oh, I guess th' campaign is doin' as well as cud be ixpicted. I see be th' raypublican pa-apers that Andhrew Carnegie has come out f'r Bryan an' has conthributed wan half iv his income or five hundhred millyon dollars to th' campaign fund. In th' dimmycratic pa-apers I r-read that Chairman Jim Jones has inthercipted a letther fr'm the Prince iv Wales to Mack congratu-latin' him on his appintmint as gintleman-in-waitin' to th' queen. A dilly-gation iv Mormons has started fr'm dimmycratic headquarthers to thank Mack f'r his manly stand in favor iv poly-gamy an' th' raypublican commity has undher con-sideration a letther fr'm long term criminals advisin' their colleagues at large to vote f'r Willum Jennings Bryan, th' frind iv crime.

"In a few short weeks, Hinnissy, 'twill not be safe f'r ayether iv the candy-dates to come out on th' fr-ront porch till th' waitin' dillygations has been searched be a polisman. 'Tis th' divvle's own time th' la-ads that r-runs f'r th' prisidincy has since that ol' boy Burchard broke loose again' James G. Blaine. Sinitor Jones calls wan iv his thrusty hinchmen to his side, an' says he: 'Mike, put on a pig-tail, an' a blue shirt an' take a dillygation iv Chinnymen out to Canton an' congratulate Mack on th' murdher iv mission'ries in China. An',' he says, 'ye might stop off at Cincinnati on th' way over an' arrange f'r a McKinley an' Rosenfelt club to ilict th' British Consul its prisi-dint an' attack th' office iv th' German newspaper,' he says. Mark Hanna rings f'r his sicrety an', says he: 'Have ye got off th' letther fr'm George Fred Willums advisin' Aggynaldoo to pizen th' wells?' 'Yes sir.' 'An' th' secret communication fr'm Bryan found on an arnychist at Pattherson askin' him to blow up th' White House?' 'It's in th' hands iv th' tyepwriter.' 'Thin call up an employmint agency an' have a dillygation iv Jesuites dhrop in at Lincoln, with a message fr'm th' pope proposin' to bur-rn all Protestant churches th' night befure iliction.'

"I tell ye, Hinnissy, th' candydate is kept movin'. Whin he sees a dilly-gation pikin' up th' lawn he must be r-ready. He makes a flyin' leap f'r th' chairman, seizes him by th' throat an' says: 'I thank ye f'r th' kind sintimints ye have conveyed. I am, indeed, as ye have remarked, th' riprisintative iv th' party iv manhood, honor, courage, liberality an' American thraditions. Take that back to Jimmy Jones an' tell him to put it in his pipe an' smoke it.' With which he bounds into th' house an' locks the dure while th' baffled con-spirators goes down to a costumer an' changes their disguise. If th' future prisidint hadn't been quick on th' dhraw he'd been committed to a policy iv sthranglin' all the girl babies at birth.

"No, 'tis no aisy job bein' a candydate, an' 'twud be no easy job if th' game iv photygraphs was th' on'y wan th' candydates had to play. Willum Jennings Bryan is photygraphed smilin' back at his smilin' corn fields, in a pair iv blue overalls with a scythe in his hand borrid fr'm th' company that's playin' 'Th' Ol' Homestead,' at th' Lincoln Gran' Opry House. Th' nex' day Mack is seen mendin' a rustic chair with a monkey wrinch, Bryan has a pitcher took in th' act iv puttin' on a shirt marked with th' union label, an' they'se another photygraph iv Mack carryin' a scuttle iv coal up th' cellar stairs. An' did ye iver notice how much th' candydates looks alike, an' how much both iv thim looks like Lydia Pinkham? Thim wondherful boardhin'-house smiles that our gifted leaders wears, did ye iver see anny-thin' so entrancin'? Whin th' las' photygrapher has packed his ar-rms home-ward I can see th' gr-reat men retirin' to their rooms an' lettin' their faces down f'r a few minyits before puttin' thim up again in curl-pa-apers f'r th' nex' day display....

"I wisht th' campaign was over."

"I wisht it'd begin," said Mr. Hennessy. "I niver knew annything so dead. They ain't been so much as a black eye give or took in th' ward an' it's less thin two months to th' big day."

"'Twill liven up," said Mr. Dooley, "I begin to see signs iv th' good times comin' again. 'Twas on'y th' other day me frind Tiddy Rosenfelt opened th' battle mildly be insinuatin' that all dimmycrats was liars, horse thieves an' arnychists. 'Tis thrue he apologized f'r that be explainin' that he didn't mean all dimmycrats but on'y thost that wudden't vote f'r Mack but I think he'll take th' copper off befure manny weeks. A ladin' dimmycratic rayformer has suggested that Mack though a good man f'r an idjiot is surrounded be th' vilest scoundhrels iver seen in public life since th' days iv Joolyus Caesar. Th' Sicrety iv th' Threeasury has declared, that Mr. Bryan in sayin' that silver is not convartible be th' terms iv th' Slatthry bankin' law iv 1870, an' th' sicond clause iv th' threaty iv Gansville, has committed th' onpard'nable pollytical sin iv so consthructin' th' facts as to open up th' possibility iv wan not knowin' th' thrue position iv affairs, misundhersthandin' intirely. If he had him outside he'd call him a liar."

13. MCKINLEY'S MODERN CAMPAIGN METHODS

In 1896 the Republican Party made great gains among traditionally Democratic voters. In order to maintain this advantage in
1900, the Republicans once again mobilized their vast campaign
resources. The efficient Republican machine successfully attempted to avoid divisive issues. Instead, it appealed to ethnic
and religious minorities, reminding them that, while the pietistic
Bryan threatened their way of life, McKinley and the Republicans meant jobs and prosperity.

Source: *Review of Reviews*, November 1900, pp. 550-55.

A visit to the offices of the National Committee in October gives an
impression akin to that made by the executive establishment of a great railroad or a great manufactory.

The enormous task of preparing campaign literature, the routine work of
the fight, went on steadily from early summer. Tens of thousands of
pamphlets, leaflets, and documents of varying sizes were compiled, setting
forth figures and arguments on the issues as they had shaped themselves,
and as they were outlined and defined in the platforms of the Republican
and Democratic conventions. The pièce de rèsistance of this matter, "The
Republican Campaign Text-Book," was ready for distribution in August.
This is a compendium of invaluable information, compiled with great care
and enormous labor, and intended primarily for the use of the thousands of
men who were to do duty as orators in the Republican cause.

It is not mailed directly from the Literature Bureau at headquarters, but
shipped in bulk, by the carload often, to the chairmen of State and local
committees, who attend to the individual distribution. In 1896, the cost of
this branch of the work was something over $700,000. This year it may get
near the million-dollar mark.

The three distinct lines of effort used to make Republican votes are public
speaking, the dissemination of documents, —leaflets, brochures, books,
posters, badges, and buttons, —and the insertion of Republican editorials
and news articles in the weekly and daily papers of the country. Most of the
committee officials consider the last rather the most effective of the three
kinds of propaganda, and the machinery for utilizing the papers is most
elaborate and ingenious.

In Chicago, Mr. Charles R. Buckland is the head worker in this field,
under Secretary Perry S. Heath. Mr. Buckland has seven assistants, two of

whom read all current literature interested in political matters for good articles worth using for campaign services, while five write the matter to be
inserted in the newspapers. There are three ways of getting these articles
and editorials in the papers of the country: the country weeklies receive
"patent insides;" about 200 papers, many of them country dailies, get stereo-
typed matter, and to the more important papers proof-slips are mailed, to
be set up at the editor's discretion. Practically all of the Republican papers
use this matter, and some Independent organs. In fact, many of the country
papers — 2,000, it is estimated — have no other political news and discussion
except what is sent out from Republican headquarters. The total result of
this effort is enormous; nearly 4,000 papers publish the articles and editorials regularly. The articles are on the most varied subjects — "Troop Trans-
ports," "Rural Free Delivery," and "Sheep in Oregon;" but the net result of
every one of them is an earnest exhortation to vote the Republican ticket.
The ingenius journalists intrusted with the task of "education" do not disdain, either devices like the "Dear Boy" letters, ostensibly containing a
father's advice to his son, but cunningly leading on into resounding arguments for McKinley and Roosevelt. . . .

Mr. Edward Rosewater, in charge of the national campaign in Nebraska,
has been reprinting in his paper, the Omaha Bee, the actual news items of
four years ago, showing the distress of the country four years ago. Beside
these notices of foreclosure, statistics of starving men, and of applications at
the soup-houses of Omaha, he prints the news of the present day, showing
the railroads searching for men, offers of money at 4 per cent, current statistics of mortgage liquidation, and other features of prosperity.

So much for the utilization of the press. The pamphlet, leaflet, and poster
work is even more enormous in dimensions and in cost. Over 70 different
documents and eight posters have been put out, — 80,000,000 copies of
them, — at a cost of $164,000. One of the illustrations of this article shows
perhaps the most popular of the posters, "McKinley Was Right," of which
550,000 copies were printed and distributed. The Republicans have kept
very honestly to their avowed purpose of using only dignified logic and discussion for persuading voters; but the campaign button, coming more
under the "notion" classification, could not be wholly omitted, and 3,000,000
of these, of three different sorts, have been sent out.

The 70 different documents range from mere leaflets to the remarkably
comprehensive and intelligent Republican "Campaign Text-Book."

President McKinley's letter of acceptance was, too, printed in several lan-
guages — 2,500,000 copies in English, 500,000 in German, 250,000 in Nor-
wegian, 250,000 in Swedish, 100,000 in Bohemian, the same in Polish, and
50,000 in Italian and Dutch, respectively.

Sectional prejudices are being carefully considered in the general dissemination of literature. About three-fifths of all the literature is sent out from
Chicago, about 18,000,000 pieces from Philadelphia, and a large part of

that which goes to the Norwestern States is issued from Milwaukee and St. Paul. For special conditions of sentiment, such as exist in the Silver States of Colorado, Wyoming, Utah, and Idaho, special arrangements are made. The regular campaign literature is edited by a well-informed gentleman in Denver, to adapt it to the tastes of the Mountain States, and is then distributed from Denver. So there is a special service for negroes and their papers, and the religious papers are supplied with sermons turning on political questions.

The third division of campaign effort is in public speaking — or, colloquially, "spellbinding."

Before the campaign, a complete list is made up of the available speakers in the country of the Republican way of thinking and those best suited for the purpose are selected. Many of them have salaries as well as expenses, while others receive only their expenses. They range in importance and dignity from the ordinary cart-tail "spellbinder" to great oratorical stars, like Governor Roosevelt, with their private cars and special trains. There are a great number of applicants for the work of political oratory; the qualifications of these are examined into by members of the committee, and sometimes they are unexpectedly called on for a sample speech to test their powers.

Over 600 regular committee orators are managed from the Chicago headquarters, and several hundred from the New York headquarters. These figures do not by any means suggest the total number of speakers, for there are hundreds of volunteers; and, when a "regular" orator holds forth at a particular town, prominent Republicans, lawyers, and officials of the community join him to make the demonstration a success. In the different States the chairmen of the State committees have in their care a large number of "spellbinders," whose selection and movements are made in the course of constant consultation with the National Headquarters. The manager of these speakers, with a hundred or more every night on his hands, with itineraries to lay out and dates to be made without conflict and with the best total effect in relation to the evening's movements — has no small task on his hands. Among the Republican "spellbinders" are 50 Germans, 25 Swedes, 25 Norwegians, 10 Poles, 10 Italians, 5 Frenchmen, and 6 Finns. There is no difficulty whatever in obtaining the necessary quantity of campaign speakers; 5,000 have sought engagement at Chicago.

In addition to the speeches proper, there are Republican and sound-money parades and rallies to be brought off with éclat, and such picturesque demonstrations as are now taking place in Chicago, where "prosperity wagons" are sent out on the streets every day, with Republican enthusiasts to give heart-to-heart talks to laborers throughout the city.

The preparation and distribution of literature, with the engagement and assignment of speakers forms the great bulk of the routine work of the campaign. What requires the acumen and experience of Senator Hanna and his immediate associates lies in meeting issues as they arise — in taking advantage of circumstances, in determining what States may be considered safe without extra effort, and what States need the concentration of party energy. It may happen, as it has happened, that a State conceded to the other side can be won by properly directed efforts. The Campaign Committee receives almost daily reports from the State committees. In this regard, the Republican organization is better perfected this year than ever before. In every State local committees are hard at work, so that not an inch of ground is left uncovered. These local committees report frequently to the State committees, which in turn report to the executive committee, so that Senator Hanna and his advisers are kept constantly in touch with the conditions all over the country as they vary from week to week.

14. TOM JOHNSON'S CRUSADING STYLE

Tom Johnson, progressive mayor of Cleveland (1901-1909) achieved national prominence for his reform administration and for his campaign methods, both of which emphasized popular participation at the local level. In his autobiography Johnson describes his tent-meeting campaign style. This type of campaign became an important element in Progressive Era politics.

Source: Tom Johnson, *My Story*, Elizabeth J. Hauser, ed. (New York: B. W. Huebsch, 1913), pp. 82-84.

CHANCE was responsible for my tent meeting campaigning. Once in one of my early Congressional campaigns when I wanted to have a meeting in the eighteenth ward in Cleveland there was no hall to be had. A traveling showman had a small tent pitched on a vacant lot and someone suggested that it might be utilized. It had no chairs but there were a few boxes which could be used as seats. Very doubtful of the result we made the experiment. It cost me eighteen dollars, I remember. After that I rented tents from a tent man and finally bought one and then several.

The tent meeting has many advantages over the hall meeting. Both sides, I should say all sides, will go to tent meetings — while as rule only partisans go to halls. Women did not go to political meetings in halls in those days unless some especially distinguished person was advertised to speak, but they showed no reluctance about coming to tent meetings. In a tent there is a freedom from restraint that is seldom present in halls. The audience seems to feel that it has been invited there for the purpose of finding out the position of the various speakers. There is greater freedom in asking questions too, and this heckling is the most valuable form of political education. Tent meetings can be held in all parts of the city — in short the meetings are literally taken to the people. It was not long after I got into municipal politics in Cleveland before the custom of tent meetings was employed in behalf of ward councilmen as well as for candidates on the general ticket, and they too were heckled and made to put themselves on record. The custom of heckling is the most healthy influence in politics. It makes candidates respect pre-election pledges, forces them to meet not only the opposition candidates but their constituents.

But the greatest benefit of the tent meeting, the one which cannot be measured, is the educational influence on the people who compose the audience. It makes them take an interest as nothing else could do, and educates them on local questions as no amount of reading, even of the fairest newspaper accounts, could do. I do not believe there is a city in the country where the electorate is so well informed upon local political questions, nor upon the rights of the people as opposed to the privileges of corporations, as it is in Cleveland. Detroit and Toledo probably come next. The tent meeting is largely responsible for this public enlightenment of the people of Cleveland.

The one disadvantage of the tent is that it is not weather-proof. And yet it was seldom indeed that a meeting had to be abandoned on account of rain. Great audiences came even on rainy nights and our speakers have frequently spoken from under dripping umbrellas to good-natured crowds, a few individuals among them protected by umbrellas but many sitting in the wet with strange indifference to physical discomfort.

At first my enemies called my tent a "circus menagerie" and no part of my political work has been so persistently cartooned; but when they employed tents somewhat later they called theirs "canvas auditoriums." The adoption of the tent meeting by these same enemies or their successors may not have been intended either as an endorsement of the method or as a compliment to my personal taste, but I can't help considering it a little of both.

15. AN INDEPENDENT CHALLENGES THE SYSTEM, 1908

Ben B. Lindsey served as a juvenile court judge in Denver during the first decade of the twentieth century. He championed the rights of youthful offenders and challenged the power of large corporations, which he called "the Beast." In his autobiography,

entitled *The Beast*, he described his fight for re-election to the
bench in 1908. Unable to gain a nomination from the two major
parties, whom he said were dominated by "the Beast," he successfully mobilized grass roots support and won as an independent.

Source: Ben B. Lindsey and Harvey J. O'Higgins, *The Beast* (New York:
Doubleday, Page and Co., 1910), pp. 306-21. Reprinted by permission.

We tried to raise a campaign fund. My friends went first among the business men — and found their pockets buttoned. All our efforts ended in raising only $450. The business men said that I was "the man for the place," but
that I was foolish to attack the corporations, and that it was dangerous for a
man of business to support me.

I then tried the ministers. I sent a letter to every preacher in Denver —
about one hundred and fifty in all — explaining my difficulties and asking
them to meet me in the Juvenile Court on an appointed evening. Four or five
sent letters of regret. Two or three came to the meeting. The others were
silent.

I talked to a number of school teachers who came to my chambers privately to promise me their support. They told me that many teachers were
eager to help, but dared not make themselves conspicuous because it was
known that the First National Bank and the Moffat-Evans-Cheesman interests controlled the School Board; and the teachers were afraid of losing their
positions.

I tried the leaders of the Woman's Club. One able and wealthy woman, of
whose support I was certain, confessed that she could not even sign my
nominating petition. She said that if any woman of wealth wished to take
part in such a fight, she would have to invest her money in another state.

I went at the beginning of the campaign to practically all the women's suffrage leaders who, at national meetings, had been telling how much the
women had done for the Juvenile Court in Denver; and none of them dared
help me.

The corporation newspapers — the Denver *Republican* and the Denver
Post — were, of course, against us. I went to Senator Patterson and asked
him for the support of his papers, the *Rocky Mountain News* and the
Denver *Times*; he replied that he would support me if I could get on a party
ticket; but his managers seemed to object to wasting the influence of the
papers in a hopeless, independent struggle. There was one other daily, the
"little" *Express*, a Scripps paper that had been established in Denver by Mr.
Scripps, at the solicitation of members of the Honest Election League, to aid
in the fight for the people. It was sold for a cent a copy — the other papers
sold for five cents — and it had gradually gained a circulation among the
working people of the city. Its editor was an incorruptibly fearless young

man, Mr. B. F. Gurley, who had had experience in Cleveland and Los Angeles. He knew the Beast and understood how to fight it.

The next aid that came seems still to me an accident that was little short of miraculous. There happened to be listening to me a lady whom I had met only a short time before. She had first heard of the Juvenile Court through Mr. Lincoln Steffens's articles in *McClure's Magazine* and she had later heard me lecture in the East. She had become interested in the work of the court; and now, after learning of our need of money to defend the court in an election, she went to one of the court officers and asked whether she might be allowed to contribute $5,000 to a campaign fund. She has never allowed her name to be made known. She has never accepted any credit for her act. But there is not a shadow of doubt in my mind that she saved the Juvenile Court.

We began to organize at once. Mr. E. V. Brake, a labour leader, took charge. He got volunteers among his followers to act as ward workers and even coaxed many away from the other parties to join with us. About two hundred women, many of them volunteers, came to our headquarters, took instructions on how to teach the voters to "scratch," and began to go from house to house repeating the lesson.

When Mr. Gilson Gardener, the Washington correspondent of the Scripps papers, came to Denver, Field said to him—in one of the most important pronouncements ever made by the Beast: "Our company is in politics? Yes. Why? By virtue of necessity. Our company contributes to political parties and for political purposes? Yes. Why? Because this is the modern system. It began years ago. It exists for the same reason that we contribute to a state fair or a Y.M.C.A. It became the custom, long since, to expect corporations to contribute to all kinds of things. And finally, it was politics. Then it became necessary. There came the unfair acts, and we needed men in office who would be our friends.

"Our company is in politics in order to have friends. We never have asked for anything improper. I speak for no other corporation or person; but our company has always been above reproach. But we do have friends. We have them in both parties. They come to me and ask advice. They come and ask me to help them lay their plans. They come regardless of their parties and they hold meetings in my office. I am not a boss. I have carefully avoided being anything like that. But I can't help it if they come to me and ask advice."

We made it plain that our fight was against the tyranny of the corporations. The unions passed resolutions endorsing our work, and the members of the barbers' union made every barber shop in Denver a centre of propaganda which their lathered customers could not escape. We sent out, from our headquarters, cards to the voters for them to sign, pledging their votes; and we received 23,000 of these pledges signed.

The women—not so much their suffrage leaders or their politicians, as the mothers in the homes and the working women in the factories and the shops — came out for us by the thousands. Our headquarters swarmed with newsboys and schoolchildren anxious to help; and some of those boys made the most effective campaign orators we had.

Denver *Express* kept on hammering; the signed pledges kept coming in; and at last Senator Patterson's two papers swung into line and things began to move with a whoop. The Christian Citizenship Union had succeeded in reaching the "church element" in spite of the opposition of those wealthy churches whose boards were controlled by the Beast. The labouring men and their wives packed our meetings. In the foreign quarters, and particularly on the West Side among the Russian Jews, the poor mothers whose children I had befriended received us with tears running down their cheeks, so that I could hardly speak to them for the choke in my throat. The people were up — with a shout — with a shout that was at once angry and tearful with anger, for we did not yet believe we could win — and the politicians shut their ears to it, and orated about their presidential candidates.

Our campaign went on gaily. It was a straight campaign against corporation rule. I made no appeals to sentiment; I often left the question of our court work out of my speeches. I was determined that if I was to be beaten, I must be beaten as the opponent of the Beast; and that if I was to be saved, it must be by voters who saw who were their masters and revolted against them. All the usual tricks of the Beast were used against us. Many Democratic and Republican "workers," in going their rounds, whenever they were asked by a voter how to vote for me, replied: "Oh, that's all right. He's on our ticket. Just vote it straight." And our workers were kept busy explaining that I was on neither party ticket.

When the polls opened, the betting was four to one that I would not get ten thousand votes. Early in the forenoon, it was known that at every polling place in Denver the people were "scratching" as they had never "scratched" before. Women wearing long white badges — "Vote for Judge Lindsey" — watched the approaches to the polling places all day long, without relief, and accosted every voter. A newsboy, on the previous night, had obtained a dollar from our committee for "campaign expenses," had bought a dollar's worth of coloured chalk and sent out a horde of boys to mark the sidewalks, the walls and the fences with "Vote for Judge Lindsey" — and the party henchmen with brushes and mops had not succeeded in entirely obliterating that "handwriting on the wall." By midday the betting gave odds in my favour, and the excitement among the politicians was breathless. . . . At last, late in the evening, I was summoned to the telephone by a call from my old opponent "Big Steve" — A. M. Stevenson — at Republican Headquarters; and he said "Ben, it's a d— miracle. You're elected, and that's about all that's certain. There's been so much 'scratching' we don't know where the h— we're at!"

Elected? Out of 65,000 votes cast, we had polled, on the official count, 32,000, which was almost as many as my two opponents had together.

16. THE STRUGGLE FOR WOMAN'S SUFFRAGE

When women first declared they should vote (in 1848) men hooted them down. Their duty was to uplift society by nurturing their families; politics was too dirty for the fair sex! By 1900 suffragists gained broad support among more modern men and women by arguing that women's superior moral influence was needed in politics, and that the housewife could not protect her family without becoming active in municipal affairs. World War One stimulated acceptance of modern ideals in both America and Europe, and women were given the vote. The last years of the suffrage movement did require effective organization to counter traditionalists in the South and among liturgical ethnic groups in the northern cities.

Source: Inez Haynes Irwin, *The Story of the Woman's Party* (New York: Harcourt, Brace & Co., 1921), pp. 197-99, 317, 319-20, 325-26. Reprinted by permission.

From the moment in 1912 that the Suffragists started their work in Washington, relations had to be established with the House and the Senate. At first, tentative, a little wavering, irregular, the lobbying became finally astute, intensive, and constant. The lobby grew in numbers. . . .

By 1914, the stream had grown to a flood. The halls of Congress were never free from this invasion. The siege lasted without cessation as long as a Congress was in session. "This place looks like a millinery establishment," a Congressman said once.

In the early days, the reception of the lobbyists at the hands of Congressmen lacked by many degrees that graciousness of which, at the very end, they were almost certain. A story of this early period taken from the Woman's Party card index is most illuminating.

Two Suffrage lobbyists were calling on Hoke Smith (of Georgia). "As you are Suffragists," Mr. Smith said, "you won't mind standing." He himself sat, lounging comfortably in his chair. He took out a big cigar, inserted it in his mouth, lighted it. The two women said what they had to say, standing, while Mr. Smith smoked contemptuously on. . . .

At all times this work was hard, and sometimes intensely disagreeable. Maud Younger in her Revelations of a Woman Lobbyist, gives some of the actual physical strain. She says:

The path of the lobbyist is a path of white marble. And white marble, though beautiful, is hard. The House office building runs around four sides of a block, so that when you have walked around one floor, you have walked four blocks on white

marble. When you have walked around each of the five floors you have walked a
mile on white marble. When you have gone this morning and afternoon through
several sessions of Congress you have walked more weary miles on white marble
than a lobbyist has time to count.

But the Woman's Party lobbyists were not balked by the mere matter of
white marble. In a week they were threading that interminable intricate
maze of Congressional alleys with the light, swift step of familiarity and of
determination. All day long, they drove from the Visitors' Reception Room
to Senatorial offices, and from Senatorial offices back to the Visitors' Reception Room. They flew up and down in the elevators. They found unknown
and secret stairways by which they made short cuts. They journeyed back
and forth in the little underground subway which tries to mitigate these long
distances. At first Congressmen frankly took to hiding, and the lobbyist discovered that the Capitol was a nest of abris, but in the end, even Congressmen could not elude the vigilance of youth and determination. As for the
mental and spiritual difficulties of the task — at first, Senators and Congressmen were frankly uninterested, or, more concretely, irritated and enraged
with the Suffrage lobbyists. It is not pleasant to have to talk to a man who
does not want to hear you. The lobbyists had to learn to be quiet; deferen-
tial; to listen to long intervals of complaint and abuse; to seem not to notice
rebuffs; to go back the next day as though the rebuff had not occurred. This
is not easy to women of spirit. Perhaps it could not have been borne, if it
had not been a labor of love. Many times these women had to bolster a
smarting sense of humiliation by keeping the thought of victory in sight. . . .
     But harder still was it to elude a something, an unknown quality — an x —
which had come into the fourth generation of women to demand enfranchisement. That quality was political-mindedness. Congressmen had undoubtedly before run the gamut of feminine persuasiveness; grace; charm;
tact. But here was an army of young Amazons who looked them straight in
the eye, who were absolutely informed, who knew their rights, who were
not to be frightened by bluster, put off by rudeness, or thwarted either by
delay or political trickery. They never lost their tempers and they never
gave up. They never took "No" for an answer. They were young and they
believed they could do the impossible. And believing it, they accomplished
it. Before the six years and a half of campaign . . . was over, Congressman
after Congressman, Senator after Senator paid tribute — often a grudged one
— to the verve and élan of that campaign. . . .
     The first picket line appeared on January 10, 1917; the last, over a year
and a half later. Between those dates, except when Congress was not in session, more than a thousand women held lettered banners, accompanied by
the purple, white, and gold tri-colors, at the White House gates, or in front
of the Capitol. They picketed every day of the week, except Sunday; in all
kinds of weather, in rain and in sleet, in hail, and in snow. All varieties of

women picketed: all races and religions; all cliques and classes; all professions and parties. Washington became accustomed to the dignified picture —the pickets moving with a solemn silence, always in a line that followed a crack in the pavement; always a banner's length apart; taking their stand with a precision almost military; maintaining it with a movelessness almost statuesque. Washington became accustomed also to the rainbow splash at the White House gates—"like trumpet calls," somebody described the banners. Artists often spoke of the beauty of their massed color. In the daytime, those banners gilded by the sunlight were doubly brilliant, but at twilight the effect was transcendent. Everywhere the big, white lights, set in the parks on such low standards that they seemed strange, luminous blossoms, springing from the masses of emerald green shrubbery—filled the dusk with bluish-white splendor, and, made doubly colorful by this light, the long purple, white, and gold ribbon stood out against a background beautiful and appropriate; a mosaic on the gray of the White House pavement; the pen-and-ink blackness of the White House iron work; the bare, brown criss-cross of the White House trees, and the chaste colonial simplicity of the White House itself. . . .

Various States celebrated State days on the picket line. Maryland was the first of these, and the long line of Maryland women bearing great banners, extended along Pennsylvania Avenue the entire distance from the East gate to the West gate. Pennsylvania Day, New York Day, Virginia Day, New Jersey Day, followed. The Monday of every week was set aside finally for District of Columbia Day. . . .

On College Day, thirteen colleges were represented, the biggest group from Goucher College, Baltimore. Then came Teachers' Day; Patriotic Day, and Lincoln Day. . . .

On Sunday, February 18, came Labor Day on the picket line. It was, of course, impossible for wage-earning women to picket the White House on any other day. They represented not only office workers, but factory workers from the great industrial centers.

In 1923 feminists Carrie Chapman Catt and Nettie Rogers Shuler sought to explain why it had taken women so long to win the right to vote. In their assessment they emphasized many of the same problems that had confronted others who sought to change the character of American political behavior.

Source: Carrie Chapman Catt and Nettie Rogers Shuler, *Woman Suffrage and Politics* (New York: Charles Scribner's Sons, 1923) pp. vii-viii, 489-92. Reprinted with the permission of Charles Scribner's Sons.

The campaign for woman suffrage in America long since ended. Gone are the days of agitating, organizing, educating, pleading, and persuading. No more forever will women descent on State Legislatures and the national Congress in the effort to wrest the suffrage from State and national legislators. The gates to political enfranchisement have swung open. The women are inside. . . .

Throughout the suffrage struggle, America's history, her principles, her traditions stood forth to indicate the inevitability of woman suffrage, to suggest that she would normally be the first country in the world to give the vote to women. Yet the years went by, decade followed decade, and twenty-six* other countries gave the vote to their women while America delayed.

Why the delay? . . .

We think that we have the answer. It was, not an antagonistic public sentiment, nor yet an uneducated or indifferent public sentiment — it was the control of public sentiment, the deflecting and the thwarting of public sentiment, through the trading and the trickery, the buying and the selling of American politics. . . .

Suffragists . . . have a case against certain combines of interests that systematically fought suffrage with politics and effectively delayed suffrage for years. . . .

That evidence tends to make clear, too, how slowly men as a whole retreated from the "divine right of men to rule over women" idea, and how slowly women rose to assume their equal right with men to rule over both. Long after men's reason convinced them that woman suffrage was right and inevitable the impulse to male supremacy persuaded them that the step would be "inexpedient." The lower types of men have always frankly resented any threatened infringement of the rights of the male and although the higher classes of male intelligence defined the feeling toward woman suffrage in other terms, at source the highest and lowest were actuated by the same traditional instinct. . . .

Superimposed upon this biological foundation of male resistance to female aggrandisement was the failure of political leaders to recognize the inescapable logic of woman suffrage in a land professing universal suffrage. On top of this, and as a consequence of it, lay the party inaction which gave opportunity to men who were far from inactive on the suffrage question,

* Australia, Austria, Belgium (municipal), British East Africa, Burmah (municipal), Canada, Czecho-Slovakia, Denmark, Esthonia, Finland, Germany, Great Britain, Holland, Hungary, Iceland, Isle of Man, Latvia, Littonia, Luxembourg, New Zealand, Norway, Poland, Roumania (municipal), Rhodesia, Russia, Sweden.

because they feared that their personal interests would suffer should the evolution of democracy take its normal course. . . .

The damage thus wrought to the woman suffrage cause, and the nation's record, was far more insidious then the loss of any election would imply. The alleged rejection of suffrage became to the unknowing public an indication of an adverse public sentiment, and tended to create rather than correct indifference, for the average man and woman move with the current of popular opinion. The inaction of the public gave a mandate for further political evasion of the question to party leaders, some of whom were certainly cognizant of and others working factors in the criminal schemes which produced the misleading result. Around and around the vicious circle went the suffrage question. . . .

Had more statesmen and fewer politicians directed the policies of parties, women would have been enfranchised in the years between 1865 and 1880 and American history, along many lines, would have changed its course. Party suffrage endorsement was won in the United States after forty-eight years of unceasing effort, but when the final victory came women were alternately indignant that it had been so long in coming, and amazed that it had come at all. Many men expressed disappointment that women did not at once enter the party campaigns with the same zeal and consecration they had shown in the struggle for the vote. These men forgot that the dominant political parties blocked the normal progress of woman suffrage for half a century. The women remembered. . . .

In spite of all weaknesses . . . no conscientious man or woman should ever have lost sight of four counter facts, (1) The United States will never go back to government by kings, nobilities or favored classes. (2) It must go forward to a safe and progressive government by the people; there is no other alternative. (3) Women have had a corrective influence in department after department of society and the only one pronounced "a filthy more" is politics where they have not been. (4) The problem of leading government by majorities through the mire to the ideal which certainly lies ahead is one which women should share with men.

17. AL SMITH ON THE CHANGING STYLE OF POLITICS

The American style of politics underwent some major changes after Theodore Roosevelt's day. Al Smith, former governor of

New York and Democratic candidate for President in 1928, reflected on these changes in his autobiography, published in
1929.

Source: Alfred E. Smith, *Up To Now* (New York: The Viking Press, 1929), pp.
52-54, 216-18. Copyright 1929 by Alfred E. Smith.

The whole conduct of elections in New York City has been completely
revolutionized in the last thirty-five years. In my earliest recollection,
Election Day was a universal holiday. Great crowds of men were gathered
around the polling places all day. Fist-fighting took place in a great many
voting precincts. About midday the small boys began to erect open fires for
which they had been gathering fuel for weeks ahead of time.

Prior to the adoption of the present form of ballot, each political party
printed its own ballots, and I remember as a boy folding election ballots at
so much a thousand. This was a form of patronage passed around in the
various districts. For years my father had the contract for trucking the ballot boxes. The various political parties set up wooden huts on the street near
the voting place and then distributed their own ballots to the electors. To
capture one of the huts for an election-night fire was to win a real prize.

Nowadays many of the retail stores do not close on Election Day. Many
men, after they cast their ballot in the morning, go out to the country, and
the city prides itself on the peace and quiet around the polling places during
the day. Yet I cannot help but feel that there was greater interest in elections
in my early days than there is now. On election night nowadays places of
amusement are packed to the doors. Moving-picture houses and theaters
have their gala night of the year. Years ago, every body, it seems to me, was
in Park Row looking at the newspaper bulletin boards. It was the only
means of securing early information on the results.

When I speak about interest in elections, I do not mean interest in the
issues or candidates alone. I mean interest in the election itself. Were I to be
asked if there is a greater interest in the issues today than there was years
ago, I would be compelled to say yes, because in 1927 one hundred thousand people gathered in Times Square to watch the returns on the vote on
amendments to our state constitution.

Another change noted by Smith involved the rise of the modern
voter, who was more interested in issues or individual candidates than with party labels. However, Smith, an old machine
politician, makes a plea for retaining the traditional style of
politics.

It is a popular impression that platforms are hurriedly drafted during the excitement and tumult of a convention. So far as the Democratic party is concerned, that is not the fact. The important constructive planks and the definite promises are well studied out in advance.

It is difficult to deny that the platform of the successful party represents the decision of the people themselves upon these questions. Of course, there are many voters who pay no attention to the platforms. They vote either the Democratic ticket or the Republican ticket year in and year out because they are convinced of the ultimate rectitude of the party to which they belong. On the other hand, a large number of independent voters study the party platforms and naturally expect, in the event of success, that the platform will be lived up to just as accurately as a man would live up to his promise.

It is a matter of fact that definite promises in the platforms of both political parties have been deliberately ignored or compromised with. The ultimate effect of that attitude on the part of the parties, plus the very apparent neglect of so many of our voters to pay any attention to party platforms, will lead us in time to a contest between individuals rather than between parties, if, in fact, we have not already arrived at that. If party government is to be successful, the rank and file of the people themselves have the responsibility of paying some personal attention to party promises, the party declaration of political principles, and the party's reputation for making good its promises.

The party is essential to our form of government. Not all the men nominated have previous political records that permit the voters to study them as individuals. In state elections few people have personal acquaintance with many of the elected officials. They must take them on the faith of the party they represent.

18. THE COMMISSION FORM OF GOVERNMENT IN ACTION

Inefficiency and corruption in Chicago in 1928 created inequalities in that city's tax assessments. Reformers sought to correct the situation by means of a special joint commission on real estate valuation. The following selection indicates the kinds of problems middle-class reformers encountered.

Source: Herbert D. Simpson. "The Tax Situation In Chicago," *National Municipal Review*, November, 1928, pp. 690-94.

The commission mapped out as its first undertaking an investigation of the actual facts of the situation, under the direction of the present writer. The board of review refused access to the assessment records, an access that was later secured through the courtesy of the board of assessors.

Meanwhile the survey of assessment methods and results for the quadrennium ending with 1926 had been completed, and a preliminary report of results was issued in June, 1927—after these results had been presented to the board of assessors and an opportunity to present them to the board of review had been requested. These results were included along with other materials in a preliminary report of the joint commission to the board of county commissioners in July.

Wide publicity was given to these results by the daily papers and by trade journals and other publications. All of the daily papers carried vigorous editorial comment upon the situation, and the keenest interest in the facts themselves was manifested by business and civic organizations and by citizens generally.

Under the auspices of the joint commission, conferences and meetings were arranged at which the facts could be presented in a plain businesslike way, with opportunity for frank and open discussion of the conditions and of means for remedying them. In this way the results of the study were presented to the Association of Commerce, to various local chambers of commerce throughout the city, to property holders' associations and community organizations, to the city and county real estate boards, to the Chicago Bar Association, the Building Owners' and Managers' Association, to various divisions of the League of Women Voters and the Federation of Women's Clubs, and to scores of teachers' associations, churches, clubs, forums, and other groups. More than a hundred such meetings were held throughout the city during the following year. In this work the Chicago Federation of Civic Agencies was particularly influential in bringing the subject to the attention of its constituent organizations and in providing opportunity for presenting the facts.

Meanwhile the state tax commission, under the chairmanship of William H. Malone, had taken cognizance of the situation at a hearing held in Chicago, November 10, 1927. At this hearing the formal complainant was the Chicago Teachers' Federation—and thereby hangs a tale of considerable interest.

The Teachers' Federation, since the days of Catherine Goggin in 1900, had been carrying on a persistent, though fruitless, fight against the tax system in Chicago. Their card of entry had been threats by the Board of Education to reduce salaries, the crowding of children in the schoolrooms, and generally inadequate provision for the needs of the public schools—all on the ground of the impossibility of securing adequate revenues through taxation. The teachers asserted that if it were not for the unscrupulous evasion of taxes and the collusion by tax officials in permitting such evasion, there would be an abundance of money to run the public schools without hardship to honest taxpayers. They had concentrated their attacks largely upon two of the more obvious forms of evasion, although unfortunately the ones most difficult to remedy by isolated treatment; namely, the corporate franchise taxes and the taxes upon intangible property. They had conducted hearings before the board of review, had taken cases before the courts, carrying them sometimes to the supreme court of the state, and had in this way kept up a running fire of attack upon these two elements in the tax system.

Miss Goggin's mantle had fallen upon the shoulders of Miss Margaret Haley, who for many years has been an aggressive leader of the Teachers' Federation and has carried on the fight against flagrant abuses in the tax system. Her criticisms of tax officials and taxpayers have made many enemies; she has commonly been classified as radical, has been charged with attempting to deliver the votes of the Teachers' Federation in accordance with political bargains previously made, and her methods and vocabulary of attack have not always been approved even by those who might not be unsympathetic toward the general objectives of the Teachers' Federation. Her customary reference to the board of review, for example, as "that rat hole" in the county building, is not exactly literary; and yet, in view of the conditions that have been disclosed, the question of precise terminology is perhaps largely an academic one.

At the hearing before the state tax commission, the Teachers' Federation, the joint commission, and other groups united in laying the situation before the tax commission and in urging the commission to take any possible measures to remove the flagrant inequalities of assessment that had been shown to exist. In particular, the tax commission was urged to direct a publication of assessments, in accordance with the provisions of a statute of 1898, which appears to have been a dead letter in Chicago since 1911.

The tax commission was deeply impressed by the facts disclosed and by the apparent indifference of the board of review and board of assessors to the provisions of the statutes governing assessment; and on January 24, 1928, the commission issued an order directing the publication of assessments in accordance with the statute. The board of review and board of assessors questioned the authority of the commission to issue such order, declaring that publication of assessments would cost half a million dollars, that no funds were available for such expenditure, and that in any case the statute implied publication by legal description of properties rather than by name of owner, street number, or other form, as had been suggested by the tax commission. The commission appeared to be without legal power to enforce its order.

Later hearings were held by the commission in Chicago, at which the evidence of flagrant inequalities of assessment was gone into more fully, and the commission was urged to avail itself of the statute authorizing it to order a reassessment in any district in which it felt that the existing assessment was inequitable. On May 7, 1928, the commission finally ordered a reassessment of all real estate in Chicago and Cook County.

Tax officials immediately questioned the legality of this order, likewise, on the ground that the assessment of 1928 would not be completed until reviewed and acted upon finally by the board of review; and that the tax commission could not order a reassessment until the present assessment had been completed. Under present conditions, the same thing seemed likely to recur year after year. Under existing statutes, therefore, the tax commission again appeared to be without authority to take any effective measure for remedying conditions in Chicago.

Meanwhile, a legislative joint commission on taxation had been authorized by the last session of the legislature, before it adjourned in June, 1927, but the governor had taken no steps toward the appointment of the commission. The Illinois Agricultural Association and other groups had for some time been trying to persuade the governor to appoint the commission, which was to be composed of representatives from the senate and house and from business and agricultural groups outside of the legislature. On May 16, 1928, a year after the legislation authorizing it, the governor appointed the members of this commission, with Senator Dailey, of Peoria, as chairman. The day after its appointment the commission came to Chicago; and a week later invited the joint commission on real estate valuation, the Teachers' Federation and other interested groups to present any facts and information bearing upon the Chicago situation.

The commission was apparently much impressed by the facts presented at this hearing and declared itself ready to support any legislation necessary to remedy the situation. Three weeks later the governor issued a call for a special session of the legislature.

The session convened on June 18. Representatives of the Teachers' Federation, of the joint commission on real estate valuation, and other groups and individuals, were invited to present the facts of the situation before a joint session of the senate and house.

The legislature remained in session only five days, but in that time, largely under the leadership of the state tax commission and the legislative joint commission, two important bills bearing upon the Chicago situation were passed. One of these bills authorized the state tax commission to order a reassessment at any time, regardless of the stage at which the local assessing bodies might be; the other provided for the publication of quadrennial assessments of real estate, specifically requiring that this publication should be by name of owner and street number or other form of address.

The county commissioners of Cook County appropriated ample funds for the publication of assessments, and the publication was promptly begun. Its effects were startling indeed. From the beginning of the publication to the time of writing the newspapers of the city have been carrying, almost daily, photographs of adjoining properties, frequently properties that appear to be exactly similar, which are assessed at totally different figures. In many cases of similar homes, sitting side by side, one has been assessed at five to ten times as much as the other. It has been extremely effective publicity and has stirred up a vast amount of discussion and of criticism.

As a result of all of these conditions, the state tax commission held a conference in Chicago, on July 19, with members of the board of assessors, representatives of the joint commission, Teachers' Federation, real estate boards and various other groups, after which the commission issued a final and specific order for the reassessment of all real estate in Chicago and Cook county.

19. ETHNO-RELIGIOUS TENSIONS IN 1928

Party discipline could not always be relied upon to keep voters in line, even in the one-party South. In the 1928 campaign Al Smith's Irish-Catholicism, big-city image, and antiprohibition stance repelled many rural Southern voters, causing them to abandon the party standard bearer for the first time in decades. This speech from North Carolina Democratic Senator F. M. Simmons clearly demonstrates just how strong the anti-Smith sentiment was.

Source: J. Fred Rippy, ed., *F. M. Simmons, Statesman of the New South, Memoirs and Addresses* (Durham, 1936), pp. 202-3, 210-17.

If you will permit me to say it, it is a damnable thing, to my mind, to say that a man's duty to his party is greater than his duty to his heart and soul.

I had the audacity to speak out and challenge the right of this pronounced champion of liquor, the most outstanding champion of the liquor interests in America today — to denounce him as the nominee and the candidate of the Democratic Party, a nomination which I say he obtained by intrigue running through eight long years, exercised by the influence of Tammany Hall and the similar boss-ridden organizations of the great cities of Boston, Philadelphia, and Chicago. . . .

When it comes to the point that men and women must give up the work of a lifetime, the dearest convictions of their hearts and their consciences, in order to preserve what they call "party," and loyalty to the nominee, then, in the language of President Wilson, when that time comes, when the Democratic Party makes that demand upon me, I shall dissent and I shall revolt. . . .

It is said, however, that everybody in the South who is against Smith is against him, not because of prohibition, but because of his religion; that they are blind, bigoted, prejudiced, ignorant. My God, my fellow citizens, even Governor McLean said we people were so ignorant down here in North Carolina that we did not understand the situation at all. (Laughter and applause.)

A Voice. We are not too ignorant to beat him the next time he runs.
— Senator Simmons.

Nobody doubts the constitutional right of Governor Smith to be a candidate for the Presidency, or to be elected President. Any man who is a citizen, and fulfills the other constitutional qualifications, is entitled to become President, whether he is a Protestant, a Catholic, a Mohammedan, a Hindu, or an atheist — provided he can get enough votes to elect him. (Laughter.) The purpose the Constitution builders had in mind when they declared for the separation of State and Church was to prevent church domination. (Applause.) You cannot misconstrue and misinterpret the very meaning and purpose of the forefathers. It was to prevent church domination. . . .

I have no doubt there is intolerance on the part of some on both sides, but in this campaign I protest there is not as much intolerance on the part of those who are opposed to Smith as there is intolerance on the part of those who favor Smith. (Applause.)

If Smith is elected, he will be elected largely by Protestant votes, but if he is defeated, he will not be defeated by Catholic votes. (Applause.) When before in all of our history was one church so solidly massed behind the candidacy of a candidate as the church of Alfred E. Smith is massed behind him? In my town we have a great many Syrians, Catholics. We have many Catholics of the Greek type. I have not heard of a single one of them who is not for Mr. Smith. They tell us that if we people in the South, we Protestants, because of our prohibition views, shall fail to give Mr. Smith our endorsement, the Catholic Church will desert the Democratic Party.

Oh, my fellow citizens, what help have the States that Mr. Smith has any chance to carry up in the North ever been to the Democratic Party? What help has Tammany Hall ever been to the Democratic Party? It knifed Tilden, it knifed Cleveland, it knifed Wilson, it has knifed every Democratic Presidential nominee. Yet Mr. Smith, their candidate now, says we are bolters down here if we do not vote to a man for him.

I am not a prejudiced man. My action in this matter is based upon my conscientious conviction. Feeling as I do, it is utterly impossible for me — I would rather die, I would rather have this right arm cut off, I would rather have my tongue cleave to the roof of my mouth, than to vote for Alfred E. Smith for President of the United States. (Great applause.) . . .

I have denounced any attempt to round up the Democratic people of North Carolina like a flock of animals under the lash of the party whip. (Applause.)

You have a right to vote for whomever you please to vote for. (Applause.) It is your duty to do that, without fear of being read out of the Democratic Party. They cannot read you out of the Democratic Party. (Great applause.) You can read them out, because they put themselves out, but they cannot read you out. (Renewed applause.)

When you come to vote, vote as you please, as your conscience tells you to vote. Vote in behalf of morality and sobriety. Vote in behalf of law and order. Vote in behalf of the church and the home and the fireside. (Great applause.)

In God's name, do not place upon the untarnished brow of the Democratic Party the brand of LIQUOR, ALIENISM, and PLUTOCRACY. (Great applause.)

I thank you.   (Renewed applause.)

20. LOCAL REFORM IN THE 1930s

In Michigan in 1934 the Grand Rapids Better Government League sought to capture control of the city government from the machine. Spearheaded by a slate of respectable middle-class candidates, the League conducted a highly organized campaign, aroused public sentiment, and secured a nonpartisan majority on the seven-man city commission.

Source: Maurice R. Quick, "The Recapture of Grand Rapids" *National Municipal Review,* June 1934, pp. 299-301.

The decision to fight was brought about, in large measure, by the fact that a full majority of the city commission would be chosen this spring. It was felt, further, that the time was ripe. Under the existing administration the city hall had been turned too brazenly into a feeding trough for lame duck state Republicans, relatives or dependents of favored commissioners, and minor political characters. Public opinion assured an overturn of some sort. If the league kept its hands off, then the pendulum would merely swing back again to another of the political factions. And so the league decided to enter the lists with a slate of its own.

But first it went after members. A series of six mass meetings was held, beginning six weeks before the primary, at the rate of two each week. These meetings were planned to be purely educational, but it goes without saying that some doughty wallops were taken at the town political leaders. Murray Seasongood came up from Cincinnati to climax this phase of the work, and an audience of well over a thousand listened to the Cincinnati story while their radiators froze in the five-below-zero winter night. . . .

No candidates were mentioned by league speakers during this phase of the campaign for the simple reason that the league didn't have any. Net results: about three thousand members, but precious little money. People were not ready to contribute to a vague ideal and told the league quite plainly that they would wait to see what kind of candidates it could produce.

Finally, William Timmers, for nine years a leader on the board of education, was persuaded to become a burnt offering on the altar of civic virtue, and headed the slate as candidate for mayor (commissioner at large). In the large third ward Harry C. Leonard, former refrigerator manufacturer and another political novice, also became a sacrifice. The patriarchal John McNabb was persuaded to accept the league's backing for re-election from the second ward. A final endorsement was given to Harry A. Hart, young language instructor in Grand Rapids Junior College, whose first ward campaign was already under way.

The primary campaign was noisy. Timmers was opposed by the incumbent mayor who had the support of the city hall machine and of the stronger county organization, by a former investment banker backed by another political group, and by four other candidates. . . .

Timmers confined himself to preaching efficient, economical government, mildly attacking the administration's financial and patronage policies.

The other league candidates took their cue from Timmers. Leonard faced a field of nine opponents including protégés of both machines, McNabb had five, while Hart had seven.

From its three thousand members, the league secured about three hundred active volunteer workers. During the last three or four days of the campaign, these shock troops canvassed about fifteen thousand homes, leaving circular material at each; a city-wide distribution was made of a circular for Timmers, accompanied by ward distributions on behalf of the other candidates. Every residence telephone in the city was called twice — once on behalf of the candidates, once as a reminder to vote. The evening paper broke all precedents and backed up the league and its candidates with a series of strong editorials. Even the morning paper backed the league candidates toward the end of the campaign.

After the primary it was found that Leonard and McNabb were elected outright, with a majority of all votes cast in their respective wards. Timmers came within 75 votes of election, receiving more than three times as many votes as Karel, who ran second; while Hart carried every precinct in his "machine" ward but failed of immediate election.

After such sweeping results, the run-off in April was destined to be an anticlimax. The league saw the real danger in a light vote and planned accordingly. . . .

With election day came the first pleasant weather of the year, but early voting was dangerously slow. About the middle of the afternoon an emergency chain telephone campaign urged people to vote, and the home edition of the evening paper did likewise. Late in the day the polls were busy. Timmers was safe, 21,627 to 8,022; and Hart won by nearly the same vote.

21. THE ARMY FIGHTS ON IN CHICAGO

Although the army style of politics was under attack elsewhere, it survived in many large cities. This look at Chicago in the mid-1930s demonstrates that a traditional politician's popularity could make him immune from criminal prosecution.

Source: Edwin A. Lahey, "Anything Can Happen In Chicago," *The Nation*, January 1, 1936, pp. 12-14. Copyright 1936, *National* magazine, The Nation Associates, Inc. Reprinted by permission.

We of Chicago have a consciousness that gives us strength. We move with the knowledge that anything can happen here, and it lightens the burden of life. The latest example of this is the case of Robert M. Sweitzer, bellwether of the Cook County Democracy, who as an indicted and ousted public official went to trial early in October in the criminal court on the charge of withholding $414,129 of the funds of the county clerk's office, which he vacated in December, 1934, to become county treasurer. Sweitzer explained genially to the jury that he hoped some day to pay the money back, and walked out a free man, "on the road to vindication."

All this was done without apparent damage to the well-fortified local Democratic machine, and it left a cynical portion of the populace with two inferences: (a) that juries are not always very bright; and (b) that if the person involved is a good fellow, the kind people call by his first name, with a record as a vote-getter for the party, no holds are barred. The end is not yet. Sweitzer, a little giddy with his "partial vindication," as he called it, is reported to be toying with the ideas of running again for public office.

Among party heelers and the open-mouthed citizens who sit at their feet there is a residue of affection for Genial Bob. Twenty-four years of public life as a good guy and storyteller have built up something hard to tear down. Public officials instrumental in exposing Sweitzer have been hissed at political meetings. An air of hostility to the state pervaded the courtroom during Sweitzer's trial.

Politicians and other observers are agreed that Sweitzer would not have been forced to undergo a criminal trial except for his own loquacity. Dazed by an exposé in the Chicago *Daily News* he confessed all to a reporter friend and the managing editor of Hearst's *Evening American*, telling them of unfortunate investments in a process for manufacturing coal briquettes, of loaning public money to unnamed politicians, and of being a sucker generally with money that didn't belong to him. This story broke while Sweitzer was shadow-boxing with the board of county commissioners over his shortage, and even in Cook County there was nothing to do but demand prosecution.

Sweitzer was summoned before the county board, in a room filled with his ardent admirers, and demand was made on him for payment. Addressing the board graciously, he pointed out that he had not had time to check Flynn's audit, and asked the board to stay its demand. He declared himself ready and willing to pay when he himself determined the amount of his shortage. At this time seven months had elapsed since he had left the clerk's office. The board gave him a week. Sweitzer made a second appearance before the board at the appointed time, and again told the members that he had not had time to determine the accuracy of the Flynn audit. Again he asked for and was granted a continuance on the board's demand for a showdown. He went his blithe way that afternoon to Terre Haute, Indiana, to attend the graduation of a daughter.

On the same afternoon the newspaper story of Sweitzer's own admission of defalcations, disastrous investments, and loans to politicians—whom he has not named to this day—appeared on the streets, and members of the county board, feeling that they had been made to look foolish, immediately rescinded the week's grace which they had that morning given him. He was summoned again to appear before the board as soon as he could return from Terre Haute. Sweitzer later declared sheepishly that he thought his intimate confessions would not be printed "until this thing blew over." He returned to town in a few days, and breezily announced to the county board that he was going to pay up immediately, that day, in fact. He had raised the money. But could the board have patience for a few hours? The money was in San Francisco banks, there was a difference in time, and it would be some hours before the transfer could be made. The board waited. The afternoon came and wore on, and old friends of Sweitzer's wanted to weep for him. Like a panicky child trying to stave off the hour of retribution, he made desperate passes, mysterious telephone calls. Late in the day the county board, finally convinced that he was faking, passed a resolution declaring the office of county treasurer vacant by reason of Sweitzer's shortage as clerk.

Sweitzer could not and would not believe that the ax had fallen. He retreated to the treasurer's office, posted an armed guard, and finally had to be ejected bodily by armed deputy sheriffs and policemen. He walked out in a daze, down a corridor lined with photographers, spectators, and scrubwomen. "We're with you, Bob," shouted a scrubwoman, tugging at his coat. Genial Bob smiled the weariest smile of his career.

Before the hullaballoo of the ouster was settled, Sweitzer was indicted by the Cook County grand jury under an old law making it a felony wilfully to withhold funds from a successor in office. No embezzlement charge was brought against him. The penalty on the withholding charge is one to ten years in the penitentiary.

The prospect of presiding over the trial of Bob Sweitzer was a nightmare to most members of the judiciary, and the case moved slowly on the court calendars. From July until October the indictment went from one court to another on all the dilatory pleas available. It was finally forced to trial in October before Judge John C. Lewe, a vigorous young newcomer on the bench. Sweitzer was represented by Benedict J. Short, a boyhood friend and schoolmate, and one of the smoothest and most ingratiating criminal lawyers in Chicago.

Short and his associate counsel, Harvey Levinson and Ode Rankin, did everything but play soft music on the violin for the jury. The adequacy of the state's audit was attacked; the indictment was a plot to wreck the integrity of the foremost political figure in the city; the defendant was being tried for the faults of a single-entry bookkeeping system. Sweitzer himself took the stand, told the Alger story of his life, of his willingness to make up any shortage if they would only give him a chance to find out what it was. (Eleven months had now passed since he left the clerk's office.) If an earnest presentation of the evidence and the sincere demands of the prosecutors, Marshall V. Kearney and Leslie Salter, that the jurors heed only facts had had any effect on the veniremen, the latter were completely melted when the defense rested.

The jury kept Sweitzer and his attorneys waiting only a few hours. The day after the verdict one of the jurors, an unemployed street-car conductor with a high admiration for Genial Bob and his works, explained: "We had trouble with one fellow for a while. He was holding out for conviction. The trouble with him was, we told him, that he had been listening too much to those state's attorneys."

Another juror, a young clerk in a downtown insurance office, paused in his work long enough to inquire timidly of a reporter who was probing the workings of the jury mind: "After all, Sweitzer said he'd pay the money back, didn't he? He's got it, hasn't he?"

He seemed a little abashed to learn that nobody credits Genial Bob with having a cent today, and the talk turned to the evidence, to the audit upon which the state based its case. "The state's audit?" said this peer of the defendant. "Was that audit the state's? Cripes, we thought it was a defense exhibit."

22. VIOLENT TIMES IN PHILADELPHIA

The methods of urban machine politics often included violence. The election episode below shows a precinct boss, in this case a saloon-keeper, in action.

Source: J. T. Salter, "An Election Episode," *National Municipal Review*, September 1934, pp. 459-60.

One night shortly after twelve in September, 1933, Spode was sitting in his fast roadster that was parked diagonally across the street from Strong Arm's saloon, and just seven short blocks from the most historic spot in America — Independence Hall. Strong Arm was the big fellow in the division and Spode was his judge of elections. Until this election they had been boon companions, but now Spode's spirit was angered to its very core, for his phlegmatic uncle had not been re-slated for magistrate, and Spode knew it was Strong Arm's work. He was there to tell Strong Arm that he would have to give the uncle a complimentary vote in the division or else Spode, as election judge, would protest at every illegal act that Strong Arm should commit in this coming primary. Spode knew just what these vote-producing actions would be — that was the reason Strong Arm had made him judge. Once Strong Arm had been in Cuba on election day, and this absentee rulership had meant disaster for him as it had done in earlier days for Hynicka in Cincinnati and more recently for Vare in Philadelphia.

The opposition candidate for judge of elections had been chosen; but when this anti-organization judge appeared at the polling place on the morning of the next balloting Strong Arm had said "git", and the duly selected judge "got". Strong Arm had then held a curbstone election. He looked at his boys and asked, "Who do you fellows want for judge?" Spode was chosen by viva-voce vote; from that time until this he has been judge of elections — the key position at the polls — with the law of the Philadelphia charter and the Pennsylvania constitution behind him.

I, too, had called to see Strong Arm but had found him gone, and his man had said, "He got a phone call. He will be right back."

Spode is short, muscular, and dark, he talks softly—as softly as the waters that lap the wooden piles at the docks in his Delaware river—and he looks Italian but he was born in a land too cold for olive trees. I leaned against Spode's fender. The uncle leaned against the car door, and Spode talked. He had often seen me with Strong Arm and he wanted to be sure that I knew what a low, yellow, traitorous cur this politician-racketeer was. From diminuendo to crescendo and back to diminuendo he spoke for more than two hours, but Strong Arm never came. When he was Spode's subject, Spode feelingly called him all the unkind names that a certain type of ward politician most easily thinks of. He catalogued every defect revealed in fourteen years of thuggery. Then he would lower his voice and talk of himself and his sad fall from grace through carrying out the orders of the inexorable Strong Arm. He repeated himself and abruptly stopped in the midst of a sentence; a half hour later he would return, with uncanny precision, to complete it. Reassembled, his story follows:

"Why, I did enough for him to go to jail four times over." And he went on to tell about a Hungarian, who was a Democratic watcher in the 1932 November election and who wanted to observe the counting of the ballots. It was about ten o'clock, the polls had closed, the Hungarian had a legal right to be present—the Democratic party had expected him to be there to watch the count.

"But Strong Arm said that he couldn't stay. He looked at me and said, 'You are the judge, put him out.' I had to use force but I got him out. A minute later he was knifed and slugged right outside the door." Strong Arm has a youth to do this sort of work—Danny, a dope fiend. Danny looks like a college freshman—slender, medium height, with high forehead, hair wetted and carefully parted in the middle, sparkle in his eyes. He has been arrested seventeen times but he has never been in jail. His employer sees to that. Danny works with a black jack and knuckles. Strong Arm buys him for a case of whiskey and a $5.00 bill, or sometimes Strong Arm just gets him a little drunk and buys him a meal and Danny does the slugging.

The injured Hungarian had been taken to the hospital where he remained unconscious for four hours. "We were afraid he was going to die; we called the hospital so often that we were afraid we would give ourselves away. Strong Arm was very excited; he put both hands in his hair and cried again and again, 'They will put this on me; they will blame me for this.' We were all worried inside. The waiting was awful."

"Three of the Hungarian's children walked into the polling place crying 'We want our father.' We put the children outside and locked the door and one standing on her toes pressed her face on the window pane—all crying and shouting: 'The murderers are in there.' Strong Arm wilted at this and said to me, 'All right, let them lock me up for homicide.' Then we got word that the man would live, so we went on with the count."

Several times during the telling of his story Spode looked at me with appeal in his eyes. Once he burst out "Professor, I am ashamed of what I did that night. It wouldn't have been so bad but my father knew that man in Hungary when he was a little boy — just so big." And there Danny stood, as Spode and I talked, just thirty feet away. While I was looking at him he smashed a beer bottle in front of a drug store; he and two companions laughed and continued their talking.

Strong Arm carried that election, and the Hungarian will always carry a scar above one eye. No one was ever arrested because of the attack. The Hungarian, Strong Arm, Spode, and Danny are living in the same neighborhood as in the past, and the police ignored the incident. These two factors tell much about the conditions under which the party process operates in a selected area.

23. THE FINANCIER IN CITY POLITICS

The depression of the 1930s placed great financial burdens on city governments. This hastened the decline of the last bastion of traditional politics, the urban machine. An article in the *National Municipal Review* in 1933 discusses the shift of urban power from the political boss to the financier. The New Deal was able to prop up the urban machines by giving them control of relief funds.

Source: William C. Beyer, "Financial Dictators Replace Political Boss," *National Municipal Review,* April-May 1933, pp. 162-63, 231-34.

It seems clear that power is shifting from the political boss to the financier. The term "political boss" is here used in a somewhat symbolic sense and stands for the political organization as well as for the boss, if there is one. Not every city has a political boss. In like manner, the term "financier," though singular, is to be understood as plural and to symbolize the financial interests, more particularly the bankers. Another way of putting it is to say that power is shifting from the political organization and its leaders to the financial interests of the community, especially the bankers.

This is happening in a perfectly natural way. City governments rely on banks for financial services: the banks market their bonds and also make loans to cities to enable them to meet their cash needs. A very common practice of cities is to borrow money from banks in anticipation of tax collections later in the year. The depression has greatly increased the dependence of cities on the banks, for as tax collections have fallen off cities have been more and more compelled to resort to borrowing in order to meet their current obligations. So long as a city is a good credit risk and may be expected to make its debt payments promptly, banks are ready enough to advance needed cash without asking questions about the city's management. When it ceases to be a good credit risk, banks become more cautious in lending money to it. If they fear that the city is drifting toward default in its debt payments, they are likely to condition further loans upon tangible evidence that the city is "putting its house in order." They may even specify what measures of economy the city shall adopt. The city authorities and the political organization back of them may writhe under this situation, but, unless they can find some other way of paying their bills, they are obliged to give heed to the terms of the bankers. Thus it comes about that the political boss must harken to the advice of the financier even though the financier may advise unpleasant measures of economy.

Those who have been giving of their time and energy, or of their means, or of both, to the cause of better city government in the United States know well that in the forefront of the resistance to better government has been the political organization. In our large cities especially, the so-called "political machine" has been held together primarily by patronage in all its varied forms, not by any crusading zeal for the public good. It has profited from jobs, from contracts, from franchises, from special privileges, from vice. Incidentally it has performed the legitimate function of operating our cumbersome election machinery, of filling our multitudinous elective offices, and of giving cohesion to our highly decentralized governments.

But the price to the taxpayer has been heavy. That price has consisted not only of the patronage exacted by the political organization, but also of the failure of his city government to employ the most economical and most efficient methods in carrying on its business. Improvements in these methods have been resisted by the political organization partly from inertia, but largely because the improved methods would interfere with patronage. Copying deeds by photography rather than by handwriting or by typewriting would lose jobs; good civil service administration would make it difficult to reward the "faithful" at public expense; classification of positions and standardization of pay would limit opportunities for giving special pay-roll recognition to the man who delivers votes on election day; better systems of controlling expenditures would interfere with easy profits for political friends; and so on *ad infinitum.* Quite naturally the political organization has resisted, and continues to resist, these measures in the interests of economy and efficiency.

Do Business Men Want Good Government?

The question now arises: Does the shift of power from the political organization to the financial group make it easier to introduce improved methods in city government? Obviously that depends on whether the financial group wants such methods introduced. In recent years there has been considerable discussion whether business men want good government. . . .

The fact is that many business men prefer to have government weak, inefficient,and even dishonest; that most of them are, or at least until recently have been, indifferent to government; and that only a minority of them, though at present a rapidly growing minority, appreciate the importance of good government and actually give of their thought, time, and means to get good government. . . .

There is, however, good reason to expect the financier to make common cause with those who are striving for more efficient and more economical government. Bankers now have a special stake in economical government. Just as the fire insurance companies find it to their interests to promote efficient fire departments in cities, and as life insurance companies find it good business policy to support public health work, so bankers at this time must find it to their advantage to aid measures that make for governmental economy. If city governments do not economize, the bankers and their clients may lose the money they have loaned to cities.

The first concern of bankers in their career of intervention has been to secure a reduction of municipal expenditures. . . .

To those to whom good government means simply economy and efficiency, the shift of power from the political boss to the financier should be altogether welcome. Not all who want good government, however, would subscribe to so narrow a definition of the term. Many would lay quite as much stress on service and on democracy as on economy and efficiency. To these the shift of power may be less welcome; it may even seem to them sinister. Certainly the financier's interest is not primarily in the service side of government. As an individual citizen he may have the point of view of the beneficiary of governmental service, but as a banker he must have the point of view of the money lender and the investor. Quite naturally he will be concerned first of all with the security of his loans to cities and with the maintenance of debt service. Non-revenue producing activities will appeal to him as of secondary importance, and may even strike him as frills. He is apt to be an easy prey to the nation-wide propaganda which falsely pictures governments as mere burdens on the backs of the producers of wealth, as though governments were not themselves wealth-producing enterprises of a high order. In this respect the political boss is likely to have a broader view than the financier. To remain in power he must please not only those who have money in municipal securities, but also the much larger body of citizens who are not investors but who are benefited by governmental services.

Those who place democracy first will also look askance at this shift of power. The political boss, heaven knows, is no democrat; but at least he must wield his power under a system that gives the people a chance on occasion to dislodge him. Periodically he must expose his candidates to the voters, and if he carries on in too high-handed a manner, his candidates may be defeated. The financier is under no such necessity. He does not run for office, nor does he place a ticket in the field with his label upon it so that the voters can defeat him at the polls. He wields his power by virtue of his control of credit, not by any mandate from the electors.

24. THE WPA BUILDS A MACHINE IN PITTSBURGH

Reform-minded citizens often distrusted the New Deal. The *American Mercury* magazine discovered that Works Progress Administration funds in Pittsburgh served mainly to finance a shift from Republican to Democratic machine dominance of that city. While the motives of the WPA director Harry Hopkins in Washington may have been honest, the money still had to pass through the hands of less-than-honest local politicians. Nationwide, four out of five of the two million WPA employees voted for Roosevelt in 1936.

Source: The American Mercury, May 1936, pp. 28-35.

Political machines are built on jobs and money, and the WPA operating program offered more money and more jobs to the political machine-builders of America, actual and potential, professional and amateur, than any appropriation struck off by the hand and brain of man since recorded history began. . . . Mr. Hopkins' desire to spread economic self-sufficiency among the unemployed might be as pure as the new-fallen snow in a social settlement patio, the actual expenditure of the WPA largesse, from Guam to Passamaquoddy, would take place under the watchful eye of local politicians as skilled in improvising chiseling operations of the public funds as a Hopkins aide is in improvising rationalizations for doubling the market price on the interior decoration of backhouses.

Now it has come about that perhaps the supreme demonstration of the WPA's efficacy as a political machine-building implement has taken place in Pittsburgh. . . .

Pittsburgh has nourished the three major ingredients of political machine activity: An economic oligarchy with plenty of axes to grind in local government; an indifferent electorate largely of recent foreign extraction and low literacy; and a municipal religion of the Main Chance. Hence, when the tip arrived last spring that the WPA pie wagon was on its way over the mountains, the Pittsburgh politicians greeted it with the happy responsiveness of an old school sultan getting news of a new Christian virgin in the harem. . . .

The incentives to use the WPA organization for political machine-building purposes in Pennsylvania were enormous. There was first of all Postmaster General Farley's somewhat romantic fancy of several years' standing that Pennsylvania could be annexed to the national Democratic strength. . . . Therefore, if a Democratic machine was to be organized in Pittsburgh to balance the irreducible Republican preponderance in Philadelphia, the job would have to be done through the WPA. . . .

As last fall's elections for the potent Allegheny County offices approached, there was a sudden dizzy acceleration in the rate of Democratic registrations. Before the polls opened, the county's 6000 Democrats of 1930 had reproduced their party identification in 112,000 voters in the city alone, 66,000 more in the boroughs (incorporated suburban cities), and 48,000 in the townships and rural districts. The word had been passed along the grapevine from ward and precinct leaders that names which would check against Democratic registrations would look well on the WPA job application lists, and practical Pittsburghers, characteristically hesitant to affront political mentors unnecessarily, obviously were doing as they were advised. All Pittsburgh realized that if ward leaders were using the WPA opening to foster a handsome registration showing, that was what ward leaders were in politics for. . . .

John H. Laboon [Allegheny County administrator] . . . emphasized, with a frankness considered excessive even in Pittsburgh politics, that New Deal political and economic orthodoxy were officially recognized as the sole tests of WPA job eligibility. Said the young party lieutenant: "I tell you right now that any WPA worker not in sympathy with the WPA program and the Roosevelt Administration will be eliminated from the WPA payroll in this district as quickly as I can act."

. . . Meanwhile new and even more startling facts about the WPA set-up were coming to light. The . . . system for the Democratic indoctrination of Pittsburgh, it appeared, was the old tried and true ward-bossed method of connecting the "good boys" with the fat jobs. Counting all the supervisors, assistant supervisors, foremen and assistant foremen, timekeepers, technical assistants, and white-collar workers around headquarters, the total number of fat jobs in the Pittsburgh and Allegheny County WPA set-up ran slightly under 5000. The fat jobs, according to their importance, paid anywhere from slightly above the $60.50 monthly scale for ordinary WPA workmen up to $160, besides the political authority which, by Pittsburgh's traditional standards of value, rightly goes with political foremanships. And the way to get a fat job, as the grapevine of political sophistication shortly spread the glad news through Pittsburgh, was to prove yourself a "good boy" by registering Democratic and getting a letter of endorsement from your ward chairman. . . .

Below the "fat job" level, the WPA, it simultaneously developed, is being geared up to function according to the old Tammany principle that if you take care of the straw bosses, the straw bosses will take care of the rank and file organization problem. Nothing crude has happened, that is to say, like refusing ordinary gang-work jobs to voters who happen to be Republicans. But once on a gang job under a politically appointed straw boss, the average G.O.P. beneficiary of New Deal humanitarianism has speedily made the acquaintance of the sharper edges of political discipline. Democratic snow-shovelers, for instance, who stayed home last winter on days when the thermometer plunged below zero, were officially cited sick or justified. In Republicans such absences have merely proved their laziness or incompetence. Democrats grousing about hard work and the stupidities of foremen have been transferred to more congenial projects or had things patiently explained to them. Republicans have been disciplined for insubordination and political agitation. . . .

In fact, acquiescence without complaint pretty well tells the story of the WPA in Pittsburgh, and there is no use being scandalized about it. When Rome committed itself to the experiment of voting bread and circuses, honest party politics vanished. When a humanitarian bureaucracy puts $24,000,000 and 5000 petty patronage jobs into the hands of expert machine politicians to create a forcing bed for Democrats, people of the political practicality of the Pittsburghers are likely to become loyal and contributing Democrats. Instead of raging about it, perhaps the most rational thing for the realistic observer in New Deal America to do is to examine WPA alignments with practical politics in his own community, hoping for the best but expecting worse and more of it.

25. FARMERS AND BUSINESSMEN ATTACK UNIONS

By 1938 the New Deal coalition was fragmenting. Two rival union groups, the old AF of L and the new, more radical CIO competed for new members and for control of the Democratic party in industrial areas. Strikes over jurisdictional issues (not wages) broke out everywhere, threatening to delay the recovery of the economy even longer. Businessmen began to fight back, as the 1938 West Coast episode shows.

Source: Richard L. Neuberger, "Ballot Poison For Labor," *The Nation,* October 29, 1938, pp. 444-45. Copyright 1938, *Nation* magazine, The Nation Associates, Inc. Reprinted by permission.

On the ballot in two Far Western states is a pair of initiative measures drafted to annihilate the labor movement. Labor unions in the region would be reduced to empty shells. Strikes and boycotts would be rendered illegal. Unions would not be permitted to collect funds for political or economic action. Even the conservative Portland *Oregonian* calls the initiative a vengeful scheme to restrict working people's rights as American citizens.

The Oregon bill, to be considered by citizens of the state on November 8, is the more all-inclusive and severe of the two, and thus the more important to analyze. Section 1 outlaws any strike or labor dispute not between an employer and a majority of all his employees. . . .

The bill is not content merely to forbid strikes. It also forbids practically all other forms of trade-union activity. Picketing and boycotting are made criminal offenses except where labor disputes exist within the meaning of the act. Obviously, no labor dispute within the meaning of the act will ever exist. . . .

Section 3 of the measure would make it unlawful for labor unions to collect funds larger than those needed for "legitimate requirements." And there is not the least assurance that strikes or political campaigns would be regarded as "legitimate requirements."

Between potshots at the Jews and apologies for Hitler, the Corvallis *Gazette-Times,* the most vociferous newspaper proponent of the measure, vilified Gill and the other Grange leaders. The anti-New Deal *Oregon Journal* featured news of the subordinate granges carried by the Associated Farmers gang. A wide variety of political sharpshooters hung around Grange halls trying to influence the election. Nearly 10,000 farmers voted. Gill and his ticket piled up a two-to-one victory. The vigilantes had their answer. . . .

A sad circumstance is that the trade unions are not entirely without blame for the conditions giving rise to the anti-labor initiatives now before the voters of the Pacific Coast states. William Green might not have to bewail the Oregon bill now if a year ago he had warned Dave Beck against the use of the prize fighters and pluguglies of the Teamsters' Union "goon squad." Louis Stark of the New York *Times* has called the bills a natural outgrowth of the bitter labor battles on the Pacific Coast.

The state's anti-injunction act would to all intents and purposes be repealed by a clause providing for injunctions in labor difficulties. Another clause makes it a crime punishable by a year in jail or a $500 fine to discourage anyone, by direct or indirect means, from going to work for an employer who wants to hire him. This would subject to criminal action a union member who voted to expel a fellow-unionist for strike-breaking. And finally, in apparent solicitude for the harassed farmer, the bill twice expressly forbids interference with the buying, selling, or handling of agricultural products, but in each instance takes care also to specify *all other products.*

The Washington initiative is similar to that of Oregon. . . .

Signatures to these initiatives were obtained during a campaign designed to spread the belief that the A. F. of L. consisted only of "goons" and racketeers and the C. I. O. only of aliens and Communists. The bills represent a new crest in enmity toward American trade unionism. A huge slush fund raised by shipping interests, department stores, lumber companies, and industrial associations is being spent to convince the people that the initiative originated with irate and persecuted farmers. Cowboy ballads and rural songs are interspersed on the radio with appeals for help that allegedly come straight from the soil. Listed as the measure's official sponsors are four so-called farm organizations: Associated Farmers, Oregon Farm Bureau, Eastern Oregon Wheat League, and Hood River Growers' Club. Actually these groups have little or no membership; Associated Farmers is a strictly vigilante outfit that stems from California. In fact, the largest organization of farmers in the state, the Oregon State Grange, is unequivocally opposed to the anti-labor measure. Ray W. Gill, master of the Oregon Grange and a member of the National Grange Executive Committee, has branded the bill a scheme to wipe out liberalism in the Pacific Northwest. In consequence the most vicious sort of abuse has been heaped on Gill by the backers of the measure.

Not long ago the biennial Grange election took place. The Associated Farmers' clique ran a slate of candidates. An amazing thing happened: all over Oregon all sorts of reactionary elements suddenly developed a vital interest in the internal affairs of a fraternal organization.

26. TRUMAN WAVES THE BLOODY HOOVER SHIRT, 1948

During the 1948 presidential campaign, Democratic candidate Harry S. Truman employed methods that had become standard for his party: he raised the spectre of Hoover and depression. It worked, and Truman, in spite of the predictions of pundits and pollsters, defeated Republican Thomas Dewey. The following is an excerpt from Truman's speech in New York City, October 28, 1948.

Source: *The New York Times*, October 29, 1948. © 1948 by The New York Times Company. Reprinted by permission.

Time and again in 1944 [the Republican candidate] told the voters that what we need is "strength and unity." He promised to displace — and I quote — "A tired, exhausted, quarreling and bickering administration with a fresh and vigorous administration." Now, doesn't that sound familiar to you? And he asked and I quote again: "Is the New Deal, the tired and quarrelsome New Deal, all America has to offer?" "Must we go back," he asked — "Must we go back to leaf-raking and doles?" Well, you people stuck by the New Deal in 1944, and we haven't had to go back to leaf-raking or the doles, or anything else of that kind. And the reason we haven't had to go back to Hooverville and bread lines and soup kitchens is because the Democratic policies of the New Deal are correct and right, and they're for all the people and not just for the privileged few.

I must say, though that some of you are partly to blame for this, because you didn't vote in 1946: That Republican do-nothing 80th Congress did all it could to start us back down that dismal road.

You know the Republican candidate is trying to persuade the people at large in the country that the elephant's got the new look, but its just the same old elephant — you can be sure of that. . . .

The record of the Repubican Party is much too bad to talk about. The Republican candidate is trying to run on the record of the Democratic Party — of Franklin Roosevelt and myself. He's a "me too" man.

Let's take a look at the record and see why he can't talk about the record of the Republican Party. Let's go back a few years. In 1928 the Republicans elected a well-known efficiency engineer named Herbert Hoover, and they promised us everything. They told us if we wanted prosperity, we must vote for Hoover. Well, the people fell for it. And I think this new candidate — well, he's not a new candidate — I think this second-hand candidate thinks the same way. You know what a bitter experience you had after that.

Many of you remember 1932. Over in Central Park men and women were living in little groups of shacks made of cardboard and old boxes. They were known as "Hoovervilles." Out here on Eighth Avenue veterans were selling apples. Ragged individualism, I suppose that's what you would call it. Farm foreclosures, homeowners' evictions, starvation wages, labor unions disrupted by company spies and thugs — that was the Republican record when they last had control of the Government. And, you know, there is a peculiar thing about this campaign. I have never heard of a single Republican candidate for office point with pride to any Republican administration or any Republican President.

Now, they made an awful mess of things when they had control back there when they were elected in 1928. And in 1932 we turned them out. The vigorous action which saved the nation and restored our faith came with the Democrats, with the New Deal, and with Franklin Roosevelt.

27. POLITICS FROM THE NEW TV TUBE

Television became a measurable force in national politics for the first time in the 1952 presidential campaign. Although its impact on the vote totals is still open to debate, "political" television did force the major political parties to adjust their campaigning techniques to "sell" their candidates. Subsequent campaigns have shown that politicians learned this lesson well.

Source: Paul Seabury, "Television — A New Campaign Weapon," *New Republic,* December 1, 1952, pp. 12-14. Reprinted by permission of THE NEW REPUBLIC; © 1952 The New Republic, Inc.

Television — A New Campaign Weapon

There is time before the next election to weigh the words of Gov. Thomas E. Dewey that "television and radio are the most effective means of campaigning."

This statement, like any other premature attempt to assess factors in this, the first Republican Presidential victory since 1928, leads us to inquire about the role which these two media of mass communication did play in the election of Gen. Dwight D. Eisenhower. Were radio and television "impartial" in the campaign? . . .

There is little doubt that the multi-million dollar campaign was the most intensive and expensive in American history. And in the distribution of the air waves between the General and the Governor — Stevenson came off second best.

This was probably to be expected. Television costs money, and the big networks — Columbia, NBC, Mutual and Dumont — are not in business for the common weal of the two-party system. The economics of this industry, not partisan preference, were decisive in determining the relative ratio of air time distributed between the two candidates and their proponents. . . .

Sidney Shalit, in the New York Daily News of November 5, has estimated that the Eisenhower "spot blitz" on radio and television ["my Mamie gets awful mad about high taxes, too!"], which blanketed the air over 50-odd counties in 12 states for 10 days before the election, alone cost more than $1 million and was originally underwritten for $2 million. The hour-and-a-half election eve GOP rally of November 3 . . . was placed on all coast-to-coast major networks at a cost of probably more than $200,000. The Democrats refrained from retaliating in kind for the barrage of "Ike" spot commercials on Korea, Communism and Corruption, not from considerations of taste or lack of prior preparation, but from last minute fiscal decrepitude. Democratic spot recordings still lie untouched in a downtown New York advertising office.

Advertising Age, the adman's bible, states without reservation in the November 10 issue that saturation of radio and TV spots seems to have paid off for the GOP. Eisenhower won in 39 of the 40 states in which the Republicans concentrated on spot announcements to be seen or heard by the voters. . . .

In Minneapolis, Minn., for example, . . . Eisenhower forces purchased more than twice as much evening radio time as the Democrats (14.5 hours to 6.5 hours), and almost twice as much evening television time (five and a quarter to three hours). In Dallas, Texas, (a bell-weather of Stevenson's fortunes in the South) the ratio was equally unfavorable to the unregenerate Democrats, Stevenson, Connally and Rayburn (14 to seven-and-a-half radio hours; 12 to five-and-three-fourths TV hours).

In Chicago, Advertising Age reports, the broadcasting industry received a real "bonanza." The Eisenhower forces "were spending $8,000 for time on one radio station as compared to $900 by the Democrats. On one Chicago TV outlet the GOP spent $25,000. Another TV station got $27,000, most of it for Ike." Volunteers for Stevenson reported that their whole Illinois budget came to $10,000, according to the magazine.

If these cities, chosen at random, are typical of how the two great political parties fared on the publicly owned airwaves of the Midwest and South, the Republicans were able to purchase twice as much air time as were the Democrats in this recent campaign.

But the potency of television as a political medium cannot be measured just by total air time purchased by political parties. At best, both television and radio merely furnish facilities for communication, not a captive audience, and it is wise to recall that Neilson TV audience-ratings of the Republican and Democratic conventions this summer showed both of them far less "popular" than the show, I Love Lucy.

Governor Stevenson's inflation speech at Baltimore on September 23 — televised by CBS in 48 "station areas" throughout the country — had to compete, not with the Governor's GOP opponent, but with NBC's Original Amateur Hour. From all reports (if the Neilson Survey is correct) he reached only an estimated 45.8 percent of all sets then in use. On September 25, General Eisenhower, speaking over Dumont, encountered similar buyer resistance: while his address was carried in 62 "station areas," it reached only 40.9 percent of activated TV sets; the other 59.1 percent, presumably, were turned chiefly to Mister Peepers (NBC) and CBS' Big Town. This congenital unwillingness of most of the listening public to forego habitual spectator habits, even in a political campaign, is a problem which neither Republican nor Democratic admen had been able to solve. . . .

Without a careful examination of the transcripts of radio commentators and a measured review of the news films used during television news broadcasts, one cannot begin to analyze bias, or fairness, in this important part of the air waves. There were complaints by many Democrats that the business-sponsored newsreels were trained for many more minutes on Eisenhower than on Stevenson during news roundups of the campaign. And that radio commentators, such as Walter Winchell, possibly violated FCC regulations by giving free advertising to the Republicans with his outright endorsement of General Eisenhower. . . . The matter is now in the hands of the Federal Communications Commission.

There is little doubt that television — the new and revolutionary medium of American politics — contributed to the unusually heavy turnout of normally non-voting citizens; it may, as has been charged, have brought irrelevant personal and emotional elements of the campaign — e.g., the Nixon soliloquy — much closer to the hearts of American voters than the rational political scientist would have desired. But heavy turnouts and irrational appeals to the citizenry are not novel in American politics. Like all other media of mass communication, television is ambivalent. Turned to a high moral and educative purpose, we have seen that it can uplift; turned to sordid expediency, sloganeering and manipulation, it can do great damage to our political process. . . .

There are certain long-range questions which our four-month experience with political television has raised. Is there a political danger in the extraordinary financial burden which televising Presidential candidates places upon our two parties? It is certain that — barring some unexpected drastic revision of our FCC regulations — the preponderance of air time will continue to go to the political party able to raise the largest campaign funds. It is also certain that, because of television, campaign expenditures will continue drastically to rise.

Who will foot the bill? Can either party ethically afford to continue entrusting its fiscal destiny to a few wealthy contributors? . . .

We also may well inquire whether the present duration of the Presidential campaign is unduly long; or whether, due to the advent of television, less physical strain need be imposed upon candidates (and their audiences) than that which now results from eight strenuous weeks of stumping the country. Pessimists among us may perhaps wonder also whether the impact of television upon political techniques may ultimately reduce the Presidential campaign to the set routine of push button warfare, managed by teams of "idea men," script writers and admen in their soundproof metropolitan offices, far removed from the voter and even the wardheeler. It has yet to be demonstrated that candidates for high office can be purveyed, like Duz, Rinso and Lucky Strikes, solely on the manipulative principle of George Washington Hill: constant repetition and annoyance. The neurological patterns of the American voter are far more complex than those of Pavlov's dogs and still are subject to many far more conditioning influences than television and radio alone.

This may be so, but it will be a long time before anyone underestimates the power of an adman. As one Stevenson supporter put it when the votes were in: "Chalk this one up for BBD&O."

28. LOBBYISTS CONFRONT THE FRIENDLY CONGRESSMAN

Lobbyists play an important part in modern politics, often exerting great influence on the people's representatives. In a letter written in the late 1950s, California Congressman Clem Miller shows how a powerful interest group with a strong lobby can get what it wants. An unorganized group of small producers, on the other hand, gets nothing.

Source: Clem Miller, Member of the House: Letters by Congressman Clem Miller, edited by John W. Baker. Copyright © 1962 by Charles Scribner's Sons. (New York: Charles Scribner's Sons, 1962). Reprinted with the permission of Charles Scribner's Sons.

Dear Friend:

In today's world most people are ready to admit that, as much as they dislike the word "lobbying," the function carried on under this name is essential to government. (In fact, the right to lobby is protected by the First Amendment.) In recent months there has been a graphic contrast here in effectiveness of lobbying activity between two segments of agriculture important to the economic health of our district: walnut growers and poultrymen. Both groups are in economic trouble because of abundance.

The walnut growers have a large carry-over from last year which, if placed on top of this year's record production, would break the market. The growers wanted the government to buy walnuts for diversion into the school lunch program, to be financed from existing tariffs on foreign walnut imports.

In the poultry industry, overproduction led by huge combines of bankers and feed companies, with million-hen farms, has broken the egg and meat-bird markets wide open. Independent poultrymen are losing six to eight cents per dozen eggs and four to eight cents per pound of meat, and are going bankrupt in droves.

The walnut industry is well organized. They have been proud that they don't have supports and don't ask the government for "handouts." This is easy to understand. One marketing cooperative controls seventy per cent of the state's production. So, when the industry got in trouble and came to Washington, they came well prepared. Each California congressman received a personal, carefully reasoned, five-page letter. It was followed up by another, shorter letter. Then, a telegram called attention to the letters. Finally, there was a telephone call, asking for comments on the letters. By this time, we were fairly wide awake. Quite properly, the group worked through the congressman in whose district the association offices and many growers are located. We received several calls from the congressman's staff, alerting us, keeping us posted, offering help in answering questions.

After this preliminary barrage, the walnut growers' representative was ready to come to town. He set up headquarters at a nearby hotel. He called on congressmen several times, accompanied by a gentleman from the packing and canning section of the industry. He talked to my legislative assistant. Then we were all invited to a luncheon at the hotel, where the plight of the industry was laid before us and it was announced that a meeting was set up with the Secretary of Agriculture. Meticulous care was taken to be sure that all congressmen and senators who represent walnut growers would be there. In a large Department of Agriculture conference room with numerous department officials present, a skillful "presentation" for the industry was made. Immediately afterward, the walnut congressmen jumped up to demand action. One was self-contained but bitter about department inaction. Another pointed out the illogical Administration position in caustic terms. In turn, each congressman added his bit to the complaint. The Administration was bland and quite self-righteous ("We have more confidence in the walnut grower than he has in himself."). The exasperation of the Republican congressmen toward the Republican Secretary of Agriculture mounted. "Would a 'shaded' market price have to become a rout before the government moved?" they wanted to know. Administration officials were apparently unshaken.

However, two weeks later, the Administration did act. The industry was delighted. The work of the lobby had been effective.

Let's contrast this with the way things are developing in the egg industry. Some time ago I received a long letter from a constituent asking
what congressional action was expected in poultry. A check revealed
that nothing was contemplated in Congress. Of the seven thousand bills
in Congress, there was not one on poultry or eggs. No hearings were
scheduled. My interest piqued, I discussed the situation with House
Agriculture Committee staff members and with the acting chairman of
the subcommittee. The prevailing view was that since there was no
leadership in the industry, and no agreement on policy, hearings would
serve no purpose. I urged that hearings be scheduled to see if policy
might materialize. A day or so later, I heard that a group of distressed
poultrymen from New Jersey were asking to meet with their government. The Georgia and Alabama broiler people also asked to be heard.

All of a sudden, we learned that there was to be a hearing. Citizens
were petitioning their government for a redress of grievances. At the
hearing a crowd of two hundred poultrymen swarmed into the Agriculture Committee room which had been designed for about seventy-
five people. Poultrymen-witnesses testified that the lowest prices in
eighteen years for eggs and chickens were bankrupting an industry. . . .

Throughout two days the same depressing story was recounted as
the farmer-witnesses, speaking for themselves and other small producers, took their turn. Technological advances, together with banker-feed
company-grower integration, were destroying the independent poultry-
man. Then the Department of Agriculture spokesman told its story. He
confirmed the growers' story but indicated that nothing could be done.
It was the inexorable law of supply and demand. Significantly absent
were representatives of the larger organized farm groups. At nightfall,
the poultrymen had to return to their farms.

What was the next step? It is up to the interested congressmen, they
told us. How come, we asked? What are we to do? The leader of the
poultrymen said that we had been told the problem. Yes, was the response, but he and his friends should go to see the Secretary of Agriculture. Testimony had indicated that Congress had already given the
Secretary all of the authority he needed to act. It would do no good to
pass more laws, particularly since they would certainly end with
Presidential vetoes.

All of the men were active poultrymen who had to get back to their
flocks. They were leaving that night. Who was to carry the ball for
them here in Washington during the next critical weeks? Who was
going to do the telephoning? Who was going to coordinate policy between New Jersey, California, Alabama, Wisconsin, Georgia, and
Kansas? The answer from them was, "No one." We had been given a
problem. It was ours now. The result to date: a resolution of the Agriculture Committee urging the Secretary to "implement such programs

of purchase, diversion, and export of poultry products as will lead toward improvement of the present critical situation." Results for the poultrymen: nothing.

Very sincerely,
Clem Miller

29. WEST SIDE STORY – CLEVELAND STYLE

Blacks comprised a majority of the voters in only one city in the 1960s (Washington, D.C.), so successful black politicians had to win at least a few white votes. This journalistic account shows how Carl Stokes, elected mayor of Cleveland in 1967, managed to win reelection. His successors in Cleveland were white, but by 1983 blacks had won the mayor's office in predominantly white Chicago, Philadelphia, and Los Angeles, as well as predominantly black Newark, Gary, Detroit, Atlanta, New Orleans, and Washington.

Source: "Mayor Stokes' West Side Story," *Commonweal* (November 28, 1969), pp. 270-71. Reprinted by permission.

Cleveland's charismatic black Mayor picked up his most surprising vote gains in the November 4 elections in two predominantly white West Side wards. The sociological composition of the area is such that some might consider it a bailiwick of Richard Milhous Nixon's "forgotten people." In Ward 7, Carl Stokes received 35.2 percent of the vote as against 28.5 percent in 1967; in Ward 8 he received 32 percent to '67s 22.8 percent. Stokes' 1967 vote in the two wards was 2411; his plurality in the entire city, 3753. The increases were achieved in a heavily European ethnic section of the city against Republican Ralph Perk, the son of Czechoslovak immigrants.

Experts had said all along that the battle would be won or lost on the white West Side. A drop in registration of 10,000 East Side Negro voters had made the West Side performance all the more critical. (The Mayor's actual vote in some all-black wards dropped by more than 7000.) The "near" West Side, or Wards 7 and 8, just over the bridge from downtown Cleveland, is still the kind of melting pot New York City was in the early 1900s. The population is a mix of Southern Appalachians fleeing the poverty of West Virginia and Kentucky, first and second-generation Europeans (Czechs, Slovenians, Hungarians, Russians, Ukrainians, Poles, Greeks,

Germans and Italians), Anglo-Saxon Protestants and Irish Catholics, Puerto Ricans and relocated American Indians. Only a possible 5 percent are Negroes.

For the most part the people are poor because underemployed or on welfare, or are slightly better-off blue-collar steel, automotive and other factory workers who live in houses with small, neat yards; the kind of people who for American journalists have become a symbol of white blacklash.

The near West Side has its share of problems: Saturday night shootings at bars, glue-sniffing and beer-drinking by minors, racial and national tensions among gangs of kids. Though the near West Side has its gentle people too, some people on the far (and more affluent) West Side consider it pretty rough territory. White liberals living in Cleveland's integrated East Side suburbs have suspected it to be a hotbed of bigotry.

Why did such a potentially hostile area (frequently hostile in practice) up Carl Stokes' margin so dramatically? Cleveland newspaper reporters have arbitrarily attributed the Mayor's success in Wards 7 and 8 to "a large influx of Puerto Rican voters" and to "the Democratic party's decision to expose Stokes to large numbers of West Side voters during the last weeks of the campaign."

Sorry, wrong on both counts. The Puerto Rican population is fairly stable, and has not experienced any tremendous upsurge in the two years since 1967; even now the total count of registered Puerto Rican voters in 7 and 8 is only 788. Though the Puerto Ricans were solidly behind Carl Stokes, worked hard for his election, and gave him probably his most jubilant campaign reception on the West Side, they comprise only 7.6 percent of the near West Side voting population.

On the second count, "exposure to West Side voters," the Mayor owes the Democratic party less than he thinks. (Most West Side Democratic councilmen avoided being seen with him during the campaign.) Weeks, and even months before Election Day, large numbers of near-West Side voters had made up their minds to vote for Carl Stokes.

In mid-October, not long after Robert Kelly's bitter law-and-order primary campaign had stirred up the old hates and the "nigger" talk, Stokes canvassers warily picked up their telephones to find out the lay of the land. What they discovered was substantial support for the Mayor, some purely on the basis of party loyalty ("My husband wouldn't care if a man was blue, green or purple, so long as he was a Democrat"), but just as much based on performance. "He's for the underdog," an elderly Italian voter said with a heavy accent. "This town had been dead for 20 years until he took over," said another voter. "He's a good man, whether he's white or black," commented a lady with a West Virginia accent. "And I surely appreciate those new lights down the street."

A resident of a Polish, Russian and Ukrainian precinct observed that services were beginning to improve in the neighborhood, and that Mayor

Stokes "is always the perfect gentleman." (Little old ladies love to watch the Mayor on television. "He's smooth as wax," one said. "I noticed Mr. Perk's collar was rumpled last week when I saw him.")

A neighborhood organizer, asked why a group of Southern Appalachians, who had been angry with the Mayor in the spring, now intended to vote for him: "It's simple. They know he's halfway responsive to their needs. They want to be sure they have the same guy to fight this time. Let's face it. Stokes has made poor people's claims legitimate. He's legitimized community control."

It should be pointed out, however, that the racists were still there, passing out hate literature, and that a couple of West Side windows with Stokes signs were shattered by bullets and rocks.

An important factor in "The West Side Story," as the *Cleveland Press* called Stokes' win, was the tight and bouncy campaign run in Wards 7 and 8 by Bill Hale, young Texas-raised director of the West Side Community House. "We didn't have any money, but we had the manpower," Hale says. The votes were there, and Hale was determined to get them. The regular Democratic party offered no help, but a grass roots corps of dedicated neighborhood workers had sprung up; swarms of college students from Oberlin, Antioch, Wooster College and Ohio State descended on the office on Election Day to help get voters to the polls. "Perk simply didn't have the manpower or the personal contacts over here in 7 and 8," Hale maintains.

30. SELLING THE CANDIDATE

As television increased in popularity as an entertainment medium, its political influence also grew. One consequence of this process was the rise of professional media experts to handle a political candidate's TV campaign. Using the same techniques used to sell soap and breakfast foods, "candidate marketing" brought new dimensions to political campaigning. It may be questioned, however, whether the use of electronic media meant any substantive change in the way voters learned about political candidates and issues. The following documents illuminate the Madison Avenue style of TV political packaging.

Source: Fred Ferrett, "Political TV 'Packager' Counts Ratings in Votes," *The New York Times,* August 18, 1970, p. 27. Christopher Lydon, "Madison Avenue's Style Varies as it Serves up the Candidates," *The New York Times,* October 24, 1970, p. 13. © 1970 by The New York Times Company. Reprinted by permission.

The selling of the candidates on television in the campaigns of 1970 is increasingly a conflict of identifiable styles and schools of technicians. It is a conflict between grainy slices of life and studio smoothness, between street sounds and jingles and movie music, between documentary film makers and market researchers from the big ad agencies and between the "look" of news and the controlled power of product commercials.

More often than not, the "structured" agency ads and Republican candidates seem to go together; the newsreel style seems to suit liberals and Democrats though there are exceptions and variations. Robert Goodman of Baltimore, an ad man who works for Republicans, designed black-and-white "confrontation" commercials for Linwood Holton in the Virginia Governor's race last year—against the moody, full-color films made by Charles Guggenheim for William Battle, the Democratic candidate. The same two media men have switched styles in the Ohio Senate race this year; the Goodman agency is warming up Republican Robert Taft Jr. in soft, color commercials, and Mr. Guggenheim is using appealingly raw, black-and-white film with Howard M. Metzenbaum, the Democrat.

Joseph Napolitan, who works exclusively for Democrats, uses both the agency-style commercials and the documentary look in the same campaigns. Yet most of the sought-after TV tacticians are settling on one or the other style. "You'll see the confrontation in '72," says David L. Garth of New York, an exponent of the "realistic" school, which, he says, is "halfway between a Ford ad and a newsclip." Mr. Garth hopes to get involved on the Democratic side of the next Presidential race. "Given a credible candidate and some money, we'll take the smooth stuff—anytime," he said. . . .

Thomas P. Losee, an executive vice president of McCann-Erickson, Inc., who directed the "tiger in your tank" campaign for the Humble Oil and Refining Company, and is currently supervising $1.5-million worth of television advertising for Governor Rockefeller, puts more value on his research tools. These include the pretesting of ads on sample audiences. Further, Mr. Losee is not convinced that voters want to pick their leaders from the blur of an earthy newsreel.

Both schools of political advertising are showing off new tricks in the 1970 campaign. Speed is one. The pace of political commercials is faster and the layers of persuasion, in sight and sound, are more subtly compressed. Thirty-second spots are more popular than 60-second spots, and five-minute spots are disappearing. Production time has also been reduced. Mr. Garth said that, through the special use of fast-developing news film, he had a spot on the air in one Senate campaign this year less than 24 hours after it was filmed. . . .

The strategic allocation of spots, an agency art, is being adapted to the peculiar problems of political advertising, in which the goal is not increased sales within a fraction of the audience but, rather, 51 percent approval across the entire market. The mass audiences and all of the specialized audiences (women, older people, men, families) must be courted.

The candidate in shirt sleeves, the most popular of the old cliches, is getting tiresome, many media men suspect. "Five years is a pretty good run for a cliche," said Mr. Garth, who started it all by taking John Lindsay's jacket off in the 1965 campaign. This year, Mr. Garth has filmed Adlai E. Stevenson 3d of Illinois in both shirt sleeves and a tuxedo. What Madison Avenue men call "the Kennedy bit"—tag football or seashore evocations of John and Robert Kennedy—is out, even in Senator Edward M. Kennedy's Massachusetts campaign, where Mr. Guggenheim has purposely excluded family symbols and references. . . .

Beyond the innovations, fads and occasional deviations of the 1970 campaign, the fact of fundamental importance is that television has solidified and expanded its role in politics. "The Selling of the President, 1968" by Joe McGinniss has made the suspicious awareness of candidate-marketing a popular theme of the new campaign year. Yet spending on political television is expected to approach 1968's $60-million and set a record for non-presidential years.

The big trend that Mr. Napolitan sees, and likes, is that the resistance of politicians and public to television campaigns is actually declining. "The mix of media is getting better all the time," Mr. Napolitan says. "That is, more people are finding that television is the best medium and they're wasting less time on all the other crap. You can't do a job if you don't believe in the guy. You can't. I mean you don't have to love him. But you do have to believe in what he's doing. No matter what anybody says, you can't sell a commodity without it being a good, commodity. You have to have something to sell."

David Garth speaks the jargon of Madison Avenue account executives and thinks in terms of comparative television ratings and of spot commercials. But he is not selling detergents. He's in the business of selling politicians to voters by the use of television, radio, newspapers and throw-aways—"the whole media package" as he puts it. Mr. Garth is a professional political television consultant, one of a small but growing band of entrepreneurs who have emerged in recent years as potent and often decisive, factors in elective races. . . . As television has grown in influence, so have those expert in using the medium's capacity to create and transmit not only images, but also emotions. Men such as Mr. Garth know that television can affect different viewers in different ways; they know ratings and demographics and what is apt to appeal to broad masses of people. These men have become indispensable in political campaigns. . . .

Mr. Ailes, whose specialty is in-studio performance, most recently produced Mr. Nixon's report on Cambodia. He is called upon often by the president to see to such things as lighting, the heights of podiums and camera angles. In Governor Rockefeller's successful third-term campaign in 1966, Mr. Tinker used the Governor's voice, but never his face in a highly successful series of commercials. But Mr. Garth said he could not do that kind of commercial. "I think people want to see the man," he asserted. "I believe you can't go in to a guy and say, 'I'm going to do this for you.' You can show him how to phrase, how to tilt his head, how to relax. But you do well when your client has talent and drive."

... With clients has come expansion. The Garth Associates offices are in the process of being redone with cork walls and Parsons tables, and sleek, stuffed Danish furniture. His staff of 12 includes Richard Kellerman, former Deputy Police Commissioner for Press Relations, and Mayor Lindsay's former speechwriter, Jeff Greenfield.

The 39-year-old specialist got his start in politics in 1960, when he organized the New York State for Stevenson Clubs and set up Adlai E. Stevenson's floor demonstration at the Democratic National Convention. Following this, he worked as a free-lance television producer. His television series with Mr. Stevenson, who was then representative at the United Nations, won a Peabody award....

"Why me?" Mr. Garth continued. "I came in with something important. There were and are a lot of good TV producers. There's also a lot of campaign managers. But not too many guys who've done both. I worked both ends. I had the background. I knew the language of TV and advertising, and politicians."

... Mr. Garth, a stocky, intense man, differs somewhat in approach from other political television consultants. Some limit themselves to television advice or technical assistance. He patterns entire media campaigns to include radio, newspaper and throwaway advertising and prefers to work with campaign managers.... He works simply with a candidate. He might begin in a studio, then as the candidate speaks, the picture goes out into the streets, into markets, parking lots, slums, housing projects, polluted waterways. "Money? Everybody talks about money," he said. "My share? It looks like a bundle for me, over a million bucks, right? Don't forget that I bought all the ads with that. I got my 15 percent, I'm not crying poverty."

31. THE MCGOVERN CRUSADE OF 1972

In 1972 supporters of South Dakota Senator George McGovern, a left-wing minority within the party, captured the Democratic presidential nomination. Gary W. Hart worked as a senior staff member in the McGovern campaign and one of the candidate's closest advisors. Hart later became Senator from Colorado and a candidate for the Democratic nomination for President in 1984. He describes how "McGovern's Army" invaded and captured California. Note how a dedicated, well-organized minority was able to triumph by countering modern political technique with the traditional army style of politics. Note also that, while it enabled McGovern to gain the nomination, it failed to win him the election.

Source: Gary Hart, *Right From the Start: A Chronicle of the McGovern Campaign* (New York: Quarangle, 1973), pp. 181-83. Copyright © 1973 by Gary Warren Hart. Reprinted by permission of TIMES BOOKS, a division of Quadrangle/The New York Times Book Co., Inc.

And so the stage was set for California. Twenty-two months before, we had felt it would be the deciding battle, the last great showdown. George McGovern against Ed Muskie or Hubert Humphrey, but probably Hubert Humphrey. And I had always felt that California would decide more than just the party's 1972 Presidential nominee. It would decide control of the Democratic Party for the future. California was Armageddon.

The Invasion of California. May, 1972. They started coming all the way from Massachusetts and Pennsylvania in late April. Traveling all the way across the country. Then after Ohio, the stream became almost a steady one. Some stopped over for a week of campaigning in Nebraska and then headed west. More continued out of the east after Michigan and Maryland. Driving, flying, busing, hiking. And, after Oregon, down from the north. More came in every day. Carloads from every state in the west.

The campaign that had begun with a few now numbered in the thousands. The army that had started with a handful was now 50,000 strong in California. The officer corps, the paid staff, numbered some 250, with more than three times that number organizing on a full-time basis without salary. They operated out of 230 offices around California. Hundreds of phones operated throughout every day from 34 phone banks across the state. These full-time phones were supplemented on the eve of the primary with hundreds of others in law offices and empty hotel rooms.

The army moved more than five and a half million pieces of McGovern literature, most of which was printed in our campaign print shop, which operated 24 hours a day every day. Local offices covered the whole range of style, from a boutique storefront in the plush Beverly Wilshire Hotel to seasonally out-of-use H & R Block tax offices. The army was everywhere.

May 20, 1972. The day after our preliminary agreement with the Humphrey representatives, I flew to Oakland to travel with the Senator and brief him on the terms for the debates and obtain his comments before completing the negotiations. He generally agreed with the position we were taking and seemed eager for a chance to counter Humphrey's increasingly strong and inaccurate charges face to face.

During the stop in Fresno, where he was headquartered, I talked to Gene Pokorny. Speaking for the grassroots people, Gene said he was upset by the way in which decisions were made and resources allocated in California. He had been in touch with other area coordinators and all had the same complaint: the state headquarters in Los Angeles was trying to run the entire canvass operation, sending out computerized voter-contact lists and requesting that canvass results (the system of ranking each voter contacted on a 1-to-5 scale) be sent back to Los Angeles so a personalized computer letter could be sent out from the main headquarters.

This system was diametrically opposed to any previous McGovern primary campaign, where all voter contact was locally oriented. Earlier, neighborhood storefront offices had been used as headquarters for local canvassing; card files on each voter contacted (the ranking system which was the nerve center of our entire campaign) had been maintained locally and used to get out the vote. The citizen-volunteers who carried the bulk of the load under an experienced staff organizer had felt a great sense of direct control and, therefore, responsibility for organizing their neighborhoods for McGovern. They prided themselves on their efficiency and dedication and felt that centralization and control from a state headquarters was a sign of lack of trust and confidence in them by the campaign leadership. And this struggle, going on in the last two weeks of the California primary, was at the very heart of the McGovern campaign.

Other campaigns, John Kennedy in 1960, McCarthy in 1968, Robert Kennedy in 1968, had relied heavily on the classic insurgency technique of rousing the countryside — the volunteers — to beat the entrenched powers. Like most political techniques, this one is based on military principles; it is New England citizens with pitchforks and muskets against George III's troops. Though the citizens need direction and leadership, it may be laid down as an unswerving law of politics that a campaign dependent upon citizen volunteers will succeed to the degree that it is able to motivate and use those citizens and will fail to the degree that it ceases to rely upon them and their judgment.

The McGovern campaign's unique contribution to insurgency politics was its grassroots character — its decentralization. The role of the national campaign leadership was to allocate resources — staff, money, the candidate's time, and media — and to select and assign the most qualified political organizers available to the states. The role of these organizers, the state coordinators, was to recruit and motivate the most talented citizens in the state to positions of local leadership and responsibility and to further allocate the resources granted from the national campaign in the most judicious manner possible. The role of the citizen leadership was to continue the recruitment process throughout the state until every block in every neighborhood in every community had a responsible McGovern supporter who would identify and deliver every McGovern vote on election day. The image is that of a pyramid with the peak as small as possible, the base as broad as possible, and the entire structure as short as possible. Reduce the number of layers of leadership. Keep the leaders at the very top in close touch with the people at the bottom. (I found out more about the overall condition and health of the McGovern campaign in a half-hour visit to a local headquarters than in a dozen lengthy ponderous meetings in the national headquarters with all the other campaign leaders. It is symptomatic of later difficulties that, as the campaign became larger and more successful, I had fewer and fewer opportunities to visit local headquarters.)

32. NEW FACES ON THE CONVENTION FLOOR

In 1972 political newcomers with reformist goals took over the Democratic National Convention. This meant conflict with established party regulars. Chicago's delegation, led by party boss Mayor Richard Daley, was barred by the credentials committee because it ignored new rules on seating women, young people, and minorities. The following two stories from the *New York Times* present glimpses of youthful enthusiasm, reform ideas, and old-line resistance to change.

Source: The *New York Times*, July 11, 1972, pp. 19, 20. © 1972 by The New York Times Company. Reprinted by permission.

Democratic Delegate, '72 Version
by Steven Roberts

The worst thing anybody can call Mike Rappeport is an amateur politician. "Hell, we've been building for this for four years in our county," said Mr. Rappeport, a 34-year-old statistician from Metuchen, N.J. "This is very much overlooked in the press. I'm a professional politician. I'm just not looking for a patronage job. My payoff is changing the direction of the country." Michael Arnold Rappeport is one of the 3,016 delegates to the Democratic National Convention that opened here today and one of the 80 per cent that has never attended a convention before. No delegate is typical, especially this year, when party reforms have opened the convention to a wide variety of newcomers. But Mr. Rappeport does represent the style and attitude of many of the new delegates: tough, intelligent, energetic, and — despite the fears of aging party leaders — rather reasonable.

The night Mr. Rappeport's McGovern slate swept Middlesex County, a delegation visited the headquarters of the party regulars. This morning, Mr. Rappeport recalled the scene this way: "We told them, 'We know we won, but we want your help.' We don't think we can rule the world, but they've got to know they can't rule it, either. We're interested in sharing power, sure, but we're not interested in throwing the regulars out."

. . . Mr. Rappeport views politics as both a hobby and a responsibility. "Life has been nice to me, and it leads to an obligation," said the father of two small children. "I know it sounds trite, but I feel that way." That sense of obligation led to involvement in the American Civil Liberties Union and a series of local elections. When McGovern supporters in Middlesex sought candidates for their slate, Mr. Rappeport's ties with the A.C.L.U. gave him a natural base to start from. Other candidates came from the peace movement, a labor union, an organization promoting better schools and a women's caucus. "People don't understand that the McGovern movement is really an amalgam of a lot of progressive things that were already going on," Mr. Rappeport said.

So far, Mr. Rappeport's reaction to the convention is a combination of frustration and elation. "It's exactly what people said it would be like — unbelievably chaotic," he said. "It's not possible to get up to-date information. The only way you can find out what's going on is watch TV — but I could have done that in New Jersey."

"But I love it, it's exciting," he added. "Good Lord! For anyone who loves politics, this is heaven. It also gives me a chance to make contacts and friends from all over New Jersey. That will be useful in the next campaign, and the one after that."

This election, and George McGovern, are only one chapter in a longer story for people like Mike Rappeport. As he put it: 'This year McGovern is the tool, the agent, in helping us build something. But I would be less than honest if I said I only got involved because I thought McGovern was a good guy. Regardless of what happens here, people like me are going to own the party in 1976."

Established Regulars Opposed Reforms
by Marjorie Hunter

The early cries for reform that have gone a long way toward transforming this Democratic National Convention into an antiestablishment gathering have been drowned out largely by the noisy fight over the Presidential nomination. But those seeking even more radical changes in the party have their patient evangelist, a quiet-spoken Minnesota Congressman, Donald M. Fraser, who has been trooping through the crowded hotel lobbies and caucus rooms, preaching the message. Mr. Fraser is convinced that the convention would approve sweeping new party reforms, heavily weighted toward "people power," if the issue ever reaches the floor.

The new reforms, incorporated in a party reform charter, were proposed jointly by two party commissions and were to be submitted for approval at the convention this week. Earlier reforms, already in effect, led to the new look of the convention delegates — more blacks, more women, more young people. The new reforms would extend the same philosophy that led to that new look to the ongoing party structure.

Established politicians, already fretting over the new politics reflected in this convention and fearful their power might be even further curtailed, have mounted a campaign against further reforms. The nation's Democratic Governors, meeting here two days ago, voted unanimously to recommend that no action on the proposed party reform charter be taken during the convention this week. Bitterly divided Democrats in the House of Representatives voted, 105 to 50, nearly two weeks ago to repudiate proposed party reforms, calling instead for "further investigation and study." And, just today, the two top House Democratic leaders — Speaker Carl Albert of Oklahoma and Hale Boggs of Louisiana, the majority leader — cautioned against convention action on reforms. While not criticizing the reform proposals, Speaker Albert said he was "not sure the time has come" to implement them. Mr. Boggs, in turn, said he felt that the reform issue should be considered when "there is more time available."

Other established politicians, too, many close to party leaders, have argued that the convention agenda already is so heavy — even threatening to run into the dawn hours — that there will not be adequate time to thrash out the party reform plan this week. Mr. Fraser, as chief spokesman for the reformers, considers such arguments are little more than "a campaign of attrition by delay."

The proposed reform charter, which would radically alter the structure and the outlook of the Democratic party, was drafted by two party commissions headed by Mr. Fraser and Representative James G. O'Hara of Michigan. The convention Rules Committee, dominated by reformers, swept far beyond the original plan two weeks ago by weighing it even more heavily against established politicians. Seeking to ease the fears of the old-line politicians, Mr. Fraser has proposed some modifications in recent days. But even these concessions appear to have made few converts.

As modified by Mr. Fraser, the proposed charter would greatly expand the Democratic National Committee to include elected members, create an issue-oriented policy conference, also dominated by elected members, to function between national conventions; establish regional party organizations, and, to a limited degree, establish a system of Democratic party memberships.

While established politicians — such as governors, state party chairmen, and certain other party leaders — would continue to have a voice in party councils, they could be outnumbered by those elected at the grassroots level. Heavy emphasis would be placed on inclusion of women, blacks, Indians, Spanish-speaking Americans and the young — the very reform elements that are so heavily represented at this convention.

As originally proposed, the charter would have created a system of national, card-carrying memberships in the Democratic party. Only those enrolled would have been permitted to vote for delegates to regional and national policy conferences. Responding to criticism that this would close party doors to those not wishing to become card-carrying Democrats, Mr. Fraser has proposed a modification that would eliminate forced enrollment as a condition for delegate voting. The state party chairmen, meeting here yesterday, voted 16 to 5 to support the revised Fraser reform charter.

33. NON-ATTITUDES OF THE NON-VOTER

The following analysis of nonvoter attitudes in 1976 was conducted by pollster Peter D. Hart. The study, made before the election, gathered data on 1,486 nonvoters, interviewed in late July 1976. It shows that the nineteenth-century ideal of mass participation had vanished.

Source: Press release from the Committee for the Study of the American Electorate, September 1976.

Over 70 million voting age Americans — more than voted for both Lyndon Johnson and Barry Goldwater only 12 years ago — will not vote in 1976. The next president of the United States will almost certainly take office with the knowledge that over 70 percent of his fellow citizens of voting age did not vote for him. In the last eight years, as many as 10 million Americans have dropped out of the political system. If they do not return by November, it is possible that for the first time in over 50 years, a majority of eligible Americans will not vote in a Presidential election.

The survey revealed significant demographic differences between all non-voters and those Americans who voted in the 1972 Presidential election (see table 3). For example, 46 percent of the non-voters are under 35, while only 30 percent of those who vote are under 35. In other ways non-voters fit the stereotype of being less educated, less affluent, more urban, and less often white than those who vote in national elections. Yet, 74 percent of the non-voters are white, 20 percent are in the upper income brackets, 23 percent live in the suburbs, and a majority are over the age of 35.

The survey also isolated a new category of non-voters which it called the "drop-out." Drop-outs are those voters who voted frequently in 1968 or before, but have since become estranged from the political process. Drop-outs tend to be older, more educated, more affluent, and more alienated than other non-voters.

Table 3
COMPARATIVE DEMOGRAPHIC DISTRIBUTIONS OF VOTERS
AND NON-VOTERS

	Voted in 1972[1] %	1976 Non-Voters %
Sex		
Men	51	48
Women	49	52
Age		
18-24	11	23
25-34	19	23
35-49	30	24
50-64	24	17
65 and over	16	13
Race		
White	89	74
Black	8	18
Hispanic/Chicano	3	7
Income		
Under $5,000	15	27
$5,000-$10,000	27	26
$10,000-$15,000	26	22
$15,000 and over	28	20
Not sure/refused	8	15
Educational Attainment		
Grade school or less	14	23
High school	45	59
College	41	18
Type of Area		
Urban	31	37
Suburban	28	23
Small town	15	16
Rural/farm	26	24

[1]This column is taken from a national cross-sectional survey of 1596 adult Americans conducted in 1973 by Louis Harris and Associates. It over-reported voters by 18 percent.

Although non-voters are no less optimistic than is the general adult population about where they expect their own lives to be five years from now, they are less hopeful than is the general population about where they expect the country to be in five years.

Among the attributes of the non-voter are a distrust of, and disaffection from major political and economic institutions, political leadership, and the media. For example (see table 4), in explaining their lack of participation,

Table 4
SELECTED STATEMENTS ON POLITICAL TRUST
AND POLITICAL EFFECTIVENESS

Indicators of Political Trust

"Do you think quite a few of the people running the government in Washington are a little crooked, not very many are, or do you think that hardly any of them are crooked at all?"

	Quite a Few	Not Many	Hardly Any	Don't Know
	%	%	%	%
All Respondents	61	24	6	9

"How much of the time do you think you can trust the government in Washington to do what is right — just about always, most of the time, or only some of the time?"

	Just About Always	Most of the Time	Only Some of the Time	None of the Time (VOL)	Don't Know
	%	%	%	%	%
All Respondents	5	27	57	6	5

"Would you say that the government in Washington is pretty much run by a few big interests or that it is pretty much run for the benefit of all people?"

	By a Few Big Interests	For All People	Other/ Depends (VOL)	Don't Know
	%	%	%	%
All Respondents	62	22	6	10

"Sometimes government and politics seem so complicated that a person like me can't really understand what's going on."

	Strongly Agree	Partially Agree	Partially Disagree	Strongly Disagree	Not Sure
	%	%	%	%	%
All Respondents	52	30	8	7	3

"People like me don't have any say about what the government does."

	Strongly Agree	Partially Agree	Partially Disagree	Strongly Disagree	Not Sure
All Respondents	33	33	18	12	4

"There don't seem to be any people or groups in American politics that can accomplish what I think needs to be done."

	Strongly Agree	Partially Agree	Partially Disagree	Strongly Disagree	Not Sure
All Respondents	30	32	17	9	12

non-voters cited attitudinal factors as more important than structural ones. . . .

Another preliminary finding of the survey is a thirsting for leadership. By a margin of 87 to 8 percent, the non-voters agreed that "what this country needs most, more than laws and political programs, is a few courageous, tireless, devoted leaders in whom the people can put their faith."

34. THE POPULAR REVOLT AGAINST TAXES

In the late 1970s the pendulum of American politics was swinging toward the right. Jimmy Carter was the most conservative of the leading Democrats in 1976. He won the nomination and narrowly defeated the conservative Republican Gerald Ford. The most dramatic evidence of a continued rightward swing was the tax revolt of 1978, especially the Proposition 13 campaign to slash property taxes for homeowners and businesses in California. Governor Jerry Brown, after opposing Proposition 13, suddenly reversed himself and became its leading champion. Brown also called for a constitutional amendment to require the federal government to balance its budget every year. Tax revolt sentiment was deep, as public opinion analysts Seymour Martin Lipset and Earl Raab reported in *Commentary*.

Source: Seymour Martin Lipset and Earl Raab, "The Message of Proposition 13," *Commentary*, September 1978, Vol. 66, pp. 42-46. Reprinted by permission; all rights reserved.

The Jarvis-Gann Constitutional Amendment, limiting property taxes in California, has touched off speculation about a conservative backlash and the ascendance of a New Right in America. But analysis suggests that the trend exemplified by the "taxpayers' revolt" confounds the traditional political designations.

In 1946, according to Gallup, Americans who wanted taxes cut outnumbered those who did not by only four percentage points (48-44). By 1963, the gap was 44 percentage points (63-19). In 1969, 54 per cent of Americans told the Harris survey that they had "reached the breaking point" with respect to the amount of taxes they paid; that figure was up to 66 per cent by 1978.

Those who are unhappy use a simple consumer's measure: in so many words, only 23 per cent of the people queried by the Harris poll in 1971 thought they were getting their "money's worth from tax dollars." In this sentiment no more than two or three percentage points separated whites from blacks, Democrats from Republicans, or one income group from another. All felt put upon. In that same year, about 7 out of 10 told Harris that the time was coming when they "would sympathize with a taxpayers' revolt," involving a refusal to pay taxes — again with little difference in view related to whether they were white or black, and whether their income was around $5,000 or over $15,000.

The pressure has increased along with inflation. About one out of three Americans ranked inflation as their chief worry in 1977; in 1978, two out of three Americans did so. The "money's worth" was diminishing rapidly. In response, public officials uniformly promised tax reduction, but they did not deliver. Then the California property tax provided the dramatic breakthrough. California real-estate inflation had been brutal, often triple-digit over a few years' span. It was common for people who had bought a modest home for $20,000 to find themselves paying taxes ten years later on a home assessed at $90,000. No one was surprised to learn that the home of a Los Angeles man had been reappraised to $60,000 in 1977, and reappraised again in 1978 to $104,000, with a jump in taxes from a little over $2,000 to a little over $3,500. It became a hardship for many people to live in their own homes, and obviously there was no point in selling for the profit to buy other inflated houses at proportionally higher interest rates.

While these and other taxes were rising so much faster than income, the number of state and city employees was also increasing faster than the population. In the period 1970-75, the number of state and local employees rose by 21 per cent, while the state's population grew by only 6 per cent. . . .

It was . . . for Californians . . . the final straw. They were obviously using the occasion to express themselves on the matter of tax burdens in general. And indeed, this is how their vote was taken, by politicians in California and everywhere else, as well as by the American public. After the California vote, a New York *Times*/CBS News poll found that the whole country was jubilant. Again by a two-to-one margin (51-24), Americans said that they supported a similar measure for their own jurisdictions.

But if California's Proposition 13 was the messenger, what really was the message? To what extent do the taxpayers just want to keep their money, as against seeking their money's worth? What services are they willing to give up? What do they expect from government?

One stream of opinion on the subject was articulated by Senator George McGovern when he said that Californians had acted on a "degrading hedonism that tells them to ask what they can take from the needy." He also saw "undertones of racism" in Proposition 13. According to others who share this view, Proposition 13 is an expression of "mean-spiritedness" and the harbinger of the conservative and/or racist backlash which has allegedly been around the corner for the past dozen years.

There is no doubt that self-interest (which, however, is not necessarily the same thing as mean-spiritedness) was a factor in the Proposition 13 vote. . . .

What is noteworthy, however, is how many voters with an apparent interest in the defeat of Proposition 13 nevertheless went for it: 44 per cent of families of public employees, 47 per cent of renters, and 42 per cent of blacks. In these categories, the majority who voted opposed Proposition 13; but in every *economic* category, it was the other way around. Thus the measure was supported by 55 per cent of those with incomes under $8,000; 66 per cent of those in the $8-15,000 bracket; 67 per cent of those in the $15-25,000 class; and 61 per cent of those with incomes above $25,000.

A similarly mixed picture appears when we look at the vote in terms of ideological categories. As might have been expected, 82 per cent of self-designated "conservatives" voted for the measure. Yet here too what is noteworthy is the large number of self-described "moderates" (63 per cent) and "liberals" (45 per cent) who voted for it.

Clearly, then, the victory of Proposition 13 represents something more complex than a triumph of selfishness and/or old-line conservatism. In trying to understand what that something is, we might begin by noting that the evidence from a variety of opinion surveys reveals that a growing number of Americans, when asked to describe themselves politically, say that they are conservatives. In 1964, according to the New York *Times*/CBS poll, the ratio of self-described conservatives to self-described liberals was fairly even (32-27); today, the gap has widened considerably (42-23).

But what do people mean when they call themselves conservatives? Evidently it has to do with distaste for a growing, interfering, and cumbersome government. Thus in 1964, according to the Gallup poll, Americans were almost evenly split (42-39) on the issue of whether "the government has gone too far in regulating business and interfering with the free-enterprise system." By 1978, . . . Americans had come to agree with the statement by a margin of 58-31 per cent. Not surprisingly, self-described conservatives now endorse this statement overwhelmingly (67-26); what is surprising is the fact that even "liberals" divide in favor of it by 45-35 per cent.

The percentage of people who think that "government is spending too much" has also risen steadily since 1973. But "too much" is a famous term of relativity. It may be considered too much with respect to the income of the citizenry; but it may also be considered too much with respect to the quality of the product. This is the "money's-worth" question. And the overwhelming tide of opinion, especially "conservative" opinion, identifies this government deficiency as "waste." In 1958, only 42 per cent of those polled told Gallup interviewers that "the government wastes a lot of the tax money"; by 1978, 78 per cent of Americans thought so. . . . A vast majority of blacks also agrees with this view.

"Waste in government" was the key phrase in the Proposition 13 campaign. Mervin Field of the California poll reports that the main comment made by proponents of Proposition 13, other than "Taxes are too high," was "The time has come to cut government costs, waste, and inefficiency." . . .

Was...the cry against "waste in government" merely a cover-up for "hedonistic" and "mean-spirited" impulses to cut services for the needy? The evidence indicates that the answer to this question is no, and that the cry against government is genuine.

In all surveys, the percentage of people who say that they trust or have confidence in the government has dropped steadily. In one recurrent poll ...the percentage trusting the government dropped from 78 in 1964 to 33 in 1976. More and more Americans think that the people running the government "don't know what they're doing."

But more significant in refuting the interpretation of Proposition 13 as pure "hedonism" is the fact that the desire for government to intervene in beneficent ways has not diminished. The New York *Times*/CBS poll reports that in 1960 63 per cent of Americans agreed that "the government in Washington ought to see to it that everybody who wants to work has a job." This year, 74 per cent of the people in general—and 70 per cent of those who describe themselves as "conservative"—approved that mandate for government. In 1960, about 64 per cent of the people endorsed the proposal that "the government ought to help people to get doctors and hospital care at low cost." This year, 81 per cent...agreed. In the fall of 1976, the University of Michigan's Survey Research Center asked a national sample whether they thought "government should spend less even if it means cutting back on health and education." Only 21 per cent favored spending less under such circumstances while 75 per cent opposed the cut. In the same year, 67 per cent of those polled by Gallup thought that government help for the elderly should be increased, while only 3 per cent said it should be reduced; 51 per cent thought that there should be more government support for health care and only 13 per cent said there should be less; 44 per cent felt there should be more government intervention on behalf of the unemployed, as compared to 19 per cent who believed there should be less. There was no significant difference between the attitudes of professional and business people and manual laborers, or among the various income classifications.

This common support of beneficent government intervention, substantiated by survey after survey, cannot be written off by saying that people are only interested in maintaining social programs of direct benefit to them. No doubt a certain amount of "there-but-for-the-grace-of-God-go-I" sentiment has always sustained liberal social programs; but the figures do not confirm the charge that it is *narrow* self-interest which motivates the well-to-do and the ideologically conservative to favor government help for the aged and the needy. Rather, Americans seem to have developed an irreversible commitment to basic government welfare programs, as they did, finally, to social security. It is now as natural to them as getting up in the morning. . . .

This attitude toward "welfare" is by no means new. In 1935, in one of the first surveys Gallup ever took, 60 per cent of the respondents said that the government was expending too much money for "relief" (the contemporary term for what later came to be called welfare) while only 9 per cent replied that the government was spending too little. The majority of Americans continued to show disdain for "relief" all during the Depression. But the same polls which produced these results revealed a considerable majority in favor of the government's providing jobs for the unemployed, and for requiring those on relief to accept such jobs.

This general response pattern has remained substantially unchanged over the years. In a 1970 Harris poll, Americans approved (46-34) the proposition that welfare should be abolished, and that welfare recipients be made to go to work. But the same respondents overwhelmingly supported (56-28) the idea that government programs should be increased to help the poor. Again, in a 1976 survey, Harris found that 62 per cent favored (and only 23 per cent opposed) "a major cutback in federal spending." However, confronted with a list of specifics, substantial majorities of the same respondents *rejected* cutbacks in spending for education, health, help for the unemployed, equal opportunity for minorities, environmental protection, and product safety. It was only on welfare that a majority (56-35) favored a cutback.

The juxtaposition of these two answers — cut welfare, increase help for the poor — poses a puzzle which turns up again and again. Thus in 1977, the white population was evenly split (39-39) on whether welfare programs should be greatly decreased, but three-quarters of them said that the government should spend money to provide job incentives for the poor. In 1977, the American public approved by 80-13 per cent the idea that all able-bodied people should be removed from the welfare rolls, but also stated by a similar majority that the government should provide public-service jobs, with tax money, for those who could not find jobs in private industry. And by about the same margin (78-15), the American public agreed that its tax money should continue to be expended on the aged, blind, disabled, and one-parent families with children under the age of seven. There was no significant difference in the answers to these questions by self-styled conservatives and self-styled liberals.

The numbers may be subject to various degrees of distortion, but the answer to the puzzle is clear. Americans — especially that growing contingent of self-identified "conservative" Americans — are willing to pay taxes to assist the needy, but they are not satisfied with the way that portion of their tax money is being spent.

There are three strikes against "welfare." It still durably connotes "relief," "dole," something for nothing, economic waste. It is connected to the sometimes exaggerated, sometimes prejudiced sense of how many able-bodied people are on the rolls, or how many prefer not to work. As a program it seems to epitomize bureaucratic government at the worst: inefficient, ornately overlaid, corrupt, unfathomable, feckless.

But helping the poor by providing jobs is another matter entirely. Thus in 1972 Gallup asked: Suppose it would cost the government less money to give poor people cash payments than to have government train them, find jobs for them, and, if necessary, provide care for their children while they work? About 81 per cent responded that they would prefer the more costly program; only 9 per cent said they would favor the less expensive one.

The message, then, is: help the poor but get rid of "welfare." That "liberal" message is consistent with the nature of our new self-styled "conservative."

This hybrid political animal has, of course, been spotted before. In 1967, for example, Hadley Cantril and Lloyd Free found that many Americans were "ideological conservatives" — that is, anti-statist in their political beliefs — and "operational liberals," in the sense that they supported government action to create jobs. The number of such people is growing. More precisely, ideological conservatism has been growing as a partner to a continuingly dominant operational liberalism. This orientation is often described as neo-conservatism, but it might just as accurately be called neoliberalism. The former designation emphasizes the belief that expansion of government services at the current welfare-state level should, in lawyer's language, be suspect — subject to proof that a real problem cannot be dealt with in another fashion. The latter term emphasizes the continuing acceptance of collective responsibility to provide for the impoverished and the disadvantaged.

But if this hybrid phenomenon is the most dynamic force in the American political culture today, it also poses a dilemma — perhaps the new American dilemma, which, like Gunnar Myrdal's old one, also encompasses a contradiction between practice and ideology, this time in the arena of government intervention. Is it finally possible to hold down the monster state while dealing with the sheer bulk of services of every kind our society seems increasingly to need?

The "tax revolt" is perched at the edge of this huge question, whose answer will probably evolve rather than be calculated. But the tax revolt raises a more practical and immediate question as well: will the politicians quickly enough recognize and accommodate to the growing neoliberal (or, if one prefers, neoconservative) mood, or will they misread it, one way or another, according to their predilections?

If characterizing the tax revolt epitomized by Proposition 13 as "mean-spiritedness," or "hedonism," or "racism" is to misread it on the one side, to interpret it as the sign of a swing to old-line conservative or right-wing Republicanism is to misread it equally on the other. . . .

The growth of tax-revolt sentiment has been accompanied by a parallel growth of identification not with the Republicans but with the Democratic party (Democrats now outnumber Republicans by 45 per cent to about 20 per cent in the polls). In practical terms, both Gallup and the New York Times/CBS polls estimate that the overwhelming Democratic majority in Congress will be renewed this November, even though the out-party usually makes a comeback in congressional contests held in non-presidential election years. In addition, the Democratic party — the party which has stood for expanding social services — has gained overwhelming control of government from the county courthouses to the state and national legislatures, and from governorships to the Presidency, during a period when the proportion of self-identified conservatives and anti-tax sentiment have been increasing steadily.

Nor are the elements of a classic right-wing extremist movement present in Proposition 13. Howard Jarvis, who has been plumping for this kind of tax measure for over ten years, suddenly found himself at the head of a parade he did not assemble. He may be a culture hero at this point, but he is not a political leader. Extra-partisan movements, whether rightist or leftist, usually make headway when they espouse a cause which is not embraced by one of the major coalition parties. Such movements have always been done in by the fact that one of the major parties, following the logic of its coalitional nature, took over their cause in a more moderate form. That seems to have happened already in California. It remains to be seen, however, if the politicians understand exactly what it is they have embraced.

The strong support of Proposition 13 by Democrats, in California and around the nation, provides the clue. As the survey data show, these Democrats have not abandoned their desire for a socially protective government. (On the contrary, most Republicans have tended to join them in that desire.) But the Democrats increasingly consider themselves "conservative" in their queasiness about the *way* government is growing and acting.

If, then, the public mood today is against enlarging the power, scope, and size of government in order to solve social problems, as advocated by George McGovern, Edward Kennedy, or the Americans for Democratic Action, it is also against returning to the laissez-faire small-government philosophy proposed by Ronald Reagan, Milton Friedman, or the American Conservative Union. Reagan, however, appears to be shifting: in a post-Proposition 13 speech he challenged his image as a "right-wing person" by pointing out that as governor he had made the California income tax more "progressive" and had increased welfare grants "by 43 per cent for the truly needy." Evidently he at least understands what analysis of the tax revolt tells us — that the predominant public mood is not "right-wing" but the neoliberal (or neoconservative) impulse to combine support of collective social responsibilities with a suspicion of growing government power.

35. CONSERVATIVES ON THE LAST FRONTIER

The resurging conservatism of 1980 was revealed dramatically in the nomination of Ronald Reagan as the Republican candidate. But the Reagan movement was only the most visible part of a large-scale grass roots movement. In Alaska, organized evangelical Protestants took control of the state G.O.P., as reporter Wallace Turner discovered.

Source: New York Times, 9 June 1980. © 1980 by The New York Times Company. Reprinted by permission.

Behind the leadership of a dynamic Baptist pastor, evangelical Protestants operating under the banner of Moral Majority of Alaska have seized control of Alaska's Republican Party.

Delegates of Moral Majority members showed up unexpectedly at party district caucuses in February and elected a large majority of delegates to the state Republican convention, who made sure that Moral Majority's candidate, Ronald Reagan, won all 19 of the state's delegates to the party's national convention.

And the state convention's resolutions went right down the line of the Moral Majority's positions: against abortions, favoring a state boycott of the White House Conference on the Family because "it is stacked against family life which is traditional in the United States"; affirmation of the right of parents to spank their children; elimination of welfare for persons able but not willing to work; opposition to drafting women.

Group Only a Year Old

The victory was the outstanding political success of Moral Majority, a national organization created only a year ago by the Rev. Jerry Falwell of Lynchburg, Va., who claims a weekly audience of 15 million for his evangelical radio and television programs. The Rev. Jerry Prevo organized the Alaska group last Dec. 15.

Established Republicans decline to complain openly about the party takeover, but privately they express dismay. Moral Majority is now digesting the takeover and advising voters on its opinions about the qualifications of various candidates, based on its stands.

"Our country is rapidly turning into a 20th century Sodom and Gomorrah because we have permitted a few amoral humanists to take over the most influential positions in our nation," Mr. Prevo, pastor of the Anchorage Baptist Temple, said in a brochure describing the aims of Moral Majority.

"Humanism, with its moral emphasis on no absolutes and situation ethics, challenges every moral principal upon which America was originally founded," Mr. Prevo's brochure said. "Advocates of abortion on demand, recognition of homosexuals as a bona fide minority, pornography, prostitution, gambling, free use of drugs and much, much more are destroying this country." He also criticized the feminist movement, the children's rights movement, television and movies.

'Free Enterprise Endangered'

Further, the brochure said, "The free enterprise system is endangered by the advent of socialism," and, "Our national defense is not what it ought to be."

Mr. Prevo's church is on Northern Lights Boulevard about 10 miles east of downtown Anchorage. This is an area where the scrub trees and brush have been pushed back rapidly in the last decade to make way for attractive suburban housing. "Government is the No. 1 Enemy" is a favorite bumper sticker on pickup trucks in the area.

The 35-year-old Mr. Prevo said in an interview that he was drawn into politics in 1977 when the municipal assembly here approved an ordinance protecting homosexuals against job discrimination. The measure was vetoed, and Mr. Prevo helped organize a campaign that led to the upholding of the veto and to the reelection of the mayor who wielded the veto. The losing candidate was backed by homosexuals.

Mr. Prevo said that he also became upset that the state Education Department interfered with the curriculum and faculty hiring at the school that his church operates for 500 students, from kindergarten through high school. "In this country Christianity has been discriminated against," Mr. Prevo said.

A group called Free Voices has begun to buy newspaper advertisements attacking Mr. Prevo's statements. One in yesterday's Anchorage Times quoted the minister as saying, "When the Bible speaks on a scientific subject it's accurate."

In his sermon at the early service today, Mr. Prevo said that he was pleased to be attacked on such grounds. Waving a Bible in his right hand, he said: "The Bible is God, and God is the supreme scientist. I believe the Book, I believe the Bible." The congregation of about 500, which would be 1,000 or more at the 11 A.M. service, responded, "Amen."

Mr. Prevo's new political force made itself felt in February, when delegations of Moral Majority members, newly registered Republicans, showed up at district caucuses and took control. When the state convention opened here on April 19, it was all over but the counting.

The achievement was made easier because of Alaska's unusual primary election system, which makes the established parties weaker than in most states. The primaries are completely open, so that voters may switch back and forth between parties as they work their way down the ballot. But popular vote has nothing to do with selection of delegates to the national convention — they are chosen by the party organization.

36. LIBERALISM AND CONSERVATISM
IN BLACK AND WHITE

The terms "liberal" and "conservative" are often bandied about without clear understanding. Charles V. Hamilton, a leading black political scientist, explains what the terms mean today in domestic politics; he does not consider the much more tangled area of foreign policy. Hamilton also succinctly reviews recent trends in the public's attitudes toward government spending, civil rights, and social issues.

Source: Charles V. Hamilton, "Measuring Black Conservatism," in National Urban League's, *The State of Black America 1982* (New York: National Urban League, 1982), pp. 115-39. Copyrighted by the National Urban League.

In the lexicon of modern-day American political dialogue, a liberal is one who favors more (not less) government intervention in the economy; one who prefers to see the government (especially the national government) enact economic programs aimed at providing employment in the public sector if necessary for those who cannot otherwise find jobs, as well as programs geared toward direct government assistance in the areas of health, welfare, housing, and education. An economic liberal, in other words, is more inclined to endorse government spending to stimulate the economy in times of recession. And a liberal clearly supports such measures as minimum wage, government regulation of health and safety work sites and of the environment, and government regulation of business practices generally.

People who style themselves liberal on social issues tend to favor such things as abortion, busing, gun control, and eliminating the death penalty. Liberals are likely to be found favoring more strict and specific enforcement of affirmative action laws. In foreign affairs, liberals generally tend to support less spending on military defense, and they put more emphasis on international negotiation through bodies such as the United Nations. They also will be more in favor of foreign aid to less developed countries, but more in the nature of economic goods and services than in military equipment.

A conservative in today's dialogue believes that less government involvement in the economy is desirable, that the society is better off relying much more on the competitive market system than on government controls. If a liberal is more prone to accept wage and price controls, these are strongly resisted by an economic conservative. Social problems covering such issues as health, welfare, and housing should be dealt with by the private sector. Conservatives are less likely to endorse government social service grants, relying instead on private efforts from the voluntary sector. On other matters, a conservative would not favor busing to achieve racial balance in schools, nor favor eliminating the death penalty. In international affairs, conservatives are more likely to support increased spending for military defense. Essentially, the conservative position on domestic matters finds its roots in the maxim: "That government is best which governs least." The minimum wage is considered harmful, not helpful, to those it is designed to benefit.

Liberalism in the current context puts more emphasis on what is considered the societal causes of poverty and deprivation, thus more collective (that is, governmental) means must be used to remedy those disadvantages. Conservatism is more prone to stress not only individual, private efforts at overcoming disabilities, but also that individuals must take greater responsibility for the causes of their conditions. Thus, liberals argue more for government social welfare programs to help people in need; conservatives believe that more people could and should work themselves off the welfare rolls into self-sustaining private-based occupations. Liberals are more likely to point to economic deprivation as the cause for rising crime rates, citing lack of jobs or, at least, "dead-end" jobs with little chance for development. This, they suggest, blunts initiative, creates hopelessness, nurtures frustration, and leads to alienation and lawlessness. Conservatives are less sympathetic to this explanation. They see anti-social behavior more as an attribute of individual failure and refusal to assume personal responsibility for one's actions.

In a more subjective vein, liberals have come to be characterized by their ideological opponents as "bleeding hearts" and "do-gooders." Conservatives, in turn, are characterized by those who oppose them as "compassionless" and "callous." Liberals are accused of seeking "hand-outs" for the poor; conservatives are accused of being "unrealistic" in their reliance on the private sector to solve many of the serious social problems facing the society. . . .

An additional factor concerns the relationship between the national government and the state and local governments. Conservatism not only champions less government involvement, but, where possible, it believes that state and local governments should have control over activities in preference to the national government. That government is best which not only governs least, but closest. Liberals, on the other hand, are wary of this approach. They prefer, for the most part, national government control. Thus, when people advocate "state's rights," liberals read this as a code term which reminds them of the days of southern state and local defiance of national civil rights laws.

Therefore, while one frequently hears politicians and others refer to "liberal" and "conservative" as mere labels which oversimplify relatively complex positions, it is nonetheless possible to discern basically central and distinguishable characteristics of each ideological view. To be sure, these broad ideological types are not always neatly found dividing the citizenry concretely down the middle. Some people might well be liberal on some issues and conservative on others. Thus, we occasionally hear a person classify him or herself as a "fiscal conservative," but a "social liberal," etc. But the fundamental categories remain sufficiently distinct to permit a reasonable analysis. . . .

As a consequence of political, economic, and social circumstances, black Americans have a history of inevitable reliance on government (especially the national government) intervention in their behalf. The very abolition of slavery and the establishment of civil and political rights were ultimately achieved through constitutional amendments, federal court decisions, Presidential decrees, and congressional enactments. From the moment they were brought to this country, blacks had to struggle to establish first their constitutional status as human beings and then their legal status as first-class citizens. These were political struggles conducted through various means but always aimed at extracting favorable decisions and outcomes from one branch or another of the national government. . . .

In the economic realm . . . heavy reliance (during Reconstruction, the New Deal, the Great Society of the 1960s) had to be placed on economic programs emanating from the government. The point to be made, of course, is that the private sector-oriented capitalist economy has always had a fundamentally different meaning for black Americans than for most of their fellow citizens. White Americans came to this country and could proceed to struggle to own private property. Black Americans came to this country and had to struggle to cease being owned as private property. . . .

If blacks are wary of a philosophy that advocates minimal government involvement and proposes policies designed "to get government off our backs," such wariness surely has a basis in historical experience. The traditional rewards of private effort in the marketplace have not been as forthcoming for blacks as for many others. In addition, the post-World War II civil rights struggle aimed a large part of its attack at state and local *de jure* segregation laws. The federal government might not always have been as responsive as it should have been, but there was no mistaking the fact that if racial segregation and voting denials were to be effectively overcome, action would have to be taken by the *national* government. "State's rights" meant permission to perpetuate racial oppression and subjugation. Therefore, *federal* courts were appealed to; the President was pressured for executive orders; Congress was lobbied for meaningful legislation. . . . Many white Americans have every reason to believe that the economically conservative theories — for them — are valid. They have been the overt beneficiaries of those theories, they have seen those theories work for themselves and their children. A set of conservative principles, in such circumstances, might well be justifiable, especially in terms of belief in the efficacy of conservative economic preferences. One has to be much less sanguine about this, however, when analyzing black social, economic, and political attitudes. . . .

Experience forms a strong part of the legacy that causes some blacks, even today, to wince when they hear someone championing state's rights. The reaction is no less acute, given the black experience, when the promise is made to "get government (meaning, especially, national government) off our backs." One can imagine a comparable Jewish reaction to the phrase "final solution," or the reaction of Irish Catholics in Northern Ireland who hear fellow Protestant countrymen invoke "God save the Queen." *Historical experiences are not irrelevant.* . . .

On the matter of success or failure of earlier "liberal" efforts, certainly one can hardly conclude their clear success. But to conclude that those efforts have been "counterproductive" is to conclude more than the total evidence warrants. The record is, at best, mixed, but there are likely few Americans, black or white, who would seriously support the contention that the combined efforts from the New Deal through the Great Society were on balance not worth the struggle.

With this historical context in mind, we may now turn to some data that show rather clearly where mass black opinion stands on various issues along the liberal-conservative spectrum.

One useful starting point is to note how people actually consider themselves. Keeping in mind that when people are asked whether they believe themselves to be liberal or conservative, they are not likely responding to a coherent set of political ideologies. . . .

As voters left the voting booth on November 4, 1980, they were asked: "Regardless of the party you may favor, do you lean more toward the liberal side or the conservative side politically?"

The responses were as follows:

	Liberal	Moderate	Conservative
Black	40%	37%	23%
White	22%	36%	41%
Other	32%	47%	20%

There was a substantial decline in support for government spending on welfare among both blacks and whites during the 12-year period from 1961 to 1973. But black respondents continued to indicate a majority in favor of such expenditures. . . .

On the issue of government spending for low-cost housing, as with education, the black attitudinal trend is opposite that of whites, with blacks favoring more spending by a considerable margin over whites. Comparing this category with welfare, one might conclude that available low-cost housing became a more important issue to blacks than welfare during the period covered. . . . Most people respond to the liberal/conservative label in terms of rather specific, concise reference points, not on the basis of broad philosophical ideas. On balance, blacks continue to prefer liberal over conservative positions in the economic realm. But not always. For example, many people would characterize a proposed constitutional amendment requiring a balanced national budget "to prevent the government from spending more money than it takes in, except in certain specified cases of crisis or emergency" as essentially a conservative economic proposal. Yet, when the question was asked in 1980 by the Roper Organization, black and white respondents were remarkably similar and overwhelmingly in favor (with blacks even 2 points more so): blacks, 89% in favor; whites 87%.

But when asked, in 1980, if the government should provide fewer services and reduce spending, only 11% of the nonwhite (most of whom in the national sample were black) respondents preferred this policy. Thirty-two percent whites preferred it.

Likewise, combined responses to questions from 1973 to 1980 elicited the following results:

- Are we spending too much, too little, or about the right amount on improving the nation's education system?

  White respondents — 50% — Spending too little
  Nonwhite respondents — 69% — Spending too little

- Are we spending too much, too little, or about the right amount on solving the problems of big cities?

  White respondents — 48% — Spending too little
  Nonwhite respondents — 53% — Spending too little

- Are we spending too much, too little, or about the right amount on welfare?

  White respondents — 14% — Spending too little
  Nonwhite respondents — 45% — Spending too little

- Are we spending too much, too little, or about the right amount on improving and protecting the environment?

  White respondents — 56% — Spending too little
  Nonwhite respondents — 66% — Spending too little

Therefore, these recent results show that overall blacks have maintained their basically liberal views on issues involving government spending for socioeconomic goals. Perhaps no better item to measure black views on the subject of the government's economic role could be found than one putting forth the following proposition in 1978 and 1980.

Some people think that the government in Washington ought to reduce the income differences between the rich and the poor, perhaps by raising the taxes of wealthy families or by giving income assistance to the poor.

Nonwhite respondents who *agreed* that government ought to reduce income differences came to 68%, while 42% of the white respondents agreed. Incidentally, only 16% of the nonwhites (and 37% of the whites) believed that government should not be concerned with reducing income differences. Clearly, then, as far as these opinion survey data indicate, mass black views on the role of government and the economy do not coincide with what is generally understood as conservative ideology. . . .

If we find that blacks hold such views on economic issues, what about in the area of social concerns? Here we refer to such matters as crime, abortion, drugs, death penalty, and extramarital sex relations. Using the definitional criteria described earlier in this article, one would define a basically conservative inclination as one that would feel that the courts should be tougher on law violators, that marijuana should not be legalized, that favored the death penalty for murder, that condemned extramarital sex relations, that believed that homosexuality was wrong, and that rejected legal abortions. Essentially, these are positions associated with the social policy stances of the Moral Majority today. Recent opinion data compiled throughout the 1970s (1972-1980) reveal how whites and nonwhites relate to these issues.

The results suggest that blacks . . . are more often than not on the conservative side on these issues. This would argue against the sometimes accepted notion that blacks support what might be called a liberal, socially permissive society. We have the following results to seven issues.

- In general, do you think the courts in this area deal too harshly or not harshly enough with criminals?

    White — 86% — Courts not harsh enough
    Nonwhite — 76% — Courts not harsh enough

- Do you think the use of marijuana should be made legal or not?

    White — 75% — Marijuana should not be legal
    Nonwhite — 72% — Marijuana should not be legal

- Do you favor or oppose the death penalty for persons convicted of murder?

    White — 70% — Favor death penalty for murder
    Nonwhite — 41% — Favor death penalty for murder

- What is your opinion about a married person having sexual relations with someone other than the marriage partner?

White — 87% — extramarital sex is wrong
Nonwhite — 78% — extramarital sex is wrong

• What about sexual relations between two adults of the same sex — homosexuality?

White — 77% — Homosexuality is wrong
Nonwhite — 80% — Homosexuality is wrong

• Do you think a legal abortion should be available if the woman is married and does not want more children?

White — 46% — legal abortion should be available
Nonwhite — 39% — legal abortion should be available

• Do you think a legal abortion should be available if the woman's health is seriously endangered by the pregnancy?

White — 92% — legal abortion if health is seriously endangered
Nonwhite — 82% — legal abortion if health is seriously endangered

On these social issues it appears, with the exception of the death penalty, that nonwhites come down on the side of what would be considered conservative views. There have been many attempts to interpret the views on crime and the courts. Blacks are some of the principal targets of crime and, general philosophical views aside, they are likely to call for more firm treatment of criminals. The marijuana issue is a similar example. Nonwhites do not want it legalized, perhaps because they are intensely aware of the effects of narcotics in their communities. . . .

Black Americans are decidedly in the economically liberal camp, and have been consistently so over the last several years. They are not supportive of economically conservative positions when it comes to the role of government spending on socio-economic issues. To the extent that the black leadership articulates policies aimed at continued and increased government participation in such areas as education, welfare, housing, and health, that leadership speaks in the same way as the masses of blacks.

On social issues, the data presented here suggest that blacks are more conservative than they are on economic matters. They do not portray a picture of a liberal, socially permissive society. They want harsher law enforcement; they are against legalizing marijuana; they overwhelmingly oppose extramarital sex and homosexuality. On such matters, interestingly, they are closer to their white counterparts, except on the one issue of the death penalty. . . .

Thirdly, on civil rights issues, as could be expected, black Americans are far apart from their white counterparts. Blacks want and expect government to ensure "fair" treatment, but this apparently need not be translated to mean preferential treatment at the expense of whites in similar economic circumstances. If these limited data suggest anything, they might indicate the extent to which blacks as a group are reasonably available for political alliances along economically liberal lines for the achievement of mutual *economic* goals. The point to be made is that some obvious divisive issues between blacks and whites (such as affirmative action and busing) need not necessarily be impenetrable barriers to effective political coalitions to achieve other goals. This, of course, is not a new finding as such, but it is one that bears repeating in a time when it is unfortunately tempting to see political strategies locked into broad fixed ideological categories.

People are — indeed, ought to be — moved by ideologies, but they are also motivated by perceptions of their own self-interests. That, at least, is both my prediction and my predilection.

37. WOMEN EMERGE AS INDEPENDENT FORCE

The suffragists who promised that when women entered politics they would have a moralizing impact on public affairs may have had a point. In the 1920s the public's support for disarmament, world peace, and prohibition rested largely on the strength of women's opinions. By the 1930s, however, the impact of women had faded; with the mood of masculinity, fighting, and destruction that characterized World War II, women vanished from the political arena. They began to reappear in the 1970s, with one large group crusading for the Equal Rights Amendment and another crusading against it. By 1980 women were voting as often as men and, more important, were voting differently. All the analysts concentrated on women — yet it could as well be argued that men were voting differently than women. Indeed, men had become more conservative in 1980, but women had not. Perhaps the men were especially outraged at the insult to national honor posed by the Iranian hostage episode in 1979-80, while women were more pacifistic.

Source: Adam Clymer, "Women's Political Habits Show Sharp Change," *New York Times,* June 30, 1982. © 1982 by The New York Times Company. Reprinted by permission.

The political habits of women appear to be undergoing deep changes that worry the Republicans and raise the long-range hopes of the Democrats. A variety of newly available statistics show that women, who in the past have voted at a lower rate than men, are now voting at roughly the same level. These statistics also show that women, whose political attitudes used to be barely distinguishable from those of men, are beginning to take positions on issues that differ sharply from those taken by men. These convergent developments are particularly significant, in the view of political strategists and poll takers of both major parties, because women have begun allying themselves more with Democratic positions.

Many public opinion experts believe that the partisan shift in the political views of women originated with distrust of President Reagan and a fear that he was too ready to risk a war. Some believe that these attitudes may outlast the Reagan Administration in their effect on his party. But others say there is no evidence that this is more than a temporary phenomenon that may vanish after Mr. Reagan leaves office. Both parties' national chairmen acknowledge the potential significance of these.

An analysis of all New York Times/CBS News Polls conducted this year shows that women 18 to 44 years old were one-third more likely than men in that age group to call themselves Democrats. They were also one-fourth more likely to disapprove of how Mr. Reagan was handling his job. And three women to every five men chose the Republicans as the party most likely to make the right decisions about Social Security, a key campaign issue this year. . . .

These differences are of very recent origin. Until the mid-1970s, polls have shown political opinions were basically undifferentiated by sex, except that women were generally less receptive to the use of force in settling international disputes. One typical view, in *Voters' Choice*, a 1975 book by Gerald M. Pomper, a political scientist at Rutgers University, was that there are "no political differences between men and women that can be attributed to the factor of sex itself." . . .

One modest ray of hope for the Republicans is that men in the youngest part of the electorate, those 18 to 24 years old, seem distinctly more likely to call themselves Republican than are older men, according to the polls. In the very long run, as Mr. Teeter [a Republican pollster] observed, this group will replace older men, who are heavily Democratic, as voters and could tilt the electorate back if they retain partisanship as they grow older. But to translate that opportunity into a political reality, Republicans must persuade those young men to vote. Among those now 18 to 24 years old who were old enough to vote in 1980, according to the Census Bureau, 37.5 percent of the 8,346,000 women and 35.3 percent of the 7,919,000 men reported that they had voted. That added up to 3,126,000 women and 2,796,000 men. Reversing that trend may prove difficult. The report also indicated that among people now 25 to 44, women increased their lead over men in voting participation from 1976 to 1980. In that group, the men's Republican leanings are less pronounced than those among younger men, but the women are still solidly Democratic, the polls show.

There are more women in every age bracket of the electorate, and by about 1964, even though they were less likely than men to vote, they cast more votes than men did. As Richard M. Scammon, the elections expert, observed, "They turn out a little bit more, and there are more of them. It adds up." . . .

The only other Presidential election in which the proportion of women voting exceeded that of men was in the wartime year 1944, when 12 million of the 42 million men over 21 were in the armed services. That was an exception to a progression in which the percentage of women voting increased steadily. This happened as more women who were eligible to vote when they turned 21, or 18 when that became the national voting age in 1972, entered the electorate and replaced those who had come of age before women's suffrage. Recent studies have shown that as more women enter the labor force, more of them vote. Moreover, increased education for women has made a dramatic difference in their voting rates, with women who have as much education as men voting in about the same proportion. The 1980 census study goes further, indicating that women 25 to 54 who are high school graduates or attended college without graduating vote more heavily than their male contemporaries by at least 5 percentage points. For those with college degrees, or without high school diplomas, the differences were insubstantial.

Thus the attainment of equality in voting percentage was a predictable milestone. But the sharp differences in political attitudes that give it such partisan significance were not. The Pomper analysis reflected the results of most public opinion polls until the mid-1970s. As Patrick H. Caddell, the leading Democratic pollster whose first national client was George McGovern in 1972, put it, "Sex was a variable that it never paid to look at." That may have been something of an exaggeration, for in both the 1952 and the 1956 Presidential elections women gave Dwight D. Eisenhower bigger majorities than men did, according to post-election surveys by the Gallup Organization. But from the 1960 through 1972 elections, Gallup found no significant sex differences. A similar post-election Gallup Poll for 1976 showed women preferring President Ford and men backing Jimmy Carter, by slight margins in both cases, while a CBS News Poll of voters leaving polling places showed no sex difference in the vote.

However, the "gender gap," as the National Organization for Women calls the disparity in voting, was a clear phenomenon in the 1980 Presidential election. Women preferred Mr. Reagan to President Carter by only 47 percent to 45 percent, according to a Times/CBS News Poll conducted on Election Day, while men gave the Republican nominee a margin of 55 percent to 36 percent. Each sex gave John B. Anderson, the independent candidate, 7 percent. With the difference in their choice and their greater numbers, women provided 58 percent of Mr. Carter's votes, but just 49 percent of Mr. Reagan's. Similar preferences were seen in some elections last fall and are projected in many 1982 pre-election polls now being taken for both parties. . . .

The Times/CBS News data on party identification, which go back to 1976, show that until the Reagan Administration men and women moved up and down in their party allegiance more or less in tandem. Both sexes shifted away from Democratic identification and toward the Republicans in 1981, but women have now returned to approximately their 1980 preferences for Democrats. Men, however, are more independent and less Democratic than they were in 1980. The net effect is a Democratic gain.

By another set of measurements, women are clearly allying themselves to the Democrats. From time to time Times/CBS News Polls inquire which party is best at handling particular problems. In August 1980, for example, when their party identification was about what it is now, 35 percent of women said Republicans would be best at solving whatever they individually considered to be the nation's most important problem. Thirty-two percent picked the Democrats. In May 1982, 35 percent picked the Democrats and 27 percent the Republicans. Even the greater shifts were recorded on several other major issues. On unemployment, for example, women divided evenly in August 1980, and again in April 1981. But in May 1982, they preferred the Democrats by a wide margin, 51 percent to 19 percent.

On the question of the parties' ability to control inflation, both men and women shifted toward the Democrats from April 1981 to May 1982, but the women shifted a bit more. Last year, men preferred the Republicans, 50 percent to 16 percent; this year their preference for Republicans was 42 percent to 31 percent. Among women last year showed a Republican preference of from 41 percent to 17 percent; this year women favored the Democrats, 37 percent to 29 percent. On the parties' ability to control government spending, a traditional Republican strength, in April 1981 women preferred Republicans over Democrats by 49 percent to 19 percent. Thirteen months later, in May 1982, the Republican edge was 39 percent to 33 percent.

On the respective ability of the two parties to keep the country out of war, both sexes narrowly picked the Democrats in August 1980, men by 40 percent to 33 percent and women by 34 percent to 30 percent. In May 1982 the men were about unchanged, favoring the Democrats by 41 percent to 31 percent. Women shifted to a clear Democratic preference, 41 percent to 25 percent.

The men in the May 1982 poll were consistently more supportive of the Republicans than were the women. Forty-two percent of the men said Republicans were better at controlling inflation, for example, while 31 percent preferred the Democrats. Among women, 37 percent said Democrats were better on inflation, and 29 percent chose Republicans. These sex differences were especially clear among people under 45. From unemployment to the military to controlling Federal spending to creating a "budget that is fair to all people," the women aged 18 to 44 were considerably more Democratic in their allegiances than were the men.

Mr. Reagan himself produced several sex-based distinctions. The total of the responses to the Times/CBS News Polls of January, March and May (see table 5) showed men aged 18 to 44 approved his handling of the Presidency 54 percent to 34. Women divided almost equally, with 44 percent approving and 43 percent disapproving. And when asked, in January and in May, if they would vote for a Reagan supporter or an advocate of different policies for the House of Representatives, the men aged 18 to 44 preferred Reagan backers, 50 percent to 38. The women went the other way, 51 percent to 39. On some issues such as abortion and the proposed equal rights amendment, there were no significant differences between young women and young men in their stated preferences. But most opinion analysts say these issues matter more to women than they do to men.

Table 5
THE GENDER GAP, 1982

	Women	Men
Approve Reagan's job performance	41%	50%
Fear Reagan will get U.S. into war	52	38
Would vote for Reagan backer for House	37	47
Consider Reagan life style extravagant	52	39
Think Republican party is best on inflation	29	42
Think Republican party is best on defense	29	41
Favor proposed Equal Rights Amendment	53	55
Would permit women to have abortions in first three months	48	53

Source: New York Times/CBS polls conducted in January, March, and April 1982; reported in *New York Times*, June 30, 1982, p. 1.

38. RACE VERSUS COMMUNITY: CHICAGO, 1983

The 1983 mayoral contest in Chicago was the most expensive, most intensely fought, and most widely watched municipal election in American history. Incumbent mayor Jane Byrne, who defeated the machine with the strong support of black voters in an astonishing upset in 1979, had proven erratic. This time she had the machine behind her, as well as a multimillion dollar campaign treasury, in warding off the challenge of Richard M. Daley, son of the late mayor. Meanwhile the black community began a massive registration drive designed to force the whites to loosen their hold on power. Congressman Harold Washington narrowly won the three-way primary by amassing over 80 percent of the black vote. But he refused to campaign among whites in the general election; they would be racists if they did vote for him, he claimed. The Republican candidate, a wealthy but obscure figure, hammered hard at Washington's inability to handle his personal affairs. If Washington had been white, commentators noted, then as the Democratic nominee he would easily have won. But if he had been white he never would have won a primary. Observers around the world interpreted the campaign as a test of racism — of morality — in America's second largest city. Washington won narrowly (52 to 48 percent), with black Chicagoans voting almost unanimously for him. Eighty percent of the whites voted against him, with moral concerns high on their mind.

Source: John Helyar, "Pride and Prejudice Aren't Only Motives of Chicago Voters: Neighborhood Fears, Distaste for the Patronage System Count, Too, in Ethnic area," *The Wall Street Journal,* April 8, 1983, p. 1. Reprinted by permission of *The Wall Street Journal,* © Dow Jones & Company, Inc. 1983. All Rights Reserved.

CHICAGO — In the heart of this city's Northwest Side, "Epton for Mayor" posters are in the windows and fear is in the streets. In block after block of tidy brick houses in the lower-middle-class neighborhood live the children and grandchildren of immigrants: mostly Polish, mostly blue collar and, for decades, overwhelmingly Democratic. Next Tuesday they probably will vote overwhelmingly Republican, for Bernard Epton, perhaps even in sufficient numbers to make him Chicago's first GOP mayor in 52 years.

This phenomenon is most readily explained by racism. The Northwest side is white and so is Mr. Epton. . . . Harold Washington is black. The area drew national attention on Palm Sunday when Mr. Washington and presidential hopeful Walter Mondale were jeered out of a Catholic church. And the slogan the Republican has used — "Epton: Before It's Too Late" — is seen by many as a thinly disguised appeal to racism.

Yet what is happening here is more complex. It involves the history of this city, which has never particularly encouraged racial or ethnic integration. It involves the fear of neighborhood change, a trauma that uprooted many current residents from their original homes and now, they feel, it threatens them again. Finally, it involves the breakdown of the vaunted

Democratic machine, which may actually prefer an isolated Republican like Mr. Epton to a loose-cannon Democrat like Mr. Washington, who vows to end patronage.

Chicago has always been a city of enclaves, less like a melting pot than a checkerboard, in which races and nationalities stick to their own areas and pursue their own interests. . . . Blacks have long been loyal sons in backing the Democratic machine here, but poor cousins in receiving its spoils. Mr. Washington owed his primary victory to no one but the 40% black minority, who overwhelmingly turned out for him while Democratic regulars split the white vote between incumbent Jane Byrne and State's Attorney Richard M. Daley.

An assumption underlies much of the fear in the Northwest Side: that its white residents would fare poorly under a black administration. That city jobs and services would go increasingly to blacks, along with city-hall influence, and that lives that aren't such great shakes now would only get worse. "I've never been a Republican; I could never afford to be one," says Doris Dempsey, a coffee-shop cashier. "But sometimes you need a Republican." Here are a few snapshots from the Northwest the week before Election Day. Taken together, they don't make an attractive portrait. "If I had to run away again I don't know where I would go," says Mirko Vukosavich, 75. He sits in his living room, telling of a different area where he and his wife settled in 1950 after emigrating from Yugoslavia. In his still-thick accent, he talks about that area's park, where the Chicago Symphony played and people could sleep on summer nights to keep cool. "We were so in love with the neighborhood," he says. But then it began changing: Hispanics trickling in and whites, panicked by real-estate agencies, moving out. As their numbers declined, so did city services. Buildings began deteriorating, then burning. Finally, in 1973, Mr. and Mrs. Vukosavich moved out, to the Northwest side. There are thousands of people like him here, some of whom have moved two and three times before, fleeing minorities, blockbusting, change. In Mr. Washington they see the specter of housing projects on the next block, plummeting property values, and another move. "I think it's more irrational than anything," says Mr. Vukosavich. "But I never thought it could happen to me the first time, either." Mark him down as undecided, he says.

More than one might suspect, there are ambivalent feelings among whites about the current political system, for many are its pawns. "If Harold Washington got rid of patronage, I'd be all for him," says a man we will call "the garbageman," who is employed by the city through patronage. He is only willing to talk anonymously and by phone, because he knows that with his bosses even race isn't so touchy a point as patronage. Mr. Washington promises to abolish the time-honored system whereby most city jobs get doled out by Democratic ward committeemen. This heresy has caused eight of the 50 committeemen to break openly and support the Republican, with others doing so less openly. They apparently feel Mr. Epton would be controllable, since there is nary a Republican to be found on the 50-member City Council. Thus, although a Republican mayor would be an embarrassment, the machine could roll on. That machine is greased by patronage. City workers are also Democratic precinct workers, who get out the vote, take care of pothole complaints or sell tickets to party fund-raisers.

"The garbageman" is a precinct captain, responsible for shepherding 510 voters. He hates it. "They keep you afraid of your job all the time," he says. "If I lose a precinct I catch hell from the committeeman, and I know I could lose my job. I've got a family to support and no protection whatsoever." He figures most people in his position feel much the same way. So is he voting for Mr. Washington? (His committeeman is playing it neutral, so the garbageman need only worry about his own vote this time.) "I don't know yet," he says. "He'd get my vote if I knew he would keep his word. But you know politicians."

It is early afternoon at the Charm Restaurant. Owner John Tragas and customer Thaddeus Godawski linger at a booth, sipping coffee, smoking cigarettes and talking politics. "They're not doing anything to talk about their qualifications or programs: they're just looking at each other's faults," says Mr. Godawski, a 43-year-old carpenter. "I feel sorry for the voters." Mr. Tragas, a 30-year-old Greek immigrant with a black pompadour, contemplates his choices in this, his first vote since attaining citizenship. To him, neither looks promising. "A Jew will very seldom help anybody but a Jew," he says of the Jewish Mr. Epton. "But elect Washington and we'll be giving the city away to the niggers. They'll feel they should be favored." He plans to vote white.

Recent Epton disclosures about his opponent's financial affairs also hit home with Mr. Tragas. It is an issue of long standing that Mr. Washington once spent a month in jail for not filing income-tax returns four years and that he was suspended from practicing law for five years for not providing services to five clients who had paid for them. More recently, court records show Mr. Washington was sued for nonpayment of bills by gas and water utilities, Illinois Bell and a law firm. Says Mr. Tragas: "I've worked and I've worked so I can pay my bills." Mr. Godawski grimaces. "That's a petty issue," he says. "It's a rotten, dirty election. If I can't vote for somebody I like I don't want to live here." He's thinking of moving to Virginia to raise horses.

During the primary, the Cicero Avenue storefront was Mr. Daley's ward office. It has been converted into an Epton office. Converted, too, are the two young men who run it, formerly Daley volunteers. "I've got a question for the media," Stanley Brisco says acidly. "How come when blacks vote together it's cultural pride and when whites vote together it's racism?" People start drifting in for an organizing meeting, many of them political novices. Consider the red-headed doorbell-pushing term of 54-year-old Marion Fleming and 61-year-old Tina Sylvestri, neighbors on the Northwest Side's southern border. "I'm not saying all blacks are bad," says Mrs. Fleming, a native Austrian, "but we cannot have them running the city." It's because their block hangs in the balance, she says, Mrs. Sylvestri nodding earnestly in agreement. Four black families have moved in, along with a half-dozen Hispanic ones. Since the primary, real-estate agents have been calling steadily, trying to entice the remaining whites to sell before it's too late. Mrs. Fleming is certain a Washington win would start a white-flight stampede, spurred by the real-estate agents, and she's also certain she and her husband couldn't afford to buy elsewhere. Only on this point does Mrs. Sylvestri stop nodding and part company. "I intend to get out," she says.

About 700 people jam the St. Genevieve's Church hall for the evening candidates' forum. Only one debater will show, however. The crowd cheers Northwest Neighborhood Federation speakers as they denounce Harold Washington for backing out at the 11th hour. Then they settle in restively to await Bernard Epton, who is running late. Bruno Sadowski helps pass the time by singing "God Bless America." They cheer lustily for Mr. Epton when he finally sweeps in with his entourage. . . . Mr. Epton answers five questions that were given the candidates in advance and now are read by neighborhood speakers. He opposes public housing without community consent. He supports ban on "for sale" signs on front lawns. Just one slipup: He vows total support for the neighborhood's anticrime blockwatch program, but that's the answer to a different question, not the one the speaker read. No matter. Mr. Epton's applause lines are in good working order, and after his half-hour stint he and his entourage sweep out again, amid cheers.

The polls say Mr. Epton has a shot at winning this thing. They show him closing the gap on Mr. Washington's once-huge lead, with lots of voters, mostly presumably white, still undecided. Even if he wins and proves controllable, the regular Democrats have problems. The blacks already have left the fold; as for the whites, says one party pro, "the problem is that once you've voted Republican one time it's easy to do it again." He pauses and adds, "I think the whole thing is coming apart."

IV
SUGGESTED FOLLOWUP

The best way to learn about the history of grass roots politics is to read old newspapers. Most college libraries have microfilm files of the *New York Times* often extending back to before the Civil War. These have a printed index that simplifies searching. Local newspaper files are usually available, too — check the public library or local historical society.

Books that try to encompass American political history concentrate on the big men and big ideas at the national level. Good collections of articles which breach this limitation are F. A. Bonadio, ed., *Political Parties in American History, vol. 2, 1828-1890* (New York, 1973); Paul L. Murphy, ed., *Political Parties in American History, vol. 3, 1890-Present* (New York, 1973); and Frank Otto Gatell, et al., eds., *The Growth of American Politics*, 2 vol. (New York, 1972). The best summary of recent scholarship is Paul Kleppner et al., *The Evolution of American Electoral Systems* (Westport, Conn., 1981). Seymour Martin Lipset, ed., *Party Coalitions in the 1980s* (San Francisco, 1981) includes both a full historical treatment and extensive analyses of recent politics. A short, very broad overview that emphasizes ethnicity is Robert Kelley, "Ideology and Political Culture from Jefferson to Nixon," *American Historical Review* 82 (June, 1977), 531-82.

On nineteenth century politics, the best introduction is Morton Keller, *Affairs of State: Public Life in Nineteenth Century America* (Cambridge, 1977). Ethno-religious forces and campaign techniques at the state level are emphasized in Richard Jensen, *The Winning of the Midwest: Social and Political Conflict, 1888-1896* (Chicago, 1971). Excellent detail on the big city machine appears in Zane Miller, *Boss Cox's Cincinnati* (New York, 1968). Lawrence Goodwyn, "Populist Dreams and Negro Rights: East Texas as a Case Study," *American Historical Review* 76 (December, 1971), pp. 1435-56, is a splendid investigation of the Populist movement at the local level.

Grass roots politics in the twentieth century can be followed at the state level in J. Joseph Huthmacher, *Massachusetts People and Politics, 1919-1933* (Cambridge, 1959); Robert Cherny, *Populism, Progressivism and the Transformation of Nebraska Politics, 1885-1915* (Lincoln, 1981); Richard Jensen, *Illinois: A Bicentennial History* (New York, 1978); John W. Jeffries, *Testing the Roosevelt Coalition: Connecticut Society and Politics in the Era of World War II* (Nashville, 1979); and the magistral *Southern Politics in State and Nation* (New York, 1949), by V. O. Key. Lyle W. Dorsett, *Franklin D. Roosevelt and the City Bosses* (Port Washington, N.Y., 1977) is useful on the machines.

The best background introduction to recent politics in each state is the appropriate chapter in the multivolume series by Neal R. Pierce covering each region of the land, for example, *The Border South States* (New York, 1975). Up-to-date information on each state and even each congressional district appears in *The Almanac of American Politics, 1984* (Washington, 1983) by Michael Barone and Grant Ujifusa. Necessary background on group voting habits can be found in Kevin Phillips, *The Emerging Republican Majority* (New Rochelle, N.Y., 1969). Just before each national election the periodical *Congressional Quarterly Weekly Report* provides a clear summary of every major race in the country. For on-going coverage, the *New York Times* is essential reading.

On campaign tactics, the weekly news magazine *National Journal* is superb. The public mood is gauged every two months in *Public Opinion*. Dan Nimmo, *The Political Persuaders* (Englewood Cliffs, 1970) and Larry Sabato, *The Rise of Political Consultants: New Ways of Winning Elections* (New York, 1981), provide thorough guides to modern campaign tactics.

On PACs and special interest groups, see Michael J. Malbin ed., *Parties, Interest Groups and Campaign Finance Laws* (Washington, 1980), and the encyclopedic *Political Parties and Civic Action Groups* (Westport, Conn., 1981) by Edward L. Schapsmeier and Frederick H. Schapsmeier. On the woman suffrage movement see Anne Firor Scott and Andrew MacKay Scott, *One Half the People: The Fight for Woman Suffrage* (Urbana, 1982). On the woman's movement in the 1970s and 1980s, see Joyce Gelb and Marian Lief Palley, *Women and Public Policies* (Princeton, 1982). The best treatment of the civil rights movement is Clayborne Carson, *In Struggle: SNCC and the Black Awakening of the 1960s* (Cambridge, 1981).

The decline in turnout is viewed in broad perspective in W. Dean Burnham, *The Current Crisis in American Politics* (New York, 1983), and in William J. Crotty and Gary C. Jacobson, *American Parties in Decline* (Boston, 1980). The rising disenchantment with big institutions is analyzed in Seymour Martin Lipset and William Schneider, *The Confidence Gap: Business, Labor and Government in the Public Mind* (New York, 1982).

Grass roots politics cannot be fully appreciated without a real life taste. College political and activist clubs provide many opportunities, especially before local and national elections.

For the indoor types, the Apple microcomputer can be used to "run" a national campaign. "President Elect" is a sophisticated computer simulation for elections from 1960 through 1980. Two or three player/campaign-managers must each allocate a war chest, schedule campaign stops, and engage in television debates. The program evaluates the effectiveness of each, produces weekly polls on who's ahead, and finally tabulates the electoral vote. One person can also compete against the computer (which seems to be relatively honest). The economic and foreign policy situations that actually existed can be used or changed, and the personal strengths and weaknesses of historic candidates can be altered. "President Elect" is published by Computer Simulations Inc. and is available (about $40) through Apple computer dealers.

INDEX

About the Contributors

RICHARD J. JENSEN is Professor of History and Sociology and Director of the Family and Community History Center at the Newberry Library in Chicago. His published writings include *The Winning of the Midwest, Historians Guide to Statistics, Illinois: A Bicentennial History*, and numerous articles.

STEVEN L. PIOTT is Assistant Professor of History at Franklin and Marshall College in Lancaster, Pennsylvania. His articles have appeared in *American Studies, The missouri Historical Society Bulletin*, and *Missouri Historical Review*. He has an article forcoming in *Labor History*.

CHRISTOPHER C. GIBBS has worked as a historian for the U.S. Army in Viet Nam and for Harvard Business School in Boston. He taught American history at the University of Northern Colorado and at the University of Missouri-Columbia. His articles have appeared in *American Studies, The Missouri Historical Society Bulletin*, and *Missouri Historical Review*. He has an article forthcoming in *Labor History*.